Look East, Look West

LOOK EAST
LOOK WEST

The Socialist Adventure
in Yugoslavia

by DAVID TORNQUIST

THE MACMILLAN COMPANY : *NEW YORK*
COLLIER-MACMILLAN LTD : *LONDON*

For Elizabeth

Contents

(ILLUSTRATIONS FOLLOW PAGE 182)

Look East, Look West

I

Taking the First Look

Even a small country like Yugoslavia presents many faces, and to make a portrait the writer must choose among them. Also, in a young country like Yugoslavia which is still boldly engaged in forming its identity, change is so rapid and various that it is not always easy to decide which features are superficial and which will become more pronounced with time. This book does not portray all the facets of Yugoslavia; it is only a portrait of those things I deemed essential in what I saw and experienced in a visit which lasted more than two years. The focus is upon what I call the "social adventure"—man's involvement in shaping the society he lives in. One part of this adventure is the effort of political leaders to fit their ideas and strategies to the reality which confronts them; the other, perhaps more important, concerns the response of ordinary men to the program and vision of society which the leaders present.

I first became interested in the social adventure of Yugoslavia through newspaper and magazine articles by men who had become convinced that the Yugoslav Communists meant what they said when they spoke of building a democratic society in which the ordinary man would become directly involved in public business. If this were true, it meant an important development away from the totalitarian state with its subdued citizens which we have grown used to expecting in the Communist world. It also meant that this little Balkan country might be solving some of the questions of democracy which concern us in the West. But I felt it was impossible to tell how much of it was true from a few scattered articles, or even from recent books on Yugoslavia, for none of them treated the surface of life, the view from the street, the world of the ordinary man. It seemed to me that a system aimed at direct democracy must be tested from that point of view. If the theories were really being put into practice, they had to appear on the surface, in the ordinary life of ordinary people. Since these things were not to be found in books, I went to see for myself.

Before setting out I learned some Serbo-Croatian, the principal language of Yugoslavia. Then I made contacts with Yugoslav officials in the Washington embassy in order to obtain long-term visas for my wife and me, and a job with which I could support us while there. I found these officials quite open in their talk and ready for me to visit their country, but their efforts to secure the visas and guarantee me a job were unsuccessful. We made the trip anyway, expecting we might have to return at the end of three months, when our tourist visas would expire and our money would run out.

Things went more easily in Belgrade. Within two weeks of my arrival I was hired by a publishing house and handed a ninety-page Serbian book on the codling moth for translation into English. Once I had a job, there were no more difficulties with the visa. I soon found that having English as a native tongue and knowing Serbo-Croatian put me in great demand. I did technical and literary translations, including a Serbian heroic ballad to be used in a film cartoon, recorded English lessons, narrated films to be exported to English-speaking countries, occasionally served as an interpreter, and edited the English text of Yugoslav laws, including the 1963 Constitution.

Having to make my living was my greatest advantage in trying to look at the country as much as possible through the eyes of the ordinary Yugoslav. Since I depended entirely on what I earned there, I had many of the same concerns as the average citizens—

money, housing, entertainment, food, vacations, fringe benefits, relations with colleagues and with the director—and people took it for granted that I would attend meetings and become involved in the problems of the society. I was left completely free by the government to go about my own business without any sort of restriction or surveillance, just as a foreigner working here would be left to his own devices. When I needed assistance or explanation, I was able to call upon my colleagues in the publishing house. Everyone quickly forgot that I was there to look at the social adventure of Yugoslavia and not primarily to work as a translator; consequently, no one went out of his way to show me anything except the countryside, or to steer me away from seeing things.

For the first eighteen months of my stay, then, I "puzzled out" Yugoslavia through what I saw and read, through conversations with Belgrade friends in every range of the political spectrum, and through chance encounters with strangers. Since I look like a Yugoslav, once my accent had improved I was frequently taken for a Serb by people I ran into, and this was a certain advantage.

During that time I arrived at the view of the country which is contained in this book. Six months before I left I arranged interviews with various officials and specialists and visited factories, hospitals, and farms like other foreign journalists. These talks and visits gave me a good deal of information I could hardly have come by as an ordinary private citizen, but they gave me no reason to change my basic judgments; in fact, they confirmed and strengthened them. This is true of both my basic optimism about Yugoslav development, and the problems and difficulties I envisage.

My first overwhelming impression of Yugoslavia was that it was following the same bent as the countries I had left: America and the Western European countries which were copying America. Even as the train from Italy made its swing through the plain toward Belgrade, the remark of a young Yugoslav girl returning home after several months in Milwaukee struck a recurring note in my first weeks in her country. "Look!" she cried, pointing out the train window toward Belgrade's tallest buildings, "They've put up many new neon signs since we left!" For her, the colored signs with their flashing figures were a solace. She had loved the glitter and gloss of America, and the fast commercialism of Italy was her idea of the good life. If she had to come back to Belgrade, it was at least not quite the same drab, dull Belgrade she had left. My own thoughts took another course. If the whole point of Yugoslav socialism was to make a fast dash toward Times Square and Piccadilly Circus, then I could hope that after centuries of economic backwardness Yugoslavs would get laundromats and supermarkets and vacuum cleaners and bathrooms, some of the truly valuable products of our consumer economies, but there was little reason why that concern should keep me long in Yugoslavia. Copies of America were plentiful enough elsewhere. I could take a look at the countryside which the Yugoslavs, being somewhat behind us economically, still had not managed to blot out with billboards. Then I could go back home to my own billboards.

Very much of what I saw in those first days in Belgrade made me think that Yugoslavia was becoming a country suited more to the girl's tastes than to mine. Yugoslav socialist commercialism had not yet caught up with the capitalist commercialism of Italy or America, but the difference was only quantitative. I had no doubt that a planned socialist economy could make up that gap and then go about the business of producing the ugliness of mass culture with a deliberate vengeance.

All the earmarks were there. If Yugoslav advertising was not as prevalent or insidiously slick as Western advertising, it was budding and spreading. The pitch was familiar: life-size photographs of handsome men and women on the walls of tobacco kiosks bore the implication *be sure to smoke if you want to be handsome and happy like us.* Feature films were preceded by slides which subjected a paying but captive audience to praise of the chocolate which was "superior to all other chocolates," the restaurant "superior to all other restaurants," and the detergent which would wash your clothes "whiter than white."

I found much elaborate vulgarity in shopwindows. The designs of cotton prints were large and gaudy and the colors clashed; paintings displayed in glass cutters' shops depicted demented allegories in phosphorescent colors; the china shops were filled with dime-store lamps and vases; and even the big cooperative stores selling folk art were showing handmade boxes and Scotch terriers labeled "Souvenir of Belgrade."

At the newsstands I found domestic film magazines on the same order as film magazines everywhere, cheap thrillers mostly translated from Western writers, inane comic strips imported from America, and an evening paper apparently modeled on the New York *Daily News* and read by nearly everyone. In those first weeks of apartment-hunting I bought *The Evening News* frequently myself because it had the most complete classified advertisements. Its headlines were sensational beyond belief. One I remember particularly well dates from the height of the Algerian revolution. It read: *Oran in Flames*. Upon turning to page four for the "text," I found only a four-line squib referring vaguely to a fire in an Oran warehouse. In the evenings crowds would collect in front of newspaper offices when the soccer results were posted; later they would line up to buy the latest editions of the sport sheets hot off the press. And there were amply illustrated weeklies to excite what we cynically call "human interest": to lead people to those mechanical conclusions such as "Isn't that nice!" when they read that two brothers have met in the street after forty years of estrangement; or "Isn't science amazing!" when they read that someone has invented a motor that can be mounted on the head of a pin; or "Isn't that awful!" when they read that an abandoned husband has shot his wife, his mother-in-law, and then himself on a street corner.

Jukeboxes had made their appearance. Besides the Western pop tunes, rock and roll, and twist which usually blare from those corpulent boxes, there were Yugoslav translations and imitations and even some original inventions in the same genre. The film announcements included a remarkable number of westerns and other popular films lacking the respectable purity of the "horse opera." One evening I heard the director of a large Yugoslav publishing house express regret that his country could not afford to import the best American films, by which he meant superproductions like those of Cecil B. De Mille. Socialism had made no evident improvement in the television fare. There were quiz shows, variety shows, and news programs with the format used in America by local stations with limited facilities. There were even imports of American mediocrities like *Tarzan* and *Dr. Hudson's Secret Journal.* In the bookstores I found the complete works of Zane Grey had been translated but many of our important classics were missing. Most shocking of all was the high price of all books. A comparison of book prices with incomes led to the unmistakable conclusion that very few people were in a position to buy books, and even those few could not afford very many. When I compared theater and opera prices with wages, I was led to a similar conclusion. Yet during my first weeks in Belgrade, the opera was usually sold out. Who was going?

There appeared to be substantial differences in wealth. The meals in the dining car of the Orient Express on which I came into the country were priced far out of the range of the Yugoslavs in the compartment with me. The range of quality in hotels was very great. There were ordinary restaurants, with ordinary food and service, and very much fancier restaurants, bars, and nightclubs. I naturally assumed that the people who could afford to go to plush restaurants with orchestras and floor shows were able to afford other things on the same scale. My window-shopping tours gave me some confirmation of this impression. There were antique stores where sofas and rugs were selling for more than a working man makes in a year. The department stores displayed imitation Persian lamb coats for under $70, while the furriers were selling the real thing for $800. Dry goods stores were selling woolens from England and Greece at upwards of $10 a yard. Refrigerators, tape recorders, and TV sets, some imported, were as expensive as in the West. Who was able to buy these things when even good Yugoslav salaries were too low for such expensive purchases?

In my long walks about Belgrade, from one end to the other, combing every street in whole quarters just to take in everything that was open to the eye, I noticed vast differences in the clothes people were wearing. The range of fabrics corresponded to the range of tailoring: from very bad to very good, from quite cheap to quite expensive. I also noticed that there was no great equality in the new apartment houses, though I did see evidence of what an earlier visitor had told me: that Belgrade was a vast work site, with construction underway on all sides. Some new buildings were definitely in better taste and of better construction than others, and even from the outside one could see that the apartments were larger in some houses than in others. I saw a correlation between these fancier apartment houses and the cars parked around them. There were many imported automobiles, particularly Mercedes-Benz sedans—often driven by chauffeurs; and it was impossible to avoid the impression that luxuries like better apartments and excellent automobiles were coming to some people not exactly by accident. Why were those chauffeurs driving so many Mercedeses and large American cars when smaller cars, including the Fiats made in Yugoslavia, would do the same job and when the balance of payments situation prevented the ordinary man from getting what he wanted from abroad? The old question kept coming back: Who enjoys these large apartments, these fancy restaurants, these elegant hotels?

One evening I thought I caught a glimpse of the answer when a chance acquaintance took me to the Publishers' and Writers' Club. We ate a pleasant meal in a lovely garden behind the club, which was a mansion on one of the most stately of Belgrade's streets. One group was dressed in tuxedos and elegant evening dresses and fur stoles. My host told me who they were: one was an editor of this paper, another the editor of that one, so-and-so the head of the theater, another the leading ballerina, and so on. "They're probably going to a diplomatic reception," he said. It occurred to me that if some of the nondescripts like me and my host were replaced by some of the American rich, no one would be able to tell the coupon-clippers from these Communist dandies. Not only did Milovan Djilas seem to be right when he wrote that a new class had formed itself to rule and enjoy the fruits of the new "socialist state," but from all appearances its style had little in it that was new.

There were other unpleasant signs of class feeling. In a hotel full of foreign journalists assembled for an international conference, the maids and bellhops, bowing and scraping, would embarrassedly refuse to go down in the elevator with the guests even when there was ample room. When I had occasion to visit apartment houses, I noticed that university graduates were as conscious of "station" as the hotel staff, for the brass nameplates which they affixed to their doors consistently gave their titles: Engineer so-and-so, Professor so-and-so, Lawyer so-and-so. And from the windows of my apartment and the want ads in the newspapers I discovered that to have women come in to do the family laundry and maids who "lived in" was nothing at all rare in Belgrade. In a government office I heard a young official scold the scrubwoman in vituperative language merely because she had not sent me to the right place when I asked directions. If the people in their evening clothes could not be distinguished from the rich displaying their "feathers," this tongue-lashing could not be distinguished from the behavior of the rich in other countries toward those who keep their world in order.

There were also suspicious signs of the party dictatorship. Every citizen had to register with the police and carry an identity card which included even a photograph and fingerprints; police cards had to be filled out for every traveler every night, even if he stayed in a private home. Signs along the highways sometimes forbade picture-taking. I found President Tito's picture in every store, every office, and every public room, absolutely without exception. The Central Committee of the League of Communists was building itself a twenty-two-story skyscraper in New Belgrade, right next to the Federal Executive Council building. At the local level I found the commune administration and commune party headquarters in the same building. Two hideous new red buildings were being built in the section of Belgrade devoted to government offices. They were mammoth and squat and glaring. I asked about them and was told they were being built to house the army and police administrations. There was universal military conscription, and a very high percentage of the federal budget went for the army; the newsreels were always showing maneuvers with some new piece of equipment. I wondered why the army was split up into small garrisons in the towns. Could they be a constant reminder to the population that the guns were in the hands of the state? And if such a reminder was necessary, then how did things stand between the citizenry and this government whose revolutionary slogan had been "Freedom to the People"?

And then, why had the revolutionary leaders chosen to reside in the villas of the former rich on the hill of Dedinye at the edge of Belgrade? This circumstance caused me a worrisome incident. A Yugoslav woman I had met crossing the Atlantic had two sisters married to government officials who lived on Dedinye. She had offered to introduce me to one of them and even gave me a letter of introduction, but I mailed the letter instead of presenting it at the door and I had not yet had a reply from her relatives when my friend arrived herself to spend some time with them. Though our close friendship on the boat had led me to expect to see a good deal of her, she called only a few hours before she was to leave Belgrade. The explanation seemed to lie not in any change of affections but in the warnings her family had her convey to me. "Perhaps it would be better," she said with embarrassment, "if you did not go to Dedinye unless a Yugoslav goes with you." Her voice dropped almost to a whisper: "Foreign journalists have written some unfair stories about Dedinye, and if you go poking around out there, you might lose your visa." No mention was made of the earlier arrangement that I should visit her sister and thereafter she refused even to answer my letters.

After midnight one evening, while I was dining in a restaurant with a friend who worked on one of the Belgrade papers, another strange incident occurred. My friend was a regular customer and bosom friends with the waiter. He also did not hold his liquor well. The only other party in the dining room at that late hour was far on the other side of the room and included one very large man, one extremely small man, and a middle-aged woman. We had been talking about Communist dogmatism, East Germany, and Khrushchev's policies, and in ordering more wine my friend asked the waiter whether he did not agree that Khrushchev was an idiot. The waiter was a wise man and only smiled at what could hardly be anyone's considered opinion of the former Soviet leader. But the large man at the table across the room stood up and protested. Such remarks, he said, should not be made in front of foreigners. My friend stood up and demanded to know upon what authority this man saw himself as the judge of what was and what was not to be said before foreigners.

"I speak in my own person," the man said. "I am not a member of the party, but such remarks should not be made before foreigners."

"And I speak in my own person and am not a member of the party and no one is going to tell me what I can and cannot say, especially a bunch of whores and fairies." This brought a roar from the woman and a squeal from the little man. From then on the argument was entirely personal and bore no relation to politics. Fortunately, it was near closing time and the waiter solved the dispute over who was to leave first by suggesting that we all leave.

There were several such bewildering and strange occurrences, so that at times it seemed impossible to see any sense in anything. From certain angles the socialist revolution appeared to have done little toward changing the overall style and forms of society; it looked as though Yugoslavia's attempt to blaze a "third way" had come down to a combination of the worst of both worlds: the commercial culture and class distinctions of the West and the authoritarianism of the East.

One reason for the suspicion and disappointment I often felt at the beginning was that my first impressions were of the surface of life and neither Yugoslav nor foreign writers have done much to convey the look and feel of the surface. From books and articles I had a fairly good notion of the ideas held by the Yugoslav theoreticians and political leaders, but when I came to Yugoslavia to see whether the reality corresponded to the theories, what I had read turned out to be poor preparation for this unique, unpredictable, and often inscrutable country.

Though my first impressions were superficial, they were all I had to start with and therefore I took seriously what I saw. Later I realized that many of the conjectures I based on these first impressions were neither sound nor complete. In general there is little use in discussing impressions which have been subsequently corrected or discarded, but first impressions of a Western visitor to Yugoslavia represent something of a political phenomenon. They tell as much about the spectacles Westerners wear when they look at things Communist as they do about Communist reality itself. I often had occasion to see this in the first impressions of other Americans. One man I met was in Yugoslavia for a few days on business. As a gesture of ordinary hospitality and business courtesy his hosts invited him to a Belgrade night spot. When it came time to order, one of the Yugoslavs suggested that they splurge and drink good French cognac, which is several times more expensive than the poorer Yugoslav article. Everyone agreed that they should give themselves the rare treat of a bit of Martell at the company's expense, but the American objected. "It's immoral to drink expensive imported liquor in such a poor country," he said; "I'll drink beer." One of those present, a woman who had been a Communist since her student days before the war, reminded him that, after all, the Yugoslavs had not fought a war and gone through a revolution in order to live in sackcloth and ashes but to enjoy some of the good things other people had, including Martell cognac. But the American, stubborn in the idea that even the slightest momentary transgression frays the moral fiber, replied, "I know what you are. You are the Communist bourgeoisie!" and he took his beer to another table where he sat glumly through the evening.

His charge was mistaken on several counts. Of the five Yugoslavs in that party, only two were Communists. The others were far from it. One of them had been a Communist at seventeen, had fought in the revolution, and been a minister in the government of one of the republics. Ten years before, he had been removed from his position and excluded from the party because of high and decadent living; he had lost all real connection with the tendencies of the society and was waiting for his pension with the apathy of a man who feels he experienced everything life could offer at a young age. Another had been a politician before the war and now belonged to that blessed group, the translators, who can earn about as much money as anyone in the country. His only political concern was petitioning local officials to find other housing for the workers who were settled in several spare rooms of his villa during the acute housing shortage right after the war. The third non-Communist was a secretary with a salary of less than $40 a month, though she had completed all the work at the university except one final examination and knew three foreign languages. The woman who defended drinking French cognac was a Communist but enjoyed no privileges. She lived reasonably well on her salary and that of her husband, a university professor. Only the director of the enterprise could be said to enjoy special privileges, but he had these as a director, not as a Communist: he had been provided an apartment by the company, had the use of a company car and the chance to travel abroad, and enjoyed an expense account for entertaining. But I recall that he had to furnish his new apartment with inexpensive furniture, on credit. His travel abroad was becoming less and less a special privilege as more and more people in the enterprise also enjoyed the luxury of business travel. The end of his personal use of the company car and the expense account was in sight, for there were already strong campaigns against these privileges of directors, and the workers' council of his enterprise could be expected to join in them.

Whatever all this adds up to, is not a Communist bourgeoisie but something far more complicated. Like most visitors, this American businessman did not stay long enough to understand the complications and judge them in the context of the whole society. Time is perhaps the most important element here. I found that when I had been in Belgrade for a few weeks I could begin to see things which contradicted my first gloomy impressions and made it more difficult to judge in black-and-white terms.

I found, for instance, that people were speaking their minds, not just in the privacy of their homes, but in cafes and offices and on the streets. The government was not telling them where to go and what to do; they lived where they pleased and worked where there were jobs. No one was being required to work in what Yugoslavs call "the socialized sector"—that is, the part of the economy which has been nationalized. Though some farms, most commercial establishments, hotels and restaurants, and all industries and health and insurance services were socialized, people were working independently in professions other than medicine, and on some of the old streets of Belgrade I saw so many privately owned craftsmen's shops, bakers, tailors, mechanics, etc., that it was sometimes hard to believe I was in a socialist country. (This "private" sector of the economy is still quite large in the towns, and it is predominant in agriculture, where nearly 90 percent of the land is privately owned.)

People appeared quite free to do as they liked. If they wanted to go to church, they went. If they could get the money together, it was not hard to get a visa for a trip to Italy or Austria or America. If the secret police watched their mail and contacts with abroad, it was not evident. I myself never saw any signs that I was suspected or was even an object of interest to the police. My Yugoslav friends showed no sign of fear that association with me would make them suspect. The people I saw and talked to were going about their daily lives with the same assurance as people in New York or Cleveland. They did not have the air of people overcome by either fear or poverty; on the contrary, the population showed every sign of liveliness, gaiety, and energy.

The signs of a rapidly rising standard of living were unmistakable. The stores were full of goods and people were buying. The system of consumer credit was highly developed, and many of the people purchasing new furniture, television sets, and refrigerators were clearly ordinary workingmen. Through the union, people working in offices and factories were going to the opera and the theater at half price to see Ionesco, Albee, Tennessee Williams, Sartre, and Beckett (*Waiting for Godot,* I was told, had a longer run in Belgrade than in Paris). The newspapers carried full-page advertisements about installment plans which allowed people with ordinary salaries to build up good libraries. The movies were cheap, and free lectures were being held every night. Everyone seemed to have enough money for restaurants and cafes.

If there were indications of differences in wealth, it was difficult to find the city slums and abject poverty that are still tolerated in many places in the West. If some of the apartment houses seemed more comfortable than others, it was also clear that most of the new ones—and there were a great many of them—were occupied by ordinary people and not by officials or dignitaries. After a time I learned that the differences in dress I observed on the street did not always reflect corresponding differences in wealth. When I began to make acquaintances, I realized that many of them looked smart because they were resourceful and invested a great deal of effort, not because their salaries were particularly high. When I went into plush restaurants, I found that the difference between their prices and those of the more ordinary restaurants was hardly enough to pay for clean tablecloths, quicker service, and better cooking.

Differences in wealth certainly do exist, and by Yugoslav standards they are large. But they are generally restricted to possession or lack of ordinary comforts; there is no accumulation of wealth, and loose spending is almost exclusively the result of advantages offered by expense accounts. People in high government circles are in a position to live well: some of them do consume conspicuously; others live with a measured comfort that befits a studious and hardworking life. In the middle and lower ranks of government service one finds people with average salaries and average comforts (the government is actually losing good people to business because its salaries are so low). People with good positions in factories and offices also live comfortably while the unskilled often live very badly. There are a few beggars who work the cafes in the center of town, but they are well fed and wear very good shoes beneath their tatters. Begging is simply a profession, illegal but lucrative. Those who are in real need are people who have left their villages and come to the city to make their fortunes without sufficient funds. In the period before they get settled or turn around and go back to the village, they do not beg in the streets and cafes but make the rounds of private apartments asking for work or a little food. Many of these people rang my doorbell during the two years I was in Yugoslavia. I was there during an eighteen-month lull in the economy and during a period when enterprises were laying off extra help to make their operation more efficient and to meet competition on the world market. The earlier boom in the economy had encouraged a faster migration to the city than the economy was immediately able to absorb. Many of these people no doubt felt like the North Carolina farmer who used to tell me how he "went off to town to get rich and came home to the farm to keep from starving."

This is only one of the many problems and contradictions which result from the Yugoslavs' predilection to let things work themselves out instead of always telling people what to do. In order to acquire a sense of the whys and wherefores of such problems, to learn what the Yugoslavs themselves think, and to judge from their context, one has to leave the tourist and diplomatic world and live in Yugoslavia almost as an ordinary citizen. For it is through all the telling chance encounters, situations, and conversations of daily life that one gets below the surface to learn which dissatisfactions and criticisms people really have on their minds, which desires for their society they consider the most important, and which failings of their society they consider negligible.

One difficulty in arriving at dependable information is that events in Yugoslavia are complicated and the foreigner must acquire a certain familiarity with things before he can put the right questions and convince his informants that he will understand the answers he gets. Yugoslavs are politically minded; they are conscious of the importance of what they say to a foreigner. Some are against the regime, and the American visitor will get an earful of the ingrained criticism of those who want a world they think they have had or a world they think exists, usually in America. I first heard this line in a small sidewalk cafe where a waiter ran over the list of his cousins and aunts and uncles in America, in our cities of steel and coal, and then leaned down and whispered in my ear, though no one was near enough to hear even had he shouted. "You know," he said, "Communism is no good." That was his whole revelation and it came out under great pressure. Such people are their own foreign ambassadors; they have their own foreign policy which amounts to establishing relations with America, even if through its humblest and most random representatives.

It is this mentality which lay behind a story a friend once told me. When one branch of his relations had a short visit from a successful American cousin, they all appeared before him in their worst apparel and talked at length about their poverty. The generous American was moved by their miserable appearance and—as his Yugoslav cousins had hoped—sent them a great package stuffed with clothes. But much to their chagrin, he did not send them the smart new things they expected from the New World, but castoffs he thought would keep them warm. They were ashamed to wear them and felt they had been insulted.

I ceased to have such encounters almost completely when my foreignness had rubbed off a bit. But I once got a close view of a disturbing example of this appeal of the unhappy to Americans who come with money and with sympathies ready to be touched by the agonized cries of the oppressed. A small party of New Yorkers I met during their short stopover in Belgrade had with them a young Yugoslav woman whom they had met in a museum. The girl spoke some English and had been kind enough to show them the sights of the city. A relation surprisingly intimate for such a short acquaintance had grown up between the girl and the two women of the party. They told me they found her the unhappiest creature they had ever met. She and her mother, she had told them, lived in one room and would never be able to move "because new apartments are built only for officials." She could not go on with her studies or get a better job because she was outside the party. When the New Yorkers bought a pocketbook for her as a little remembrance, she took the purse and began to cry. "The secret police," she said, "will come to ask me where I got this."

In a half-hour conversation I had with the girl in her own language, she talked only of her personal unhappiness. She was indeed wretched but her misery had nothing to do with the party, the secret police, or the privileges of officials. Her mother had lived in darkness and mourning since April 1941 when the invading Germans aimlessly shot her father and brother. Now, she said, her mother no longer mourned her own but grieved "for all those who died and left no one behind to grieve for them." She herself had married a successful young man six months before, but now she had left him to return to mother's gloomy company. "Mother is right," she told me, "it is a mistake to live in the world."

I learned from occasions like this that those who present themselves as opposed to the regime gauge the accosted foreigner's reactions very carefully. As soon as they discover that a foreigner knows enough to see the absurdity in remarks like "apartments are built only for officials," the spiel changes. With some, like this girl, it changes to personal sorrow. With others, like a tailor I talked to, it becomes more complicated.

One afternoon as I stood captive at a fitting, the tailor began, "The Communists are great and could stay in power forever if it weren't for certain details of their system." I asked him to give me some examples. "Our people are working hard to develop the country," he said, "but they [the Communist leaders] are spending money on nonsense." Again I asked for specifics. His idea of "nonsense" turned out to be picking up the check when foreigners came on business and were taken to dinner at a modern hotel near his shop. Then he got down to matters closer to his heart. "In this commune," he said, "there are ten tailors; four of us work and are on top, why must we have competition from those other six who do not work?" At this I mentioned that in America the tailors had virtually disappeared in my lifetime for purely economic reasons and the present economic trend in Yugoslavia would surely eliminate the six and leave the four. Then he switched to taxes—the income tax rate, he said, went as high as 50 percent. I remarked that it went higher in America. "But that is only for industrialists. I am just a poor man who works in a little shop and if she works overtime"—he pointed to the young schoolgirl who was always sitting in a corner of his shop stitching or ripping seams—"I have to pay a fine of fifty thousand dinars. Besides, the tax people make me add fifty percent to my ordinary tax payment, in order, they say, to make up for what I put in my pocket." I pressed him and he admitted that all the artisans, including himself, put their income in two piles, one to be declared for taxes and one to keep all to themselves.

Unfortunately, it is not simply those who are against the regime who watch carefully what they say to foreigners and gauge their reactions. Those who support the regime often act as if they feel an official responsibility for the impression gained of their country. At first they can be exasperatingly noncommittal or so full of easy praise for the system that they give exactly the opposite impression from the one they desire to give. The reaction of a foreigner to one of these encomiums is that the problems must be so horrendous that everyone is afraid to admit them. I met many such people, both officially and unofficially, and each time they gave me a gloomy feeling about the country, a suspicion that something worse than anything I knew must be going on. What always made me feel most optimistic was a lively conversation with some thoughtful man who knew the country's problems and did not need to hide them in order to maintain his belief that things were going ahead and that the ideals of socialism and democracy were slowly coming into reality. Fortunately I had the opportunity to talk with many people in and out of the government, in and out of the party, important people and unimportant people, who found themselves in a peculiarly complicated agony about aims and ideals, about the quality of the revolution and the ideas of the present, about the new creations and the new responsibilities of the future—and who were open in their talk and in their ranging criticisms of the way things stood. A country with such ideals as the Yugoslavs have set for themselves cannot go forward without this agony on the part of serious and conscientious people who are not afraid to recognize and admit their problems. And these are the people from whom a foreigner can learn something reliable.

Perhaps the essential thing I learned was that Yugoslavia is not a ready-made society patiently standing still to be cataglogued and described but a society whose every feature is in the process of continuous change. If this process were simply quantitative—raising the standard of living, increasing the number of schools, hospitals, factories, roads, and bridges, improving the skills and knowledge of the people, and the like—then we might still be able to gauge quickly and easily what is happening there, for the quantitative revolution is universal or soon will be, and we are now so accustomed to it that it might be taken as a constant and reasonably predictable characteristic of the present world. What makes Yugoslavia unique and contradictory is the fact that in a country just emerging from underdevelopment and with a bloody and complicated past, a Communist Party built up during the Stalin era has begun to organize society on the basis of ideas which grow out of and continue the traditions of Western democratic and socialist theory. A new kind of democracy which may contribute to solving the contemporary problem of concentration of power exists alongside a familiar kind of dictatorship. But their coexistence is not static. The dictatorship is no longer the seat of all the power, and the democracy is no longer an empty form. Nor have the state and party become figureheads and the people independent rulers. Real power is being constantly transferred from the center outward. The commune, the business enterprise, and the individual citizen and worker are daily finding more possibilities open for their initiative. Partly, in fact, the dispersal of power seems to be delayed by the slowness of these basic social units to take up the responsibilities that are offered. Partly too, of course, many people at the center have found it difficult to give up their power. There are hesitations and shifts and obstacles and difficulties on all sides. Extremely advanced ideas and possibilities are enmeshed with some of the most old-fashioned Marxist notions. One sees every kind of undemocratic practice alongside evidence of a new kind of democracy. One finds everything to criticize, and yet, as one American professor put it, "There are no criticisms the Yugoslavs haven't already made themselves."

II

The Epic Once Lived

The Balkans have never been simple—particularly that flank of the peninsula now occupied by the Socialist Federal Republic of Yugoslavia. Two of my Yugoslav friends were rather bitterly amused when their son in the second grade wrote the following description of the Nazi occupation of Yugoslavia in his school notebook: "Our country is very large and very rich, and that is why the Germans wanted to take it from us." Unfortunately, conquest cannot be explained so easily. In reality, the history of this half of the Balkan peninsula is one of horrible poverty, bitter division, and pitiable fragmentation; the helplessness of its under-development drew in outside forces like a vacuum; it sat like a bird's egg in the nutcracker of East and West; it lay open and it lay between.

Of the six republics which make up what is now Yugoslavia, three were under the Turks for over four centuries: Serbia, Macedonia, and Bosnia-Hercegovina. After several rebellions, Serbia gained full independence in the nineteenth century. Macedonia was freed only fifty years ago by the Balkan Wars. Bosnia-Hercegovina was released by the Turks in the 1870's, only to become part of the Austro-Hungarian Empire (it was here that the explosive brew of World War I received its igniting spark, when a Bosnian patriot shot the Archduke Ferdinand in Sarajevo, the capital of Bosnia).

Two of the other republics—Croatia and Slovenia—belonged for centuries to the Austrian Empire, and part of Slovenia was later taken over by Italy and held until World War II. The Adriatic coast was at various times under the Venetians, the Austrians, and the Italians. Only the high barren mountains of the tiny republic of Montenegro remained independent.

In the First World War the Serbs fought heroically with the Allies, suffering great losses; after the Armistice the Kingdom of South Slavs, Yugoslavia, was formed, covering almost the same territory as the present Yugoslavia—a territory about the size of Virginia and North Carolina combined. But in the new nation the Serbs behaved much as rulers over the rest of the country, aggravating nationalist feelings. In this kingdom of 16 million people there were three religions: Catholic, Orthodox, and Moslem; and two languages: Slovenian and Serbo-Croatian. Serbo-Croatian included not only its present three dialects and two alphabets but also—much to the disgust of the strongly nationalist Macedonians —the Slavic tongue spoken in Macedonia, which was not recognized as a separate language until after the Second World War. Mutual hatred divided Serbs from Croats, Macedonians from Serbs, Croats from Slovenians, and all of them from the large minority groups of Hungarians, Rumanians, and Albanians. The cultural differences covered the whole range from West to East— from the Germanized Slovenians to the Moslem Macedonians.

These unique confrontations of East and West, the great natural beauty of the country, and the quaint backwardness of its inhabitants made Yugoslavia a marvel for tourists, but few came. There were no roads or railroads except for the few built by the Austrians in their former territory. There was little industry except for a few minor factories owned for the most part by foreigners; a few large farms in the plains north of Belgrade were mechanized with steam tractors; there were mines owned by foreigners—British, French, Austrian, German; and for the rest there was subsistence farming, illiteracy, poverty, filth, disease, superstition, and confusion.

The Kingdom of the South Slavs was incapable of solving its

problems. The constitutional monarchy degenerated into a royal dictatorship; the jails were filled; the leader of the Croatian Peasant Party was murdered on the floor of the parliament; and in 1934 the king himself was shot by a Croatian fascist. The country was ruled by a small clique who profited heavily from transactions in which foreign industrialists gained access to the country's natural resources. The end of this period came with the most brutal of all the occupations of Yugoslavia.

The four years 1941-1945 brought the bloody and complicated history of the Yugoslavs to a climax of horror and heroism. The Germans invaded in April 1941; the Yugoslav army was promptly defeated and the government fled to London. The Italians took over Montenegro, the coast, and part of Slovenia; the Bulgarians moved into Macedonia; and the Germans occupied the rest of the country. In Croatia, a puppet state was set up under a Croatian fascist group called the Ustashe.

A few Serbian army officers under a colonel named Drazha Mihajlovich took to the woods. These people, known as the Chetniks, were the first to offer resistance to the occupiers. Then, in June of 1941, Tito and the Yugoslav Communist Party called for general armed rebellion, and the call found response in varying degrees over the whole country. The heroic example offered by members of the Communist Party, and the incredible organization and administrative energy of the party itself eventually made a disciplined army out of spontaneous uprisings and popular bitterness against the occupiers. This force, known as the Yugoslav Partisans, fought both occupiers and collaborators, at first working with the Chetnik army officers but later fighting many of them when they turned out to be more anti-Communist than anti-Nazi. After 1943 the Partisans had the material support of the Allies and later they received fighting assistance from the Russians on the Eastern front near Belgrade. But the liberation of their country was properly their own, and with their victory Yugoslavia became a socialist country under the revolutionary dictatorship of the Communist Party.

In that struggle the Yugoslavs lost 10 percent of their population; the material loss in factories, railroads, bridges, farm stock and produce, tools, and machinery was equal to three-and-a-half times the country's annual income—the largest loss relative to national income of any country in the war.

After the liberation it took two years of hard labor to bring the economy back up to its prewar level; at the same time the Yugoslavs had to begin constructing an industrial base in order to develop what was fundamentally an extremely backward economy. And the new socialist government had to consolidate its hold over a country torn apart by old dissensions and by a war and revolution. Meanwhile, though the country was no longer occupied, it found itself in a new and surprising subjection to the socialist colonialism of the Soviet Union.

In 1948 the Yugoslavs broke with the Russians to make their own independent way as a nation and to build socialism according to their own lights. The successful resistance by the postwar government to the pressures of Russia and the Cominform countries, the desperately needed military and economic assistance from the United States, and the government's firm policy of suppressing division among Yugoslavs along the old lines, whether national, religious, or political, laid the foundations for stable development. In the twenty years since the war the country has not split apart along any of the old seams of division, the government of the Communist Party has been consistently stable and progressively more liberal, and since 1956 economic development has been very rapid.

Much of the credit for these successes belongs to a Croatian named Josip Broz, one of whose conspiratorial names was Tito.* In 1937 he was chosen by Moscow to head the Yugoslav Communist Party. When Tito took over, the party was a tiny faction-

---

* There are two excellent biographies of Tito in English: *The Heretic; The Life and Times of Josip Broz Tito* by Fitzroy MacLean (New York: Harper, 1957), who was the chief British liaison officer to the Partisans; and *Tito* by Vladimir Dedijer (New York: Simon and Schuster, 1953), a Yugoslav journalist who is the best chronicler of the war in Yugoslavia. These two books also give the best descriptions of general events in Yugoslavia during and immediately after the war.

ridden underground organization whose leaders were not even in Yugoslavia but in Vienna. He gave the organization new life, and by the time the Germans invaded, its 12,000 members were capable, disciplined, and devoted.

Without the war Tito's name might never have become known even to most Yugoslavs. But soon after the 1941 uprising the Germans posted his picture all over the walls of the major cities and towns with an offer of a reward for his head. And suddenly he was known to everyone. Belgrade friends have told me that when people saw the picture their reaction was exactly the reverse of what the Germans expected. They said to themselves, "A man with such a face cannot be bad"; and many who would otherwise have remained uninvolved were moved by the posters to set out and join the Partisans.

What the war made of Tito is less important than what Tito made of the war. His strategy was such that an overwhelmingly superior German force was never able to defeat his Partisans; and they drew ever increasing support from the population—partly because of their heroism in the face of fantastic odds, partly because of their rigid discipline, which punished stealing or looting by death, and finally because the Partisans stood consistently for Yugoslav unity at a time when the country was literally being torn apart.

Fighting the war and making a revolution went hand in hand for the Communists, but it was not Tito's policy to put the revolution ahead of national independence. When it came to the test, though he had been trained in Moscow and was committed to its policies, he proved to be a Yugoslav first. In 1943 he took steps to form a provisional government on liberated territory in spite of Russian objections. He obtained an agreement from Stalin that Soviet soldiers who brought the Eastern front into Yugoslavia would not remain after the Germans retreated. When in 1948 the choice lay between an independent Yugoslavia and a Russian-dominated government, Tito chose independence, though a large section of his own party opposed him. This was the final proof for most Yugoslavs that, Communist or no, Tito was a great patriot.

The decisions Tito made in those years of crisis during and immediately after the war laid the foundations for present-day Yugoslavia. The critical years are now long past, and his role in domestic affairs is no longer so important. Now in his seventies, he spends more time at his villa on the Adriatic island of Brioni than in the capital; and he appears in the news mainly when he is entertaining foreign dignitaries. But he continues to be revered by Communists and non-Communists alike as a great national hero and as a living symbol of Yugoslav unity and independence. Though Yugoslavs are full of jokes about socialism, I never once heard a joke directed against Tito, even from the most determined opponents of the regime. And indeed, many people talk as if he had nothing to do with any of the mistakes or failings of the postwar government; somehow they seem to think he is "above" politics. This reverence for Tito cannot be explained by assuming that he is "running" Yugoslavia today or dictating all the major decisions; rather, I think it makes sense only in the context of what the war meant and what it continues to mean for every Yugoslav over thirty.

Those four years were much to suffer even for those who did not fight. Nearly two million people were killed, and it was a rare family that did not lose someone. Hundreds of thousands of Yugoslavs were transported to labor camps in Germany and other hundreds of thousands were forced to work for the Axis war effort in Yugoslavia itself. Even the mildest form of civilian involvement—the shortages of food, clothing, and fuel—went far beyond the use of substitutes and rationing. It meant disease, hunger, and cold.

The collapse of the Yugoslav Royal Army was immediate but the occupation was never calm. The occupiers deliberately fanned all the flames of nationalist and religious hatred and distrust, with devastating effectiveness. There were massacres of religious minorities in Croatia and in Bosnia-Hercegovina. There was constant sabotage, terrorism, and demolition. Trains were blown up with regularity; field crops and full barns were burned; bridges were destroyed; whole villages were razed in the guerrilla fighting or for reprisal. Citizens were snatched from the streets or their homes to die as hostages—100 Yugoslavs for every German soldier found dead, 50 Yugoslavs for every German wounded. In Kraguyevats, a town of 40,000 people, 7,000 men and boys were grabbed up and hastily shot in the course of a single day. Public hangings were staged in parks and on main thoroughfares to frighten a rebellious population; and Jews, Gypsies, and political prisoners were executed as fast as graves could be dug. Even at its most ordinary, the occupation meant uncertainty about one's fate and about the fates of all those from whom one had been separated. For four years the war was always there, showing itself in ever more horrifying forms. This experience cut very deep into people's lives and it is there today, not far beneath the surface. No one escaped it all and most Yugoslavs knew a great deal of it.

I encountered it in everyone about whom I learned anything personal, for people almost always spoke first of those years. Mirko, a student of electrical engineering, was eight when the war began. His father and older brother were among the Communists rounded up in the first days of the occupation, and they were both shot in a concentration camp on the edge of Belgrade. Mirko's father-in-law, a political leader in his village, was shot from ambush at the end of the war. The family still does not know whether the motive was political or personal; perhaps it was both. At the age of thirteen, Mariya, a secretary now, spent her days searching for food to take to her parents and older sister, who had become implicated with collaborators and had been placed in three different jails many miles apart. Mariya's husband once told me how, early in the war, his older brother had criticized a comrade in the Communist Youth Organization for being reluctant to take a message to a nearby town when the Germans had been alerted along the route. "I'm not afraid," he said, "I'll go." He was captured and transported to Germany; there he succumbed to experiments with injections of kerosene into his bloodstream. Rado, a typist, was left an orphan at the age of ten. His only close relative, an older sister, was killed in one of the vicious battles at the end of the war when the retreating Germans slaughtered the Partisans, who were unused to fighting on level ground. Dragan, an accountant, was fourteen when a German ammunition dump exploded in his town of 12,000, killing one-third of the population. Dane, a research chemist, recalls walking to school at the age of ten and seeing corpses so frequently that he eventually thought nothing of it. Slavko, a painter, was put in a concentration camp with his mother at the age of nine. Bora, a psychologist, was nine when the Germans entered his family's apartment in the dead of night and took his father away. When Ratko, another psychologist, was returning to Belgrade from the country, a bridge under his train was blown up. His car, untouched by the explosion, was pulled off the damaged bridge to safety. Looking back, he watched the train's last car, filled with German soldiers, drop into the river below.

Such things shape a generation, and few members of the present generation were spared them. Even now most Yugoslavs between thirty and fifty begin with what they suffered during the war when they want to explain how they have become what they are.

The war also shaped this generation by what it called upon them to do. Though in 1941 Yugoslavia had been a nation for less than a quarter of a century, it underwent one of those deep spring changes in which old kings and counselors topple from decrepitude and then new kings and counselors rise up to lead a people.

That generation was terribly young for the task it undertook. In the museum of Mostar in Hercegovina, where the fighting was extremely vicious, there is a permanent exhibition of documents from the war. On one wall the black letters of a simple memorial stand over snapshots of the hundreds from that immediate region who died in the fighting. The small photos are ranged in rows of thirty or forty. A man who could not read the memorial might think these were the annual pictures from the local high school. The older men and women are so few they might have been the teachers. And in Mostar, which is not a big town, the young people who took an active part in the war must indeed have represented an entire high school generation.

Pero, one of my first acquaintances in Yugoslavia, was not yet in high school when he began to fight. Now a sophisticated young man in a gray flannel suit, showing many traces of his five years spent in England, he often mentioned one thing and another about the Partisan war during our long conversations. But even when the bits and pieces had fitted into some coherent whole, it was difficult for me to imagine him as he had been twenty years before, though I once saw a snapshot of him at fourteen holding an automatic rifle which looked too big for such a small boy even to lift.

He was one of five children of a police official whose job before the war included putting Communists in jail. His oldest sister was a Communist student at the time of the invasion. She had already participated in hunger strikes and other political protests and then had gone into the Partisans and become the first woman commissar. At one time she was a commissar to a legendary commander who died heroically in a crucial battle in 1943. He was a mountainous Montenegrin who would not take shelter in battle but would answer enemy fire standing fully exposed in front of his men. It was important for the new commissar to establish her authority by overcoming the traditional Montenegrin feeling that women are inferior, and in their first battle she exposed herself beside the reckless commander. He ordered her back but she insisted on standing with him. When she was wounded in the leg the commander wept, and thereafter he took cover.

Eventually all seven members of Pero's family joined the Partisans, but for the first year or two the younger children were still sometimes at home. They were allowed to pass the Italian checkpoints to go into the mountains for firewood and could therefore serve as couriers to take food, messages, and even ammunition to the Partisan detachments in the woods. Pero once told me how they would rob the Italian ammunition stores kept in the cellar of one of the town's public buildings. The barred cellar windows were even with the ground. Pero, who was then twelve, would stand with other boys of his age by one of the windows while his fearless little brother of eight entered through the bars. The older boys would grow jittery while they waited, but the eight-year-old, his shirt bulging with grenades, would come squirming out calmly like a boy who has been stealing apples. Not all the stolen munitions reached the Partisans: from every lot the boys took a dividend of live grenades for their war games in the rocky hills. Later, when wearing uniforms and carrying rifles, they sometimes spurted bullets around each other's feet for fun. Pero marvels now at this recklessness and at how little they seemed to know about military things. They thought it was safer, for instance, to run toward the noise of a falling bomb than to take cover. And they thought if they did not look up at airplanes they would be invisible to those in the plane.

But these stories come from the fringes of the war. Though there were women and children and old people in the Partisans, the real brunt of the fighting was borne by young men in their late teens and twenties and early thirties. Many did not survive. Those who did were more profoundly affected by the war than any child could have been. They experienced incredible privations and witnessed the slaughter and sacrifice of their generation.

One morning in a modern office I heard a veteran tell a story which illustrates very well the hardships and heroism of those years. There were long periods, he said, when his detachment lived on meals of one spoonful of porridge or cheese, and sometimes there was but one meal a day. They were constantly on the march to avoid the enemy offensives. Every day was another long step toward final exhaustion and starvation. Every man had suffered more than he could stand, so that there was no question of anyone still having a reserve of physical strength. Yet when it came time to share out the pitifully small rations, the men did not all behave alike. Some would rush toward the pot to get their spoonful, unable to bear those last few minutes of restraint. Looking at them, one could not but think of the way men act in crowds, when they have abandoned their self-consciousness. There was, of course, no reason to hold back any longer. They had borne the privations and sacrifices as well as any, and now that the time had come to eat, there was no shame in admitting the weaknesses of the body. Yet some men, mainly uneducated workers and peasants with little knowledge of ideas or of what are considered the sophisticated decencies, would walk slowly to one side and stand easily with their arms folded, deliberately ignoring the pot of food and the rush the others were making for their rations. This, said my friend, was their moment, when they showed their sense of what it meant to be a man. For many of them, that struggle, in which a man's life was not a very large possession, must have meant their one opportunity to show their sense of nobility and their ability to live up to it. "You should have seen the way they stood there with their heads up high," he said, "they had the pride and dignity of kings."

That was the end of the veteran's story, but it is not quite the end of mine. He was an impressive teller of tales and when he reached the end he had rendered his audience silent and fully appreciative. As he stood there in the center of the room, representing to us the majestic pose of those who did not hurry for their food, the door opened quietly and a man entered from another office with some papers. He paid no attention to what was going on, and with those noble Partisans right there before our eyes we paid him no notice. He put down his papers without a word and retreated, passing the storyteller as if he were not there. Only as he opened the door did he say under his breath, as if to himself, "Yes, that's the way it was. In those days it was the thing to be a hero." And then he smiled at me, probably the only one who had not heard the story before. I was not, his smile said, to take his irony for bitterness, but neither was I to forget that it was irony.

Sometimes the irony can be disquieting. One evening a group of drunks were sitting at adjacent tables in one corner of a crowded Belgrade restaurant. Suddenly the voices from that side of the restaurant went up in pitch and volume and when we all turned we saw what might be called an inebriated circus: the drunks were doing tricks like monkeys. The audience frowned in disapproval but continued to look on. One big fellow in the center of this chorus line was in that rare phase of drunkenness which is near madness, when a man seems literally to be possessed of some devil. What was most interesting about his performance was that his subconscious had chosen to pour out an ironic survey of recent history. "Long live Stalin!" he shouted, and then in a singsong recitation he passed on to the feats he performed in the war. "My sister is a national hero! . . ." he yelled, in a voice which shook the remaining diners out of their privacy, ". . . and we gave birth to this country." And then with an audience of two or three hundred under his complete command, he began to chant a tune much resembling "Onward Christian Soldiers," all the while crossing himself, doffing his beret like Maurice Chevalier, and executing the vaudeville step once called "Shuffling off to Buffalo." His song went: "Workers are we, the educated workers, the best people, the tested people, the workers, the educated workers—dee dee dum, dee dee dum, dee dee dee." And we all looked on, residents of a world much further removed from his than the distance between sobriety and drunkenness. In the messy denouement the audience showed its annoyance but nevertheless paid him a certain respect, for like the holy and protected idiot of Russia in Boris' time, he spoke some truth. His irony was aimed at the history of that audience, and though he was mad drunk and drowning in that drunkenness, the audience knew his madness touched something true about them.

Was he mocking the oversimple slogans of an earlier time, or was he suggesting that the revolution and its ideals were being forgotten? I was not certain. Both attitudes were common. And to be sure, as the revolutionary ideals are becoming more complex and realistic, life is becoming more comfortable.

Twenty years have passed since the war and Yugoslavia has come a long way. Times have changed both outside the country and within it. Now it is even amusing to read the Partisan slogan and password "Death to Fascism—Freedom to the People" at the bottom of bank notices which declare that checkbook No. 12345 has been lost and will be invalidated if not found within thirty days. In the inconspicuous places where it has stuck fast, this anomalous war cry has come to sound like bombast. The Fascists are gone now; men die of old age in their bed; and freedom to the people means solving the housing shortage, raising personal incomes, getting more buses for city transportation, inventing a better marketing and distribution system for farm produce, and moving along the slow, complicated process of building a new kind of democratic society—none of which can be done with either slogans or guns.

The inflexible attitudes of wartime or immediately afterward will no longer do. Peaceful development demands an essentially different atmosphere. It is time to be judicious, to penetrate to the fine points, to register all the complications, to find fruitful compromises. Now it is not the shock worker who is needed but the man who does excellent work in a reasonable time, whether he is a lathe operator or a politician. But this demand for essential change in work and attitudes comes upon a generation which has known only crisis in its entire adult life. Crisis, it turns out, can become a habit and emergence from crisis a spiritual difficulty of great proportions.

Pero, who had only reached his middle teens when the war ended, is one of those who have kept up with the changing needs of his country. One Saturday evening he told me he was going out to shoot crows the next day. "This will be the first time," he said, "that I've touched a gun since the war." He went on to explain that he had changed completely in temperament in the last twenty years. As a youngster, he said, he hanged dogs and cats for amusement. In the Partisans he served as executioner and had no difficulty whatsoever in shooting the enemy prisoners who were put before him. One incident had stuck in his mind very vividly. He was crossing a street when a retreating German threw himself under a truck right at his feet. The skull collapsed and the brain spurted onto Pero's trousers; yet he stood there calmly and continued eating a roll. Not until an old woman came up and asked him, "Son, how can you be so callous?" did he realize that there was anything odd in his behavior. Now, he said, he felt faint at the sight of blood or when he had to see someone in pain. Firearms and explosives frighten him. He has reflected a good deal on war and believes he could not fight again. He feels he would be tortured every moment by something that never occurred to him as a boy: that the enemy soldier is an ordinary man like himself, wishing no one harm on his own account, going into battle like himself with frightened thoughts that he might be killed, with longing for his family.

Pero has changed in other ways as well. During the war he thought the victorious revolution would immediately open the doors to paradise. He soon learned that a change in ownership could not in itself develop the country's economy or educate its population or establish the complicated systems by which societies manage to operate smoothly. During the war he imagined a world divided into black and white, into Communist and anti-Communist, into imperialist and socialist. He soon learned that though capitalism and socialism are clearly distinct principles, a man needs many other categories if he is going to compare the world's various economic and social systems realistically. Pero is now one of those who see that the development of socialism in Yugoslavia depends on increased democratization and liberalization and is hampered by authoritarian and illiberal measures. He has the optimism about people that is the basis for all democratic feelings. He is one of the young who are anxious to solve the complicated problems of creating modern socialist society; often they are impatient with the older men who have held responsible positions since the war and are less educated than the young and less enthusiastic about what can be done.

There are many others like Pero who know that dogmas and holy memories will not help to make democratic socialism; but there are also many who find it difficult to keep pace with the changes in the society they fought to create. At times since the war's end some men have doubtless wondered whether they might not better have died young and innocent, doing the simple good and brave thing that had to be done. Their names would have enjoyed eternal glory and gratitude, and they would have known nothing of the revolutions that followed the first one. There is only one death, but after the first revolution, there is always the second revolution, or at least the revolution's second phase, its second wave—which is followed by the third and the fourth until the revolution has become so complicated that some of its old defenders lose their bearings. They have to be told they are blocking the road. Attitudes and measures which once served become not only ineffectual but even destructive with the changing times. That moment of the first revolution, 1941-1945, was a moment of great clarity for those who fought on the Partisan side. They—particularly the Communists among them—felt the rightness of the cause to be as far beyond doubt as the evil committed by their enemies. They knew they were right and they knew who their enemies were. All the rest was tactics, and they devoted themselves to the struggle without dividing their energy or their certainty.

It is tragic how little is won by fighting, no matter how or why it is done. The victor gets only the victory and that little bit of the future he might have created as he fought. All the rest has to be created in a never-ending struggle. And often a man who has been precisely with the times during the war and revolution afterward finds himself left behind in the new struggles, no longer with the right rhythm, confused and out of step. I knew a number of such men in Yugoslavia. Some of them were still young, in their middle forties; they were men who had borne the brunt of the war and afterward were put in positions of responsibility—mayors of communes, directors of factories, and the like. They have worked conscientiously and honestly and have always tried to follow the line set down by their party leaders, but very often they come short of the spirit of their leaders' attempts to move toward a more liberal society, and as a result they hinder those attempts. These are people who cannot conceive of the party's becoming less important, who think that a non-Communist is necessarily less worthy than a Communist, who believe that when President Tito makes a speech to the country he is really only issuing directives to them, who still see the world in the black-and-white terms of wartime, and who are bewildered by the present. I once heard such a man address a sizable meeting called to elect delegates to the commune assembly. Although the manner of election and the assembly's functions had been formulated upon new and complicated democratic theories, the man who got up to speak on these very new matters could find nothing so timely to quote as Tito's speeches from 1943.

I heard many remarks in this vein: "When I was a boy I set out with my grandfather's old pistol and used it to assassinate the local chief of police under the occupation. When I was in my teens I ate grass to live, and all my son knows of hunger is choosing whether he will eat veal or pork. There's something wrong with this generation." Or "During the war we thought only about making a good society. Now people think only about themselves," or "In the war we cared about ideals; now the world we created cares only about the dinar."

The connection between too great attachment to the war and an illiberal influence in Yugoslavia's present development is elusive but very important. Perhaps what distinguishes the "conservatives" most clearly is their desire for simplicity and their tendency to compare the present only with the past rather than also or primarily with the possibilities of the future. These are the traits of conservatives everywhere. But Yugoslav theories have no place for conservatism; they envision an "imaginative" society, permanently oriented toward the future. The past served that vision by opening up possibilities to be exploited in the present; the task of the present is to open up the way to future possibilities. This view rejects not only the past but also simplicity, and the conservatives, living already in a world that is no longer simple, appeal sentimentally and sanctimoniously to the war.

These people are not the only war remnants. There are others who feel that their past heroism and sacrifices entitle them to everlasting respect and rewards. They feel they deserve high positions and good salaries; and if they act autocratically or stupidly or even misuse their positions, they should be excused, for the country owes its very existence to them.

All these people, the honest and the dishonest ones, were given responsible positions right after the war, when the country was torn by the divisions and hatreds of that war and the new regime understandably wanted men it could trust in positions of power, whatever their other qualifications. Something else is required now, but it is not so simple to get rid of the incompetent. The society cannot condemn them unless they break its laws, nor can it refuse to recognize that their sacrifices do deserve something. And certainly the society cannot simply throw out of their jobs thousands of fairly young men—often still in their late forties or early fifties —who do happen to be the people who helped to make that society possible and who support it entirely, even if their support is sometimes embarrassing.

The army, whose postwar officers were largely men who had proved themselves during the war, made perhaps the earliest and most resolute effort to solve this problem. Skill in the primitive warfare of the Partisans could not continue to be the sole criterion of the fitness of officers in an army whose function was changing rapidly. Modern military techniques and equipment had to be mastered. The country's young men had to be given training which would make them useful in modern warfare if the country was threatened. Roads had to be built and power lines set up for the country's economy. And young men from the backward countryside had to be given some notion of the aims of the new Yugoslavia and some education which would make it easier for them to contribute to the country's development. Many of the officers promoted during the war were unfit for these new tasks. So a system of examinations was established. Every officer had to take periodic tests to qualify for the next higher rank. If he failed to earn promotion, he was pensioned off. Those who remained in military service were thus forced to make a special effort to keep up with the times. As one of my friends in the government remarked: "That's the decent way to get rid of the know-nothings. Cover them with medals and send them home."

In the spring and summer of 1963 there was a mass turnover in the government. A new constitution enacted in April provided for broader civil liberties and more political democracy, and the elections which followed brought a very high percentage of new and frequently younger people into the federal, republic, and commune parliamentary assemblies (the average age of deputies is now about forty). This was the signal for similar changes in the administration. "After the war," a high government official told me, "it was natural that the Partisans should move into the top positions of the government. They stayed in those positions a long time since they were still young men. Without the new constitution, which offered a good excuse for making changes, they would have stayed much longer. Now eighty-five percent of the old guard have taken their pensions. This was a serious blow to many, for they are not old. But I can tell you that this has brought an enormous change in the atmosphere in government circles. Many important jobs are now held by young intellectuals who've gotten better educations than the older leaders and who've sloughed off many of the dogmas of the past. Besides, they've traveled abroad and learned what makes society run in other places and that helps them to think more practically."

Factories and offices are now establishing new requirements for various jobs and pensioning off their old heroes as soon as they can afford to do so. But this moves gradually, and there are complications. In one office I knew of, the standards set for a particular job were met by everyone except one man; he was not penalized for doing less work and this caused great dissatisfaction among the others. As one man resignedly told me, "What's to be done? He's an old hero, you can't throw him out or cut his salary; you can only wait two more years until he's old enough for a pension. But in the meantime his example doesn't encourage the rest of us to work harder."

The complications brought by war heroes are equaled by those which have resulted from the polarization of the revolution. Though many Yugoslavs who opposed the Communists left the country after the war, many others did not, and like some heroes, they often continue to think in the black-and-white terms of the past. I knew one young man, a brilliant psychologist, who was doing very well in this new society but who hated it bitterly because his father, a prewar army officer, had been put in prison right after the war and had died there. This personal tragedy discouraged the young man from doing what he might have done to help make the kind of society he wanted. I knew other people whose careers had come to a halt because they were on the wrong side in the war. They had been trained for the diplomatic corps or the army or the civil service and then suddenly the posts were given to people on the winning side. Many people remained permanently embittered, and by losing their talents, training, and support the society has suffered. One of my acquaintances, the son of a wealthy family, was studying law at the Sorbonne when the war broke out. He fought with the Chetniks—against the Partisans— and after the war, though he was not put in jail, there was no question of finishing law school. His family lost its wealth and the new regime was hardly likely to finance Paris schooling for one of its opponents. The young man ended up doing nothing with himself, working as a clerk, his sense of reality distorted by the past and its bitterness. One day he started off too quickly when a traffic light changed, and he rammed a car in front of him. Though clearly at fault, he insisted over and over again that he was fined only because the man he ran into worked for the secret police and had "pull."

But just as the war heroes are gradually losing their importance, such people as he are slowly overcoming their hatred. If the clearest sign of the first was the announcement in 1963 that no more applications would be accepted for the coveted medal given to people who fought with the Partisans from the first year of the war, the clearest sign I saw of the second came in a conversation I had with a bright young teenager from an old wealthy family. His father and uncle, he said, had become implicated with the Chetniks during the war and had lost everything they owned. His uncle left for America. His father stayed, but he remained an opponent of the Communists. The boy went on: "I'm against socialism too; I think capitalism is a better system, but I don't think we can go back to capitalism here, because I don't think history is moving that way."

The bitterness of the opponents and the vainglory of the heroes are dying away first with the young. Older people still feel they have to justify themselves, to explain what they were and did during the war. Men who were no longer young when the war came and did not fight, also talk about the war a great deal, perhaps because it robbed them of a clearly defined place in the new society at an age when they normally would have been in positions of responsibility. They are not of the new nor are they its enemies. They feel superfluous.

Two such men expressed to me sharply contrasting attitudes toward the war and revolution. One is a shrewd old fox who came from a prosperous family in the provinces and studied abroad; he returned to his country in the twenties "to enlighten his people" with a degree in psychology from Edinburgh. He was involved in prewar politics and interested in socialism, but the prewar parties, he says, were going in circles. "We were all exhausted," he told me. "None of the parties had anything to offer the people. We couldn't solve the prewar problems, much less the problems brought by the coming of war." During the Popular Front days immediately after the liberation, this man held various official posts. Once a government ministry sent some clothes to the national press agency where he was employed, and he was put in charge of distribution. "I found I had something to learn about socialism," he said, "for when I began to give the suits to the chauffeurs and messengers, those who were the poorest dressed, I got a telephone call from the minister himself. He told me to distribute the clothes first to the officials of the agency, for those in positions of responsibility—who would have to meet foreigners—would need them most, and there was no telling when any more would be available." This gap in outlook between the prewar politician's hankering for an idyllic socialism and the Communist's appeal to realism has never been entirely healed. This man, now over sixty, cannot but take a broad and often ironic look at the events taking place around him. Though in general his criticisms reflect his anomalous position in the new society, he said one thing which gave me great amusement. "This government," he said, "is bringing us many things we needed and in a great many ways the atmosphere of the country is changing for the better. One's objections to the political prohibitions must always be put against the multitude of opportunities which men are given in this society to

be political; but one element of this atmosphere makes things very
difficult for me: the taboo on black thoughts. I would feel ten
years younger if I could just enjoy some downright rotten cyni-
cism."

The man prospers at present as a scholar. But he is out of touch
with new developments. He is overcautious in his talk and imag-
ines that the government is still interested in the activities of those
who were involved in politics before the war. And somehow,
though he admits the dynamism of postwar Yugoslavia, he has
never fully recognized that the Communists met the challenge
which he and his contemporaries in prewar politics could not meet.
One day he said to me, "Socialism is a fine thing but not such a
fine thing a man would want to die for it." To a man who has
never had to fight, the statement seems nothing more than good
sense, but in Yugoslavia—with its fresh memory of hundreds of
thousands of young people who gave their lives generously and
bravely out of the hope of socialism—it is a thought which most
people would find black and cynical indeed.

Another elderly acquaintance, a peasant in his sixties, looked
upon much the same experience from a very different point of
view. "I have friends in important positions now," he told me,
"and they often say, 'You see, Slavko, what a mistake you made in
not setting out with us. Think where you would have been today!'
And do you know what I think? I think that nine chances out of
ten I would have been dead if I had gone with them when they
asked me to join in 1941. Why didn't I go? There it is, I didn't
want to die. I love life too much; it is my weakness, and I just
couldn't give it up."

His sense of shame for his weakness is reflected now in his
refusal to join the party. Not having had the courage to join them
in the treacherous days of 1941, he is too proud to join them now
that it is safe. "I tell them I'm too old now to join," he says. "But I
respect what they did and what they are doing. They are doing a
good job of leading the country; they are taking it forward. I try
to do what I can to help them. I am for them and I tell people so.
How can you be opposed to people who come into your village

and ask only that you let them work to make things better? Even if I objected to them, I would not speak against them. I would only be silent."

The point is not that the war and revolution should be forgotten; it is that they must be seen in perspective. When those who owe their positions only to services rendered in the war have been awarded their medals and are drawing their pensions; when men no longer think they are suspect for their wartime actions and others do not strive for recognition of theirs; and when the bitterness is erased and the polarization has been resolved, then the war and revolution will take their rightful place among the violent and heroic exploits of a people with an old epic tradition. The saga of those ragged barefoot men with red stars on their caps will always fill a central place in the annals of Yugoslavia, for they not only united their country and kept it alive, they laid the foundations for a new society and provided that society with the vision and energy for building an independent future.

III

The Vision and the Daylight

THE DESCRIPTION Yugoslavs give of the political atmosphere in their country in the years between the end of the war and the break with Stalin and the Cominform in 1948 corresponds in most essential points to the conception we Westerners typically hold of "the Communist state." The new revolutionary government took all power into its own hands and ruled by decree. The state managed the economy to the last detail; decisions made at the top of the government administration were transmitted down a rigid chain-of-command which extended to the lowest official in the smallest office of the most remote commune. The party organization reinforced this structure and made state power even more complete and effective.

When in 1948 Yugoslav leaders began to inveigh against Stalinism, bureaucracy, and centralization, they were in effect overthrowing the founding principles of the government they had set up and were running at that very moment.* But 1948 did not mean an abrupt change in ways of running things. One Yugoslav social

* There is debate about whether the present Yugoslav ideology developed as a result of the break with Stalin or whether Yugoslav views had developed by 1948 to the point where conflict was inevitable. The point is very interesting, but one can appreciate the intimate connection between Yugoslav socialist theory and the break with Stalin without saying definitely that one was cause and the other clearly effect.

scientist estimates that as late as 1950 the federal government was more involved in making specific decisions and issuing executive orders than in formulating policy and drafting laws. The abortive hard-line policy to force private farmers into cooperatives came over two years after the break with Russia. In the early and middle fifties Milovan Djilas was making criticisms of Yugoslav conditions which coincided with those which he and other Yugoslav leaders were making against Stalinist bureaucracy. Today there is no question that the dominant trends in Yugoslavia are toward freedom, local self-government, and the rule of law. But whenever a new step is made in any of these directions, it is always furthered along by new admissions that, after all, many aspects of the old bureaucratic period have hung on.

The changes since 1948, then, have been gradual, but the conflict with the Cominform signified a fundamental change in principles and approach which has put the Yugoslavs in a separate class among Communist countries. In its purest, most idealistic form, the theory of Yugoslavian government was explained to me by a federal undersecretary.

"One important reason for rigid centralism," he said, "is the intellectual's illusion that he can make society operate more rationally and justly if he has all the power centralized in his own hands. He lets himself believe that society is like a laboratory and he is the benevolent scientist who will set everything right and will solve all problems scientifically. I can remember the day, for instance, when fifteen pairs of shoes were lined up on the desk of the minister of the leather industry so that he could decide which styles would be mass-produced for the population. This wasn't science but autocracy. At one time we thought people's needs could be met in this way, but reality taught us otherwise."

He leaned forward and took up his pencil and a pad of paper. "Here is that idea," he said, scratching a doodle onto the paper. "Now we have put this idea in the archives." He tore the sheet from the pad and made as if to file it away. "For us that conception of society has only a historical interest. We have learned that the intellectual never knows enough to run society humanely and rationally from the center, no matter how great his power. Society is not a laboratory but a great sea; like the sea it has certain overall patterns, but there are too many variables and unpredictables. And the intellectual's desire to make society his laboratory leads in but one direction: toward greater centralization of power. For he attempts to explain each of his failures by the liberties someone else has taken, spoiling his plan. Men do not act or react in the way the intellectual-scientist or philosopher-king expects them to. In his supreme vanity and arrogance he lays the fault to them instead of to himself, and his idea of a remedy is to gain even greater control over them. That pattern of thinking leads to Stalinism and nowhere else. We have left that road.

"In our view socialism cannot be created by merely assuming power, nationalizing property, and managing the economy in the name of the working people. True socialism must be democratic and it cannot be so until socialist governments solve the problem of putting the ultimate power into the hands of the ordinary citizen and worker. In attempting to solve this problem the revolutionary party and government must help him to become a free, competent, and responsible agent in social life. Forms must be set up so that he can act on his own to change his living conditions, his economic situation, and the public decisions which affect his life. This cannot be done if we tolerate a huge bureaucracy with all the power concentrated at the top. Power must be decentralized and decision-making must be brought down to the local level where the ordinary citizen and ordinary worker can actually become engaged in public and business policy. The key, then, to our thinking is decentralization, for we believe that rationality and humanism, energetic economic activity and democratic freedom all lie in that direction."

"This view is bound to appeal to most democrats," I said, "but aren't you really talking about the virtues of anarchy while the dominant forces today are pushing us toward bigness and central control?"

"No," he answered, "we are not anarchists, and we are definitely trying to make a place for ourselves in the modern world.

We of course don't suppose that every individual can go his own way or that society can be broken up into little independent and unconnected communities. Modern techniques of efficient production, organization, and communications require complex interrelationships and these interrelationships lead to social organization in a pyramidal form with a broad base and a narrow summit. In other words, the need for efficiency leads to integration in political, social, and economic life. But decentralization and integration need not be contradictory processes. The important thing is to decide which powers and functions should be exercised at the local level and which should be delegated to central or higher bodies. In Yugoslavia we are organizing society so as to decentralize the power to make specific decisions; the power to plan, coordinate, and set standards and procedures is integrated. The individual departments of a factory, for instance, are coordinated by an overall production plan, but the departments are given wide latitude in deciding themselves how to organize their share of the work. Individual economic enterprises are allowed to compete freely on the open market, but through social plans, investment policies, and tax laws the society as a whole exercises a general influence on the shape of the economy. In principle, tax revenues are collected at the local level and spent there, but the specific expenditures of local communities are guided by a plan which sets the proportions for the total national expenditures according to the general needs of the country.

"We hope that this combination of integration and decentralization will provide efficiency and at the same time help to reverse the chain-of-command—so that orders go from the bottom upwards, and not from the top downwards. We are trying to make those who plan, coordinate, and regulate at the higher levels responsive and responsible to the people below them. Their function is to check excesses and lend guidance; they must not be allowed to become power elites, in whatever mixture of bureaucrats, managers, and politicians. The essential power of decision must be kept as close as possible to the individual worker and citizen. It is he, after all, who has created the social wealth; it is in his interests that social decisions ought to be made in a democratic society; and he is in the best position to know what his needs are and to see that they are met."

The undersecretary's remarks contain the kernel of the thinking that has guided Yugoslav development in the last fifteen years. Decentralization has been the general trend in both the economy and the government. The process of reducing the power at the top and encouraging independence and responsibility at the bottom has gone faster and further in the economy than in government administration, since the Yugoslavs consider the economy to be the dominant and determining force in society, and they therefore consider economic democracy more urgent than political democracy. The economy has been decentralized in three principal ways: industries formerly grouped together under the supervision of government ministries have been broken up into individual enterprises; financial regulations on economic activity have either been removed or reduced to encourage independent initiative on the part of enterprises and market competition between them; and management has passed to the enterprises themselves.

The enterprises are run by a workers' council elected by the whole labor force of the enterprise and a professional staff hired by the workers' council (though it acts on the recommendation of the commune in hiring its general director). The professional staff, whose job is to conduct day-to-day business, is equivalent to management in an American company. The workers' council supervises the enterprise's general activities in the interests of the employees, much as a board of directors in an American company outlines long-range policy in the interests of shareholders. The workers' council also elects a smaller group called the managing board, which oversees the details of the business and works directly with the professional staff in carrying out the policy established by the workers' council.

This system, called "workers' self-management" has been instituted in every factory, office, and store; in very small enterprises, the whole labor force may act as the workers' council; in very large enterprises, there may be not only a central council but also councils for individual departments, or "economic units," as the Yugo-slavs call them. The same system has been instituted in hospitals, schools, universities, and even government agencies, as well as on socialist farms and in farmers' cooperatives. Recently a variation of the system has even been introduced into banking: instead of being controlled by the central National Bank, local banks are now to be managed by a council of depositors, formed to oversee the work of the bank staff and to make long-range policy.

The theory behind workers' management is that it makes no sense to say that "the people own the means of production" if they have no control over them. Furthermore, since a man spends a large part of his life at a job, and since his job is his most vital association with society, the effort to give him some influence over the conditions of his immediate environment must begin at his place of work. Finally, in an age when much of the work in factories and offices is dull and repetitious, workers' management is a counterbalance to the dehumanization of technological processes, in that it gives workers the power and responsibility to make business decisions.

In the federal government power is gradually shifting from the close-knit group of original leaders to a broad circle of younger people. The Federal Executive Council, composed of the top men, was until recently all powerful. That small group drafted nearly all the laws passed by the parliament, enacted countless executive decrees and resolutions, and controlled the whole administrative apparatus of the federal government. Now the parliament is being encouraged to pass legislation more independently and the administration is being put under its authority.

At the same time that power is shifting from the executive to the legislative branch of government, federal authority is undergoing a gradual process of dispersal to the six republics; from there it is filtering down to the districts and communes. As a rule, the federal parliament now passes general laws setting standards for the whole country; the republic parliament passes more detailed regulations, and the commune then interprets and implements these regulations and adds its own, according to its particular situation. The commune has thus become the basic administrative unit of government. Its political authority and independence are becoming greater as its share of tax revenue increases and as economic development brings more varied and complex local problems and possibilities. The commune not only handles communal services and utilities, police and fire protection, schools, social security, medical care, and welfare, but in many cases it has the money to make large investments in housing, factories, stores, and tourist facilities. The commune thus plays a very important role in shaping the local economy and local social and political development.

Each of the country's 581 communes is small enough to allow all citizens to understand and participate in the public business done in it (in size and population a commune corresponds to an average American county). Each commune is run by an assembly with two houses. One house deals with general communal matters and is elected by the whole adult population, by precincts. The other house deals with local commercial and economic matters and is elected only by those people who are employed: they send delegates from the places where they work. The two houses meet in joint session to decide on matters which concern them both. Assembly committees have direct authority over all appointed administrative officials. The police force of the commune, for example, is ultimately responsible, not to the mayor or some appointed administrator, but to a committee of the assembly.

The commune assembly is nominated and elected directly by the local citizens, who may recall their representatives. The members of the assembly elect delegates to the republic and federal parliaments. Thus, above the commune level the citizens are represented only indirectly. Below the commune assembly there is a body even closer to the citizens. This is the meeting of electors, held at frequent intervals in every precinct. At these meetings the voters hear explanations of important legislation, discuss current issues, and put questions and suggestions to their local representatives. There has been serious talk of giving the meeting of electors official status and legal power to instruct their delegates to the commune assembly, but this idea has not yet been acted upon.

The system of political self-government at the commune level and workers' self-management in business is designed to give the ordinary man an active role in shaping his society. The theory is that when society's business is carried on under his eye and within his reach, he can influence the decisions on how much money his commune collects in taxes, how those revenues are spent, how his office or factory is run, and how his children are educated. Through his participation in public business he can become more than a reader of large-circulation dailies and a voter in periodic mass elections; he can enrich his life and become the master of his fate.

For over fifteen years the Yugoslav leaders have been drafting and enacting laws to systematically apply this theory of participatory democracy to all areas of social life. But devising a theory and making it work in practice are two quite different matters. As a Yugoslav sociologist has put it, "We could pass a law tomorrow saying that every Yugoslav ought to live well, but that in itself wouldn't raise the standard of living for a single citizen."

Some of the obstacles standing in the way of decentralization and direct democracy in Yugoslavia come from the past, while others are being created by the present. It is difficult to say which are harder to overcome, but those associated with the initial backwardness of the country are in many ways the most painful, both for the society and for the individual citizen.

Until the end of the Second World War, traffic in Yugoslavia meant buggies and oxcarts on dirt paths. The streets of towns were wide seas of mud in spring and fall. The farmer's plowshare was often made of wood; his pitchfork was merely a tree branch with the bark peeled off. As late as the 1930's there were still houses which had greased paper instead of glass in the windows. Farming was done on tiny scattered plots; industry consisted of artisan workshops rather than modern factories; illiteracy was high; diseases like tuberculosis and typhus were widespread; average life expectancy was low.

Since the war every energy has been channeled toward building a prosperous modern society. But the struggle to develop economically and to bring about social and political change is played out against the weighty and frequently obtrusive background of the crude and primitive past. The working force in the growing industries and services is coming largely from overpopulated and backward peasant villages. The new workers are men and women whose entire working experience has been in an agriculture which was virtually untouched by modern agricultural science. An engineer in a Zagreb machine tools factory once told me that the greatest problem with these workers was that they did not understand *why* their work should be precise. "Once they understand the reasons for precision they're capable of achieving it," he said, "but getting them to understand is the harder part. After all, in the world they come from everything is imprecise: the weather, the crop, the harvest, and all of their farming methods. Many of them have never used any kind of machine."

And many of them have grown up in a world governed by traditions and superstitions which have hardly changed since the Middle Ages. A recent documentary film on the construction of the main highway to Greece contained a pathetic scene. The road was to pass through a deep bog to which the local Macedonian peasants attributed healing powers. As the bulldozers plied back and forth, plowing great drifts of dry dirt into the bog, the peasants, who had waded out into the bog as a sign of protest and were standing in mud up to their necks, were forced into a slow retreat. The wry commentary was "Sometimes it is easier to move mountains than people."

The migration is thus not simply from village to town, from field work to factory, from a farmer's to a worker's schedule; it is a migration across boundaries of culture and over perhaps as many as four or five centuries. A man in a train once said to me, "We're going so slow you'd think we were crawling over eggs." The disproportion in the image of a diesel locomotive "crawling over eggs" is a measure of the distance between the Yugoslav barnyard——where even now half the population resides—and the modern industrial society coming to birth with its laboratories, complicated economics, technological marvels, and sophisticated theories of workers' management.

A peasant who sells his little plot of worn-out land in the village and moves to the city is taking the first step toward modern life. But once he gets to the city, the difficulties he confronts are immense. Since he usually starts out without any of the skills needed in the cities, he must take a job at the bottom of the wage scale. As a newcomer he also starts out at the bottom of the waiting list for a socialized apartment. During the first few years in town he has to work forty-two hours a week (until recently it was forty-eight,) adjust to an entirely new kind of environment, and—unless relatives take him in—live with his family in the cramped quarters of a rented room for which he pays the landlord a sizable part of his salary. To make ends meet, even on the poorest diet and with no luxuries, his wife may also have to take a job, leaving no one to take care of the children. If the newcomer is going to get out of this situation he will have to go to night school in order to acquire the skills required for better jobs with better salaries.

With time and perseverance most of the economic difficulties can be solved. The towns—and the factories themselves—provide many opportunities for both husband and wife to get more education and technical training. In a few years they will get to the top of the waiting list for apartments; once the housing problem is solved, they can live reasonably well on their combined salaries. Meantime, they do have social security benefits and free medical care, and their children are going to better schools and becoming assimilated into city life without their parents' difficulties.

But the psychological strain of adjustment to city ways is very great. Many of these people have never seen a television set or used a telephone; they are frightened by city traffic and unaccustomed to the complex technicalities of city life which can be handled informally in the rural village. Without the customs and traditions of the village or the long-established patterns of big agricultural families to provide a framework for their individual lives, many of them are quite lost. A professor of psychology once told me the story of a woman recently from a village who lived high up in a city apartment building, surrounded by people she did not know. The woman sank into a depression and was sent to a psychiatrist. The psychiatrist, who was apparently more alive to Freud than to the social realities of the case before him, tested the woman and talked with her and finally said that basically she hated her husband and wanted to kill her baby. The diagnosis so shocked the poor peasant woman that she really did lose her mental balance and was taken to a hospital. There, a more sensible psychiatrist examined her and said, "The trouble with you is that you don't have neighbors to drink coffee with or a cow to milk or a garden to tend; isn't that right?" The woman nodded. "I thought so," the psychiatrist said. "There's nothing wrong with you. Go on home and keep your house clean; the rest will take care of itself." Other stories reflect the peasants' pathetic efforts to hold their world together. One family housed a cow in its second-story apartment in Sarajevo. Two goats dwelt on the thirteenth story of a Belgrade apartment house. The family kept them in the bathroom and milked them regularly. They even chopped up the tile floor so that the animals would not find it so slippery underfoot.

Inevitably, some of those who come to town from the country are not up to the great effort and strain required to make the full transition from a backward agriculture to responsible jobs in modern factories and offices. Although economic incentives are used to encourage men to improve their skills, they do not always work. Sometimes men are uninterested in trying to improve their lot because even the marginal existence provided by the lowest factory wages seems comfortable compared to the misery they were accustomed to on the farm. For others this marginal existence in the city is so difficult and discouraging that they haven't the energy to try to push up. Still others simply try to "beat the system" by doing as little as possible and getting as much as possible, honestly or dishonestly. In one of the most common jokes in Belgrade, a former peasant tells his foreman: "You can never pay me so little but what I can't work less."

Beating the system by idleness and deceit became an engrained habit in those parts of Yugoslavia which were under the Turks for centuries. Then it was the only way to survive; now, when it is far from the best way to get ahead, it causes untold problems. The messenger at the publishing house where I worked—a man in his fifties—was a fairly typical case. He was paid the lowest salary in the publishing house for delivering messages and manuscripts and doing other errands around the city. Since the publishing house lacked funds to build apartments for its employees, he had to rent from a private owner. His wife was not well enough to work and he had two children to support. When I once asked him where he was going on his vacation, he replied, "I'm going to stay home in bed. I haven't got the money to do anything else." His situation was pitiable indeed. But on the other hand, he never to my knowledge made any efforts to learn any skills and he was not even a reliable messenger. When told it was urgent that he deliver a manuscript on his way home, he was apt to wait until next day to deliver it. If there was any trouble, he would declare with a bland smile that the person was not at home the day before. He made little profits on the bus tickets the publishing house provided him for traveling around the city. When he entered a bus, he would hide from the conductor in the crowd and save the ticket for his own use. Once when he and I happened to get on a bus at the same time and I stepped up to pay the conductor, he said, "Don't do that; only fools pay."

Factory workers who still live in the country and do some farming constitute another problem. Many of them take jobs in the factory not to change their way of life but simply to keep their farms going. The low salary they are paid as unskilled labor is regarded as a supplement to the income from the farm. More important, the job assures them free medical care and other fringe benefits which cut down expenses at home. They spend their leisure hours and many working days doing farm work. In the summer they come to work with their scythes, already tired out from cutting hay in the early morning. Their rate of absenteeism is high all year round, and since they are not really interested in factory work but still consider themselves farmers, they make mistakes, have a high accident rate, and are not interested in new skills and advancement.

These people inevitably make problems in a society trying to industrialize rapidly and do away with a primitive past. The problems have very little to do with ideology: the difficulties a Yugoslav plant engineer experiences with peasant workers sound very much like those of American textile mill managers when the industry moved south and started hiring farmers. I often heard old residents of Belgrade talk about the slovenliness of new families in from the country in the way that proper middle-class people used to talk in this country about southern Negroes or West Virginia coal miners.

The impatience of educated townspeople toward the peasants sometimes leads to comically desperate efforts to implant new attitudes. In one factory I knew of, where many of the workers were coming from the peasantry, the workers' council bought shoes for them and ruled that no one could wear peasant sandals to work. These handmade slippers were too clear a sign that the workers were not modern. Another factory built new apartments to house its workers and offered to get consumer credit for everybody to buy new furniture, but no one was allowed to bring furniture from the village to put in these modern apartments.

As is always the case with comprehensive and hurried assaults upon the old and exaltation of the new, there are excesses. An American forester who spent a summer advising the Yugoslavs on their timber resources told me that when he said geese were used in the State of Washington to rid pine seedling plantations of insects, his Yugoslav hosts only laughed. Few things are as easy to come by in Yugoslavia as geese, but the proponents of the "new" must have insecticides and a mechanical sprayer. The forester got a similar reaction when he mentioned that some American timber crews were going back to mules because they found them more economical than diesel tractors. Again the Yugoslavs laughed. Getting rid of the goose and the mule was precisely what building the new Yugoslavia meant to them.

I found much of this impatience with the "old" very understandable, for the technicians, the accountants, the electricians, and doctors and engineers and teachers who complained most about the primitivism of their country were contributing more than anyone else in order to bring up the rest of the population. Their salaries were much higher than those of messengers, ditchdiggers, janitors, and street cleaners, but they were still low even though these people were supplying the skills most needed to develop a modern industrial society. If the factories and offices did not have to set aside large funds for training new workers and providing them with social security benefits, medical care, and apartments, these people would get higher salaries. Likewise, the high taxes their factories and offices paid in order to finance new schools, hospitals, housing developments, and factories in the most backward parts of the country were coming partly out of their pockets.

Frequently I felt that people blamed far too much on the prewar past. Many of the country's most serious problems are part and parcel of the present and even specific to the kind of development the Yugoslavs have planned for themselves. If they were less resolute about their vision of society, they might use models from East and West with only minor adaptations. But in neither direction can they find forms designed for the combination of socialism, decentralization, and democracy which they envisage. When they take ideas from other places, they must thoroughly rework them to fit the Yugoslav context. In attempting to solve problems on their own, they have had to take an experimental, trial-and-error approach. This has meant a merciless succession of changes in systems and procedures, so that people sometimes become dizzy and fatigued with the sheer effort to keep up-to-date.

Another serious problem is that decentralization has sometimes stimulated local self-interest to the point where the country's overall needs are neglected. For example, in order to compete on foreign markets Yugoslavia must become engaged in mass production. Related enterprises all over the country must therefore work out joint production plans. But the resistance, sometimes based on economic self-interest and sometimes on local chauvinism, is fierce, and the federal government no longer has the power to settle the matter.

Furthermore, breaking down the bureaucracy of the federal government through decentralization has led to the formation of smaller bureaucracies at lower levels—in the republics and communes. Complaints about abuses of power at the local level face the country's leaders with a dilemma. Should they try to exercise control from the top and thus retreat from the goal of decentralization? Or should they wait until democratic pressure from below becomes strong enough to correct these abuses? Now they generally choose the latter course, but the strong government of the past created a kind of dependence which is hard to break away from. Now, when faced with a local political problem, people do not think first of solving it themselves; their first idea is to demand that some stronger force from above solve the problem for them.

Whenever my friends felt gloomy about the way things were going, they would recite endless tales of officiousness, collusion, corruption, and injustice: officials were receiving consultant fees not because they did any work but because they had power and connections; store managers were falsifying inventories, embezzling large sums, and escaping to France; directors of enterprises were misusing company cars and the money allowed them for entertaining foreign customers; in some places workers were being fired for daring to criticize the management; one official had connived with a construction company to get himself a villa in the country with a fishpond and a special road to the property—all out of company funds; restaurant managers were watering the wine and brandy to cheat both their customers and their enterprises; personnel managers were using police methods to spy on employees; and petty local officials were often ignorant, arrogant, and highhanded. But my friends all too often blamed these things on "too much democracy." Instead of thinking about using democracy to solve the problems from below, they wanted Draconian measures from above.

If decentralization is to work effectively, the problems must be solved from below. But this means that the people in the commune must be familiar with the complicated problems of social security, urban planning, education, housing, and economic development. The workers in enterprises must understand business law, market research, investment finance, personnel policy, international trade, and labor productivity. They must all be trained in the procedures of democracy; they must learn to distinguish their interests as individual citizens from their responsibilities to society as a whole; and they must learn to see where their interests and the interests of society coincide. Obviously, people will actually run things only where and when they have developed their capacities as managers. And the process of developing these capacities is delicate and slow in a country where people who have inherited little of the social discipline of the industrialized countries are attempting to run factories and schools and communes.

The Communist Party (in Yugoslavia it is now called the League of Communists) is supposed to play a "leading role" in making decentralization and self-management work. Although workers' councils, managing boards, assemblies, and other public bodies have the legal right to manage all public business, the party is in a position to exercise a certain control, or at least surveillance, over their work. The party has its basic organizations in every factory, office, school, hospital, commune, and precinct; and it is involved through these organizations and through its individual members in practically every public decision. On the one hand, the local party organization is supposed to help develop the system of workers' management and local self-government and to see that it is not held back by officials and bureaucrats who wish to retain the power they once had; on the other, the leadership of the Communists is supposed to prevent the kinds of foolishness, irresponsibility, shortsightedness, and outright corruption which are bound to appear when a large part of the decision-making in society is turned over to a population which has had little experience with democracy, business, or modern technology.

The party organization in a factory, for example, is supposed to act as a check on a factory director who tries to railroad his policies through the workers' council. It can either fight him openly or exert pressure behind the scenes, pointing out that he is bound by party discipline (almost all factory directors are party members) to respect the independence of the workers' council. At the same time, party members on the workers' council are supposed to argue for efficiency and wise business policies and to oppose decisions which are against the interests of the factory and the larger community. For example, they would be expected to fight against a council decision to raise everybody's salary before money had been set aside to invest in new machines.

Party members are not always a majority on the council, but since the party is a well-organized group, it can usually push its policies through even when its members are in a minority. Perhaps inevitably, the basic party organization frequently abuses this power. In theory, party activity is supposed to reinforce workers' control and set the workers on their own feet as active and responsible managers. The party program clearly establishes these goals for its members. But whether the basic party organization follows these principles or not often depends on the personal and political makeup of the people who run the organization. The character of the factory director is particularly important, since he is the key individual in the factory. He will almost certainly be a Communist, but there are all sorts of Communists. He may be either an optimist or a pessimist regarding the potential strength and ability of the workers' council in his factory. He may be well trained and competent at his own job and be glad that the workers' council is capable of doing its job, or he may be incompetent and afraid that an independent workers' council will oppose him and lay bare his shortcomings. He may be devoted to the principles laid down by the party or he may be a man who does not give a damn for any principles, for the workers in his factory, the economic success of his enterprise, or even the laws of the country.

An autocratic director may get control over the party organization in the factory and then use it to control everyone else. In drawing up the nominations for the workers' council, the director, the union secretary, and the party secretary may pick only yes-men as candidates. Then the director can present his recommendations to the workers' council as if they were commands. Even the managing board may function as a unanimous yes-man. The labor force of the enterprise may be given so little information about how the business is being run that they are not in a position to

oppose the director. He will consult only with the party organization and together they will manage the enterprise. They may manage it well or poorly, but in either case they are placing their own
power before the goal of workers' management.

Ultimately, party activity in factories and offices depends on the
self-confidence and responsibility of the labor force, and specifi-
cally on the strength of the workers' council. Legally, the council
has the right to make the decisions. But in some places the workers
are ill-prepared or even reluctant to take on the responsibility of
managing the business, or they are afraid of the director and his
professional staff; in these places the party organization usually
takes a very active role in workers' management. Ideally, the effect
of the party's activity is to make the workers independent. Once
the non-Communist members are not afraid to stand up for their
rights and are able to establish successful business policies, the
Communists become less important. In some enterprises the basic
party organizations have already become superfluous and inactive.
One friend of mine who was the secretary of the party organization
in his office said that they had so little to do they acted primarily
as a discussion group.

This "withering away of the party" has not happened in very
many places. Yet progress is being made. It is now ten years since
the workers' councils were established as the first new form of
direct democracy. In these ten years more and more people have
been drawn into the management of the economy. More recently,
increasing numbers of people are being drawn into the work of the
commune. The process of dispersing power and responsibility
downward and outward is not smooth. Much depends on local
situations and even on the very personalities of the people involved, both the Communists and the ordinary citizens who are
supposed to assume responsibility. Perhaps, however, we can take
the fact that the making of democracy in Yugoslavia does not go
smoothly or without headaches as an indication that the Yugoslavs
are facing some of the essential difficulties contained in the democratic ideal.

IV

The Social Adventure

Y UGOSLAVIA'S international role as a leader of the nonaligned nations and as an independent voice in the world's ideological contentions is much better known than its unique and lively internal life. The reasons for this are obvious: most of what is written about the domestic situation is locked in a little-known language, and Yugoslav thinking is embedded in a complex tradition and context which are frequently misunderstood by outsiders.

Furthermore, it is extremely difficult to define the elements which give Yugoslavia its liveliness. Partly this liveliness must come from the character of the people themselves. The South Slavs have long been known for their fearlessness and emotional excitability, and for their shrewd sense of reality. Yugoslavs enter recklessly into difficult situations and relations; they are realistic enough to expect as a matter of course that one and the same man will show at some moments exalted nobility and at others dastardly, equally extreme baseness; and they are sensitive, expressive, and maneuverable enough to enliven ordinary conversations with unspoken implications and tact.

The rebellious independence which kept them alive as a people during centuries of occupation is as evident today as ever. Sometimes it shades over into an exuberance and unruliness completely foreign to Anglo-Saxons. The Yugoslavs tell a story on themselves to illustrate the difference. A dozen Yugoslavs, the story goes, entered a London bus. As the bus moved along they began to sing to pass the time. None of the Englishmen in the bus said a word in protest, but all quietly left at the next stop. I have seen two men come to blows over who was to descend first from a nearly empty Belgrade streetcar. Waiting for movie tickets or trying to get on a bus can be infuriating because so few people have any concept of standing in an orderly line. The absence of an established social discipline has made it easier to introduce the completely new ideas of Yugoslav socialism; at the same time, needless to say, lack of discipline hampers improvement of the system.

Perhaps the national trait which offers greatest support to the new economic, social, and political system is the openness of Yugoslav life. A quarter of a century ago Rebecca West noted this trait in her great journal of a trip through Yugoslavia, *Black Lamb and Grey Falcon,* remarking that nothing was concealed, neither sickness nor fear, sorrow nor anger. Daily life in Yugoslavia today is full of illustrations of this openness and outwardness, which lead to a deep engagement with life. Old women in Belgrade, for instance, are notoriously nosy. They stop and offer advice to any passing young pregnant woman, with no sense that they are violating the young woman's privacy. One day as my wife was returning from the market with some lettuce in her reticule, an old woman astonished her with the question, "Oh, do you have a bird?" She explained that she had noticed the lettuce and assumed it was for a parakeet. Then she asked whether she could have a leaf or two for her bird since she hadn't seen the lettuce in the market and it would be something of a trip to go back. In the market strangers freely ask each other how much they paid for the merchandise collected in their baskets and where they bought it, or give advice about where to buy.

I first witnessed the remarkable ease with which Yugoslavs who have never seen each other before drop into conversation—and even intimacy—on a Yugoslav freighter crossing the Atlantic. Half the passengers were Americans, half Yugoslavs. Though Americans are famous for "getting acquainted," it took five days for us all to call each other by first names, while half an hour out of New York the Yugoslavs were strolling the decks in twos and threes, arms linked, or gathered in little knots of conversation. By dinnertime, passengers, officers, and crew were friends.

Even with its twenty million inhabitants, Yugoslavia is small and the cities are few. Most people are familiar with much of the country and easily find common ground with strangers from the other republics. After nine months in Belgrade I spent a short holiday in Montenegro. The first evening there I chanced to have dinner with a man who knew many of my Belgrade friends through three different connections: he knew the family of one friend because they had grown up together in Chachak, a town in central Serbia; he knew another group of friends because they had done translations for his magazine; and he knew the people I worked with because his magazine had once been located on the floor above my publishing house.

The very terms of address Yugoslavs use with each other seem to be an extension of village familiarity and intimacy: "kinsman," "countryman," "brother," "comrade," "friend." A child who stops someone in the street to ask the time of day says "Uncle" or "Auntie," and older people call anybody younger than themselves "Son" and "Daughter."

Sometimes the old women see themselves as social monitors. One day as my wife parked the car in front of the apartment house next to our own, a woman passing by spoke to her and said, "Why don't you park your car in front of the next house where there is no one living in the basement? Your car will block the view from the basement windows of this house." Not only did this woman not live in that basement apartment and not in that house, we never saw her again on our street. Men also feel free to interfere in certain goings on without being asked. Perhaps one of the reasons why juvenile delinquency is not a great problem in Yugoslav cities is that men are quick to butt into anything suspicious on the part of young boys. If a man sees a boy handling a parked motorcycle or scooter he will tell him to get away without even a break in his step, although he has no idea what the boy's intentions are or who owns the vehicle. One of the best examples I saw of this universal vigilance of adults upon the activities of the young was at an open-air film in the Belgrade soccer stadium. In the section where we were sitting, far up in the stands, a dozen boys in their late teens were amusing themselves by flipping their lighted cigarette butts down into the crowd. Since the stands were crowded and dark, the people down below could not reach the boys and had to suffer this annoying and even dangerous breach of public decency. Then a man of perhaps forty-five, two rows behind the boys, reached down and shook one of the boys so violently by the shoulders that the whole thing was stopped instantly.

In short, the Yugoslav has little of the spectator about him. His primary instinct is to become involved in any public incident he happens to come upon. Everyone who has ridden Belgrade's problematical city transportation for a time has seen how quickly a misadventure or one loud word can turn a crowded bus into an open forum.

This openness and outwardness are such an evident part of one's everyday impressions that one can ask whether the character of this people has not played a part in shaping those socialist institutions which characterize Yugoslavia's independent route toward modern society. There are, after all, other ways of arranging socialist societies. One man can take all the power into his own hands and run the country like a classic dictatorship; or the party can function as a collective dictatorship, managing the government and the economy in the name of the people while discouraging most of them from taking any part in decision-making; or duly elected representatives can wield all the power while allowing the citizens to make decisions only at election time. How much did the previous existence of a strong degree of social outwardness and responsibility figure in the formulation of Yugoslav democratic theories in which the citizen is expected to become directly involved in public business on every side? And, on the other hand, how much have these theories affected the national character? These are not questions I can answer; I pose them only to indicate my suspicion that the Yugoslav character and their new institutions are inextricably entwined.

At the very least we can say that the Yugoslavs are too independent, active, and outgoing to take a passive attitude towards society, and the general political developments since the war have encouraged their outwardness and social involvement at every level. I was often surprised to find that even in the tiniest matters individual citizens were quick to act against anything they considered unjust, instead of patiently submitting or closing their eyes. I was even more surprised to see how often they got results. One of my favorite examples is a man on the trolley car which made its first stop right by a popular restaurant near the center of Belgrade. According to the posted schedule the late night trolley was supposed to arrive at one minute to twelve, but it always came at 12:05—five minutes after the fares were doubled. One night a man got on and refused to pay the double fare. A tremendous argument ensued, with the conductor taking the usual line of petty officials: "I leave the roundhouse when I'm supposed to and it's pure accident the trolley is late; I'm not responsible; I'll throw you off the trolley unless you pay." The rider was adamant: "Your company is consistently and deliberately delaying this trolley in order to make us pay double. I refuse to do it any longer and I shall report you personally and complain to the company." Thereafter the trolley arrived at one minute to midnight.

Many things which in other countries would be accepted as inevitable social ills, such as bureaucratic waste and inefficiency, highhandedness on the part of officials, patronage, and the like, are in Yugoslavia matters of explicit and general public concern. Everything of course is not acted upon, since the dynamics is not always loose enough for much individual action. But the political tension, the desire to act, the consciousness of frustration, and the resentment against constraint are all there. Indifference, apathy, and alienation do exist—sometimes based on bitterness and sometimes on complacency—but they are becoming less important as the scope of individual action expands. Nearly every political speech and declaration asks for more individual participation in the affairs of society, and though there is often a sizable gap between those speeches and what ordinary politicians and officials actually do, the political forms now developing not only require more individual action, they make it harder and harder to set limits to it. Expanding participation by citizens is indeed the keystone of Yugoslav democratic theory; and the whole success of the system depends on the parallel development of forms for individual political action and the readiness of individuals to take a responsible part in public life.

It is not just the political elements of socialization which have been encouraged. The Yugoslav working day, for example, which ends in early afternoon, has been accommodated to the national custom of a large family dinner about three o'clock, two or three hours of rest, and an early evening promenade along the main streets of towns and cities. The life of the coffeehouses and cafes has not only continued but has flourished in a time when funds for luxuries were hardly abundant. Neighborhood cultural centers with auditoriums for films, lectures, adult education, meetings, concerts, art exhibitions, visiting theater troupes, and dances are considered a necessary part of what the Yugoslavs call the "social" standard of living.

To explain the peculiar publicness of Yugoslav life we must note not only the inherent character of the people and their old institutions, but also the kind of policies and programs with which the leaders have sought to evoke the responses of the national character. It is fair to say that for nearly a quarter of a century now this people has been *led*. This is not to say that they have liked everything done by the leaders or that they are entirely happy with the present state of things: at times they have been pushed and they are still prodded on occasion. It is not to say that all the government's efforts, even all those which have been accepted by the people, were the right ones. None of the leaders has ever made such a pretense. Finally, it is not to say that the government's policies have always been deliberate and clear, that it has not wandered or muddled along. Two of the regime's most outstanding qualities have been its ability to rebound and try a new course and its capacity to wade through a sea of embarrassing and worrisome contradictions.

To say, then, that this people has been *led* means none of these things, and yet it means something important. In the first place, it means that the leadership since the war has given the Yugoslavs a feeling of cohesion they did not have before. The Yugoslav Communists made their move to lead the nation before there was any great certainty the Yugoslavs *were* a nation and at a time when the most powerful force in Europe, the Third Reich, had announced its express intention to prove that they would have no future. In twenty-five years of Communist leadership, a national solidarity has developed which, to be sure, is not free of tensions and tests, but which does outweigh the regional, religious, and class antagonisms that split the country apart before the war.

Not only has the postwar leadership given the Yugoslavs an idea of themselves as a nation but it has also provided them with a focus for their unity—the construction of a new kind of socialist democracy. This in turn is giving them a complex social education. However much of Marxism one may wish to question, it is a profound and comprehensive philosophy. A citizen cannot but become more aware of social, political, and economic workings from a familiarity with Marxist terms, concepts, and explanations. And however much Communist politicians use ideology to justify decisions made for reasons unmentioned and pledge allegiance to values which have no part in their actions, they perform an important educational function when they refer constantly to an integral system of explicit ideas and values and explain all their important policies not only in ideological but in technical terms. I have heard men in the Yugoslav government complain that the speeches and articles of the leaders are too theoretical and technical for the ready comprehension of ordinary people. They do indeed make difficult reading matter. The thinking is often tortuous, and the phrases are sometimes obscure. I would even venture to say that some of the jargon represents nothing real in this world. But in spite of the scarcity of plain talk, the political speeches, resolutions, and declarations do convey real thoughts, policies, and interpretations and give at least some of the principal reasons why the government is or is not following a particular policy. These difficult "tracts" (explanations of policy never err on the side of brevity) do offer some dependable link with the consistent body of ideas and values which constitute the Yugoslav "vision," even though the decisions themselves may frequently be presented to the populace as *faits accomplis*. The number of Yugoslavs who can read these long analyses, who know which parts are deadwood to be disregarded, and who can see the real state of things behind the abstract phrases is not small. I talked with a surprising number of ordinary people who could discuss intelligently the problems of industrial growth, labor productivity, decentralization, and self-management.

But the more important role of the government in educating the populace has been indirect, at the grass roots level. Local chapters of the Socialist Alliance of Working People (the mass political organization which serves to rally broad support for government policies) are constantly arranging lectures or discussions on current domestic and international problems in every neighborhood and every community center. Intense public campaigns, during which citizens' meetings are held almost daily, seem to follow one another at very short intervals. Someday there might be a reaction against this large amount of publicly important business. On the other hand, democracy does ultimately mean that ordinary people must take on the burden of public business, and the Yugoslav theory of democracy is based on the idea of spreading the load out to the last reluctant citizen. Before the new constitution was adopted in 1963, the campaign to inform people and encourage them to discuss the draft version, which went on for months in thousands of gatherings large and small, was so intense that few citizens could have remained ignorant of its provisions and problems.

Political speeches and neighborhood discussion would of course be hollow and ineffective if the system itself were not forming the attitudes and exciting the energies which make responsible self-government possible. Unlike the leaders of most other socialist countries, the Yugoslavs have relied very little on coercion or on demagogic posters and slogans which fire up enthusiasm for "building socialism." They have not painted everything in capitalist countries as evil and everything in socialist countries as liberating and good. They very seldom attempt to soften the present reality by appealing to an illusion of future paradise. (A popular Yugoslav joke shows very clearly what these people think of such illusions. Khrushchev was encouraging his people and said, "The Communist society is on the horizon." And a man in the audience spoke up: "I believe you, Comrade Khrushchev. But the thing about the horizon is that no matter how far you go toward it, it always stays the same distance away.") In Yugoslavia dogmatism has been put on the defensive; criticism and admissions of unpleasant realities are increasingly treated as a vital necessity.

This, I think, is the key to the success of the social adventure in Yugoslavia. Instead of pressuring people or using outright force, the Yugoslavs are trying to further the building of socialism by a consistent effort to give the "builders" themselves real incentives and real responsibilities, while at the same time expanding their individual liberties. Authority, decision-making, and financing are being constantly decentralized to encourage every man to take part in the running of his society. The power of the central government is gradually but steadily being dispersed. That power is being taken up by ordinary citizens who are becoming involved not just in political discussion but in political action. Literally hundreds of thousands of people are serving on the councils, boards, and committees which make real decisions in apartment houses, businesses, and farm cooperatives, and thousands of others are sitting in the assemblies which have been set up at every level of the political system, from the federation down to the commune.

Probably the Yugoslav vision of socialist democracy has never been more clearly defined than it is now. It has taken time to work out a set of ideas flexible enough to keep pace with a complex and rapidly changing reality, profound enough to promise long-term validity, and noble enough to excite men's idealism and focus their energy upon building an equitable, sane, and decent society. Until recently the flaws in the ideas and the shortage of real possibilities in the Yugoslav situation were too great to bring the vision and the reality to a bold confrontation. It would be foolish to suggest that the Yugoslavs have even now found the key that opens all doors, but their tentative solution to the problem of power and responsibility in modern society has passed many of the preliminary tests and they are depending upon it with increasing confidence.

Though this is an exciting and important experiment, the atmosphere is not apocalyptic. Yugoslavs take these developments in their stride. They take workers' management very seriously—even soberly. In places where it is not working well, people are tense and resentful and they worry about whether they will ever make anything real of the abstraction. In places where it is working well, people think about it not as an abstraction but as the normal way of dealing with the problems they confront in their business.

But when a man is trying to solve a problem in his factory through argument and discussion with other men, he finds this far more complicated and difficult than simply doing his job according to orders. The opportunity to take part in decision-making unquestionably enriches and broadens a man's life, but at the same time it makes things more difficult because responsibility is after all a burden and must be borne by extra work, through study of issues, and through the complex art of political maneuver.

Making the new democratic forms work and facing the responsibilities which they bring are complicated and difficult tasks. It is only natural that Yugoslavs should sometimes feel nostalgia for the early postwar days when, in spite of the chaos left by the war and the difficulties imposed by a new revolutionary government, it was easy to know what had to be done. What Yugoslavs mention most often from that period is the solidarity they felt in digging themselves out of the rubble and getting the country in working order again. After work, people labored until midnight repairing the damages of war. Later these work brigades, composed mostly of young people, began to lay railroads, build highways, and raise factories and dams. Much of the work was done by hand; concrete was mixed with a shovel and transported in rough hods. In these later days when the situation is not so desperate and when much more thought is given to private luxuries and pleasures and to social problems far more subtle than disease, hunger, and bombed-out buildings, people remember how hard they worked then, but they think more often of the fact that it was easy to work together.

The nostalgia for that spirit of solidarity does not go completely unsatisfied even today. There are still emergencies—like the blizzard I saw one winter in Belgrade—when citizens participate in "work details." One Sunday morning the residents of every apartment house in the city went out to clear the streets, roofs, and sidewalks of three feet of snow which would otherwise have tied up the city for days. Not everyone participated, but enough did to make the individual's share of the work light. And though Yugoslavs guard their private lives as people do in most other places, I am sure it did not occur to anyone that being called upon in this emergency was any sort of invasion of privacy. Most people seemed to enjoy the opportunity to work with the rest of the citizens of their city to do what only such a mass turnout could have done. I heard many people say that they were sorry the spirit one could feel in the city that morning had become so rare.

Aside from general emergencies like blizzards, floods, and earthquakes (of which the country seems to have more than its share), I have seen the "work detail" used for local projects for which there was no money. My apartment in Belgrade overlooked a vacant lot where old bricks and lumber lay in scattered piles. The local youth organization saw the lot could be turned cheaply into a soccer field for the younger boys if the debris were piled neatly to one side. One Saturday the boys carried around mimeographed notices to every apartment in the neighborhood announcing that a work detail would assemble at eight o'clock next morning to clean up the vacant lot; all residents of the quarter would be welcome and their work would be greatly appreciated. Next morning several dozen people formed lines to pass the scattered bricks from hand to hand toward the corner chosen for stacking the debris. Men of fifty on their one day off from the office carefully passed the large bricks to little girls who had turned out even though the bricks were a little heavy for them and the playground was not for them but for their older brothers. The work was not completed for a month or so and, except for the boys who were to use the field, the faces changed every Sunday. The only expense was for the bulldozer which came one day to level the ground.

The youth brigades still go off every summer to work on the highways, but now there are machines to ease the labor and speed the work. Though the brigades are now of little economic importance, they have become a special social institution. Teen-age boys and girls from poor mountain villages and modern city streets, from farms and from factory towns are brought together in a kind of glorified camping expedition. There is a great deal of campfire singing and guitar playing along with the work; young people from backward areas are taught skills; and the old nationalist divisions are softened by the mixture of boys and girls from all the republics.

The country has outlived the time when its solidarity could be founded on collective action in times of distress. Hereafter, self-interest and the general welfare will rarely coincide completely, and the test of the system will be whether or not it leads to satisfaction of both the general and the private. At the moment the emphasis is swinging from public to private because the great common experience of the war is now retreating into the past and because Communist ideology has abandoned many tendencies toward oversocialization and is supporting traditional concepts of the family and the individual; the aim is not to exalt the general over the private but to set up a democratic mechanism which will help individuals to see that much of their private welfare lies in the direction of a general effort toward general improvement.

The passage to a system of direct democracy based on individual initiative is being made as a postwar generation comes of age. Older people show considerable distrust of the youth, who are said to be self-seeking, antisocial, cynical, and apolitical. They see a reflection of this in the young people's attraction to Western films, rock and roll, dungarees (made in Yugoslavia with "Texas" and [counterfeit] leather "Lee" labels), and bouffant hair styles. And the

young people do feel a certain kinship with the despairing and cynical attitudes sometimes voiced by Western youth. It is difficult to estimate the depth of this feeling of living in a world gone wrong: how
much is the result of shallow copying and how much is a true
reflection of what the youth feel about Yugoslav society. Though
many do call themselves "apolitical," they respond to specific issues with great interest, involvement, and determination. They are
concerned about how their universities or factories are run, and
they do not intend to be pushed around. Their attitudes are very
different from those of young people twenty-five years ago, when
"politics" meant a desperate militancy, revolution, and war. But
much of their elders' concern about their attitudes seems simply
the eternal stuffiness of an established generation toward the "up-
starts" of the new generation which is coming along with its own
slant.

This Yugoslav "problem of the generations" is sharpened by the
fact that the older generation, which fought a very bitter war and
revolution and has since that time brought the country such a long
way, is itself still young. These two generations very close in age
are yet very different in the experience through which they have
lived. Each of them feels it has something to teach the other, and
the next decade or so will probably be something of a tug-of-war
between their differing temperaments. But that tug-of-war will be
only a part of the larger struggle of democratic and liberal tendencies against authoritarian and conservative conceptions. This is by
no means only a question of generations. There are old liberals
and young conservatives, and everyone has something of both in
him.

The struggle for accelerated democratic transformation of the
society is a power struggle between these two tendencies but in a
sense it is also a struggle for a new atmosphere, which means that
changes in attitudes are as important as changes in laws. Frequently the letter of the law is applied before its spirit. The change
in attitudes seems to spread by osmosis, independent of large-scale
political action. It seems, for example, largely accidental that the
press is boldly critical in some areas and timid in others: I saw

many cases of sharp criticism springing up in new quarters; usually it was not only unopposed but was supported. A play which turned a Serbian heroic ballad into a slashing attack on the operation of the party and upon "reasons of state" won a prize in Novi Sad for the best dramatic text of the year. A film script which exposed the way in which workers' management is subverted in many Yugoslav enterprises was held back by the council of a film company for more than a year. But when finally produced, the film won first prize at the Yugoslav Film Festival.

There are also reverses on the wide front of the struggle to make lively criticism an accepted element in every area of Yugoslav life. Shortly before I left Yugoslavia, a very sophisticated, up-to-date, and critical weekly on literary and intellectual subjects was denied its government subsidy and had to dissolve. But the paper's final issue was a splendid blast-off, hardly the gesture of men who were very frightened or afraid for their futures. And I learned from one of the editors that they were actually approached to resume publication but refused. Talking to him about problems of public criticism and censorship, I asked what would happen if a novelist treated the still "forbidden" theme of the Cominform split in 1948. He supposed that nothing would happen but doubted that anyone would touch the subject for some time yet. "But," he said, "I've been talking to some younger literary people [he himself is in his early thirties] and they're saying things which shock even me."

The struggle to transform the atmosphere is gradual and local, and frequently it depends on the efforts of individuals to change the situation in which they find themselves. For example, when a friend of mine, the editor of a magazine published in English for foreigners, asked for informal photographs of President Tito, the official photographer offered him only the usual stiff and formal poses. The editor, a very resourceful and insistent young man, sent his own photographer and got poses of Tito sitting with his wife in the backyard swing, standing in shorts with a fish he had caught, filing a piece of metal in his workshop. As soon as they were published, the editor of Belgrade's afternoon paper called to ask how he had gotten those photographs. His paper was always asking for just that kind of pose but had never managed to get one. My friend allowed him to publish some in the paper and a short time later he heard that the official photographer had taken a new position where the pay was better. "Maybe the pay is better in his new job," my friend told me, "but I know he left because his conservative policy on pictures of Tito was finally swept away and he went with it. Tito's new photographer is twenty-three and just out of school. That's significant."

This same friend also told an amusing anecdote to illustrate how the atmosphere depended on people's habits and experience. When he took over the English-language magazine, it was dry and dull and gave a poor impression of Yugoslavia. He felt it should be lively and colorful; he also felt it could win no friends for Yugoslavia if it solemnly repeated slogans instead of showing things as they actually were. Convinced that foreigners would look more kindly on Yugoslavia if they were told the truth, including the difficulties, he set out to find journalists who could write in the way he wanted. Somehow, when they wrote for foreigners, even the most lively and critical of Yugoslav journalists seemed to resort to facile praise. During his initial shortage of writers, the editor asked for an article from a high government official. "I understand what you want to do," the man replied, "and I'm in favor of it, but I can't write that way myself. I can write a government report or an ideological essay, but it's not in me to write what you want. The old habits of mind and style are too strong."

The old habits of mind have taken many people out of the social adventure. A man I worked with in a Belgrade publishing house was a pathetic example of how people can fail to adjust to the rapid tranformations of society. Now in his fifties, Veljko was a young journalist before the war; aware of what was preparing for Yugoslavia, he joined the Communist Party in 1938. He had an uncomplicated faith in the Communist cause, and he told me the hardships of war were far easier to bear for those who believed than for those who were fighting only because there was nothing else for them to do. For some, he said, heroic death for the Communist cause was truly sweet.

After the war Veljko was director of Radio Belgrade and then director of the largest Yugoslav film company. But his pro-Stalinist attitudes cost him his job in 1950, and he was excluded from the party. He did not go to jail, but his troubles broke his spirit. Since then he has worked halfheartedly as a reader in the publishing house.

One day at work I mentioned to him that a French journalist had said there were no coffeehouses in Russia. The coffeehouse is one of Veljko's favorite institutions, and he could not settle it in his mind that socialist Russia did not have them. "That journalist is lying," he replied. "Why should he?" I asked. Someone else in the office added that a friend recently returned from Russia had made the same observation. Veljko scowled.

His criticisms of the present Yugoslav system are contradictory. He bemoans the vanity and greed which prevail, he says, in some of the higher circles. But his idea of a solution to all such problems is "less freedom." Clearly he still hopes to be proved right in thinking that public criticism and democracy will lead to commercialism and dissipate the ideals of the revolution. He has had to give up defending Stalin, but his faith in authoritarianism has not broken. Veljko's rhythm is no longer in time with the prevailing social developments in Yugoslavia, for he no longer shares the spirit which is shaping them, the spirit of more freedom and more democracy. The man who feels nostalgia for the old ways of Stalinism or a hankering for the illusion that rationality can be achieved by central control cannot take the risks or make the efforts necessary to push forward the frontier of openness and press back the frontier of old authoritarian habits.

My friend Ibrahim accepts the vision, but he has not been able to adjust the humanity and rightness of what he believes to the hard daylight of reality. He comes from an old and wealthy Moslem family in Hercegovina. Like so many other young people during the war, he joined the Partisans and at twenty was a colonel. In the early postwar days he was one of the two top leaders of the Communist Youth Organization. Though his position was important and demanded full-time attention, he refused a salary.

Here he got his first lesson in the difference between the timeless idealism with which a man fights a revolution and the realism necessary to transform ideals into practical accomplishments in a postrevolutionary society. His superiors simply reminded him that he would have to have money to live and told him to take the salary. Later Ibrahim became a professor of Marxism in the Advanced Political School, where young men were trained for government service. He lost his post in the middle fifties for encouraging open discussion of Milovan Djilas' criticisms. That was the beginning of his unhappiness. He was thrown out of the party, his wife divorced him, and he went to jail for two years. He came out penniless. And then he had a nervous breakdown.

After a time he put the pieces together again and went to work in a government publishing house, where he became a senior editor. But after a controversy over publishing policies, he quit in anger and moved to a commercial publishing house. There he worked as a junior editor, was elected to the workers' council and the managing board, and made a reputation for himself by his efforts to put some life and force into the discussions and decisions of workers' management. His work was so good that there was serious talk of making him director of a new publishing house. His social and personal rehabilitation appeared complete, and he resolved to go into politics again.

Talking to me about it one day, he said, "You know, I live up near Kalemegdan [the old fortress over the confluence of the Sava and the Danube] and I often walk in the park very early in the morning. I see the workers going off every day to their jobs like a great wave; and one day I thought to myself, 'This is supposed to be a workers' country; there's much yet to be done.' So I resolved to petition the party to be reaccepted, for there's a fight to be made and it will be fought inside the party, not outside. This will be our third revolution," he went on. "The first was in the war and the second was in 1948. This one is the democratic revolution and it's just beginning to move. This time we have to fight in a new way. We couldn't have made the first revolution without faith. This time we can't make it with faith—it's too complicated."

Ibrahim himself was not to fight in the new revolution. Perhaps all the sudden changes and expanding possibilities in his life were too much for him. He suddenly stopped coming to work and began to sit in the cafes day and night, borrowed money from his friends and then avoided them, went off hitchhiking to Hercegovina, fought with his family, and refused to come back to work. After Ibrahim had been absent for a month, the director of the publishing house, who feared and disliked him for his efforts to make workers' management effective, now had good cause for firing him and did so. Ibrahim's hopes of becoming director of the new publishing house vanished. He didn't even bother to petition the party. There was no longer any question of personal success or political action; the question was reduced to simple survival. Somehow he recovered and found part-time work at the government publishing house he had worked for earlier, but the fight for more democracy went on without him.

Ibrahim's great weakness lay in his inability to be a politician. He could not do what a man must do if he wishes to move from ideals to practice; he was not stronger, smarter, and more stable than his opponents. Nor could he maintain the inner tension that comes from constantly squaring vision against reality. And he lacked that determination to see things through which is one of the remarkable qualities of those who are in the mainstream. For an idea of the desirable and possible is not enough to make a social adventure unless men accept the idea that the only way out is the way through.

I heard dozens of good political jokes in Yugoslavia; the intensity of political life and the native ability to look at things from unusual angles makes the country a good breeding ground for them. One is a good illustration of the idea that the only way out is the way through. It is brief and yet gives a very good picture of the tension and the burden of the social adventure. It runs: "Socialism is like an airplane ride; you have broad horizons; you are always a little sick; and you can't get out."

There are two ways of taking the joke. One is the bitter anti-socialist attitude—where the broad horizons represent a futile

Utopia, the nausea represents a stifled hatred, and the confinement is meant literally. Taken in this way, the punch is gone. The joke makes sense only if one applies it to the feelings of a socialist in socialism. Here the airplane ride is a striking image of the extent to which one's imagination, intelligence, and even physical strength are taxed in the building of the good society. The broad horizons are the vision of what could be, the possible and desirable. The nausea is the anguish a man feels in trying to shape the not-very-tractable material of society into something which resembles his vision, and the confinement represents political and intellectual obligation. There is no other where to go. There is no way out, there is only the way through.

The social adventure in which neither Veljko nor Ibrahim was participating—the transformation of Yugoslavia into a democratic society—is being shaped by intellectuals who see their position in the society as one of engagement. They find enough looseness in the political atmosphere to maneuver intellectually and find plenty of problems to work on. At the same time they find that their basic political ideas are being manifested enough in practice so that they can recognize the socialist vision as a premise for thinking about society.

I had a good many conversations during my two years in Belgrade with such a man, Milan, a successful mathematician whose books have been translated into Russian and English, who has lectured in Italy, taught in America, and who is now a member of the Federal Parliament. Milan sees the roots of the present going back to the high schools and universities in the thirties, when exceptional boys were Communists at twelve and thirteen and great numbers were some sort of Marxists at sixteen and seventeen. Even at that time, he says, their Marxism was not dogmatic. Milan himself came from a solid bourgeois family, and in spite of the emptiness and futility he felt in their way of life, he hesitated about going off to the Partisans, until he was finally in the woods one night and his decision was irrevocable. He had chosen to risk his life and there was no way back to the comfortable security of his well-to-do family. Everything, he says, has been different from that moment.

The effect of taking that risk has not died away with the years after the war. It is that decision which each of them took alone twenty years ago, he feels, which gives men like him their special stamp today.

"It may seem paradoxical," Milan once told me, "but we felt that our revolution would make it possible for Yugoslavia to rejoin Western civilization. Now we're feeling the contradictions of this desire. For while the West has the culture, humanism, and democratic traditions which we want to preserve and extend, these values seem threatened in the West itself—by commercialism, a growing division into elites and masses, a stultifying anticommunism, and a reluctance to face the socialist proposition that private economic power throttles democracy."

Though Yugoslavia is still many years away from the affluence which comes with technological development, intellectuals like Milan are already moving on to the problems of humanizing modern industrial society and improving the quality of life, problems which concern many Westerners. Milan is a clever politician and now that he is a member of parliament, he has the power to put some of his ideas into practice. He is typical of the energy of this society. There are many like him, young government officials, scientists, technicians, and professors—Communists who were in the Partisans as boys and were given a good education after the war both in Yugoslavia and abroad. They are the people who are pushing liberalization of the system.

But as the society changes, more and more people with another history and other attitudes are becoming involved in the push. My friend Ratko illustrates the success the Communists are having in getting the support of trained and educated non-Communists and the extent to which the ideas of the theoreticians have penetrated down into the lives of ordinary men.

Ratko's family was never rich, but it has a tradition of education and culture. His father was a judge before the war and after the war was made assistant director of the national lottery. He is now on a pension. He is a jolly old man in whom the new politics never conquered the old, but his complaints, which are never bitter, are mainly against inflation. It is not easy to live on a pension, and a man with training and culture, a man capable of taking on responsibility in a society where so many are not, might well feel disappointed that his last years should be so spare of luxury. Though I have noticed no adamant opposition to communism in any of the family, they are all moved more by nostalgia for the past than enthusiasm for the world being built now.

Ratko is the middle of three brothers. The oldest is a doctor who studied in Paris and then went abroad where he has stayed to do heart research. Ratko's younger brother is a cellist and a graduate of the Music Academy. He calls himself apolitical and says all a man can do is find his own quiet niche and fill it with as much decency and culture as he knows how.

Perhaps Ratko's original leanings were not very different from those of his brothers, but his profession has brought him closer to the politics and social problems of this country. He is an industrial psychologist in a large factory, and his ideas about politics are very realistically bound to his professional training and experience.

He is serious and hard-working, and his work is unquestionably in line with the directions set out by the League of Communists. Some of my most interesting conversations with him were about his refusal to join the party. Party members have for years encouraged him to join, but his refusal is deep-seated. His basic belief is that an individual should remain an individual and not be drawn into a political organization of any kind, for membership in such a group takes from a man his individual responsibility. He once told me that he strongly opposed the establishment of a two-party system in Yugoslavia, for the country had all the political parties it needed. Another time he declared that it had one too many.

He feels that the most crucial problem of his country at the present moment lies in the primitivism of its people. His view is that all the difficulties with the economy, the political system, and the social arrangement stem from this one single fact: the country is still short of educated, cultured, responsible people and the skills, training, and discipline of the average man are below those in the highly developed countries. The political polarization caused by the revolution, he says, put many incompetent people in important places while many capable people were demoted or left in unimportant positions. This political turnover further aggravated the country's shortage of trained people. It is inevitable that the party should be one force holding the incompetents in power and the capable people out of power.

"Look," he told me, "I know the party and government leaders still feel they must have party people in positions of responsibility; they want people they think they can trust to work within the framework laid down by the Central Committee. But like any other artificial social criterion, the requirement of party membership for certain positions makes problems. When party membership is necessary to advance beyond a certain level, many people join solely to further their careers. Others get advancement through their services to the party or through party connections rather than through professional competence. At the same time many good people refuse to join because they don't want to advance that way or because, like me, they feel that the obligations of party membership contradict their duties as citizens."

Ratko feels that competent people outside the party now stand for something and are in a position to exert pressure. One example he gives is that of a friend who is president of the managing board of a construction firm. "Look at Jovan," he says. "He's not a member of the party, but he's gone to an important position in his enterprise. One day he will be director—mark my words."

The only way to combat the imcompetents, he says, is for non-Communists to take on more and more responsibility for doing every job right. He has found that in order to put over his ideas about what is right he does not have to join the party, but he does have to take an ever more active role in meetings and discussions, forums and boards. There are many who think like Ratko. If the ultimate goal of the tranformation going on in Yugoslavia is the withering away of the party and the instituting of direct democracy, these men will make it possible.

V

Daily Life

THIS BOOK focuses primarily upon only a part of the daily life of Yugoslavs and their country—that part which is affected by the ideas and programs of Yugoslav communism—the part I have called the "social adventure." But this social adventure by no means encompasses the entirety of daily life in Yugoslavia, which is neither all adventure nor altogether social. The mundane and personal, the job one goes to, and the leisure one is free to use figure large in Yugoslav life, as they do in any country.

Though Yugoslavia's standard of living and general social wealth are quite meager by American standards, the difference is becoming less noticeable. Many Yugoslavs are now enjoying what might be called the modern minimum: a steady income, an apartment, enough furniture, a radio, decent clothes, and some pocket money for cigarettes, liquor, restaurants, and the movies. The most obvious signs of the country's relative backwardness are disappearing from the towns and cities and from those parts of the countryside which have already been affected by the drive for modern agriculture. A new class is forming, though it is not the class of bureaucratic elitists we usually think of as the exclusive beneficiaries of Communist economies. It includes virtually everyone who is "up with the times"—everyone with education or skills; and within it the range in the standard of living is small. On the street it is difficult to distinguish the waiter from the novelist, the director from the clerk, the ship captain from the machinist, the actor from the taxi driver (some caution is needed here, since Yugoslav taxi drivers are notoriously prosperous), the doctor from the accountant, or the scientist from the railroad engineer. Some of these people have been able to acquire more household goods than others, but the greatest distinction is that some can afford one of the little Fiat automobiles produced in Yugoslavia (where they cost about one million dinars, or $1,300).* Above this group there exists only a diminishing group of high government functionaries; below it there is the great mass of the little-schooled peasant population and the lowest-paid workers—those with meager skills or none at all. In a sense this "middle" class represents the new society which is emerging from the old. It is growing fast because the opportunities are multiplying for both young people and adults to acquire education and training.

Like its counterpart in other countries, this new class is caught up in the revolution of rising expectations—with a special accent because the war and the first years of reconstruction and economic development constituted a long period of scarcity, and the availability of modern consumer goods is therefore still quite new. Everyone is short of money because there is so much everyone wants to buy. Once a family has gotten an apartment and managed to furnish it, they set their sights on a refrigerator, hot-water heater, vacuum cleaner, washing machine, television set, new clothes, a trip to Italy or Switzerland, and one of those little Fiats.

Though food prices and rent are very low, incomes are also very low. A simple comparison of average earnings with these basic budget items would lead one to conclude that most men's salaries are no more than barely adequate for food and shelter and occasional clothing purchases; but the department stores, furniture stores, and appliance stores are always crowded, and on the first of the month the aisles become impassable. For a time it seemed to

---

* In 1965 the dinar was devalued from 750 to 1250 per dollar. However, since prices and incomes rose correspondingly, the equivalents given in this book are still approximately accurate.

me very reckless for my colleagues in the publishing house to run out every month with their pay envelopes and return with their arms full of packages. I did not see how the remainder from their purchases would feed them for the rest of the month, even on a diet of bread, cheese, and onions. And indeed they were forever talking poverty. Then I realized that there is a certain pattern in the way families, which usually have more than one source of income, budget this "getting and spending." One person's income is set aside for living, and the other incomes go for the luxury of high-heeled shoes, material for a new suit or dress, a new lamp perhaps, or a new gadget or two for the kitchen. When they complain about their finances, people like to forget the household's other sources of income. For instance, I was given the impression that one family I knew—husband, wife, two children, and mother-in-law—were living entirely off the wife's low salary as a draftsman. The husband was in school; the mother-in-law was too old to work, and the children were small. But then I discovered that the wife's salary of 24,000 dinars ($32) a month, which certainly was just enough for the bare minimum, was only the start. The husband had a stipend of 12,000 dinars ($16) from a factory on condition that he work for the company for two years after getting his engineering degree; the mother-in-law had a pension of 9,000 dinars ($12); they received two monthly child supplement payments from the government totaling about 3,000 dinars ($4), and they rented out a room to two students for 10,000 dinars ($13.30). The family's real income was thus something more than double the salary. This was true of almost everyone I knew. A husband would spend his money on the first of the month and complain for thirty days that he could not support himself and his wife, and then it would turn out that his wife worked and made a large enough salary to afford them a very decent living.

Many people with special training and education are able to supplement their regular incomes by doing work for fees. Journalists sometimes make as much in fees as in salary by writing feature articles for their own or other papers. Engineers and architects do special projects and designs at home. A factory psychologist collects small fees for writing an article for the factory newspaper or teaching a course in the factory school. A draftsman earns a fee by taking home drawings which are not part of his ordinary job. A set designer does posters for a company which is preparing an exhibition, or decorates a restaurant. Artists, translators, and specialists in all fields do more or less of this contract work to supplement their low salaries and achieve a standard of living that in some ways equals the average in the West.

Though these people can often afford to spend more for restaurants and entertainment then the average Westerner, they cannot equal him in the purchase of durable consumer goods. Yugoslav prices of television sets and hi-fi equipment, washing machines, refrigerators, stoves, and electrical appliances are not only very high compared to Yugoslav incomes but often even higher than Western prices. (The reason for this is that imports carry heavy duties and the domestic manufacturers have not yet achieved the efficiency of mass production.) No Yugoslav's salary is large enough to allow him to buy such things on the first of the month. Nevertheless, more and more people are buying them through the Yugoslav version of installment buying. This is a form of low-interest (about 2 percent) consumer credit obtained from banks through the enterprise a man works for. The monthly payments are taken out of his salary. I have known people to borrow an amount equal to their annual salary through this system. The arrangements for financing automobile purchases and the purchase or construction of houses and apartments provide for even larger credits. Although credit for installment buying is given in the form of coupons, there are ways to turn these into cash. When a friend of mine needed cash for a vacation, he took credit and then sold the coupons at face value to a young bride who was about to spend her savings on furniture. The one snag in getting credit is that the application must have two cosigners, one of whom must be a man who has not taken credit himself. So many people take credit that it is sometimes almost impossible to find a cosigner who is not in debt. I know of one case where a girl who worked in a large office had not a single acquaintance without credit. Finally she found a man who was in the same predicament, and they signed for each other, since technically neither of them had credit at that point.

With private contract work, with two people working in almost every family, and with consumer credit, people are acquiring more and more of the goods of this world. And with this comes a rising degree of sophistication. All of this happens first and fastest in the big cities, but it is spreading, slowly, everywhere; and even where it goes slowest, the move toward sophisticated modern society is rapid and involves great cultural changes.

The exaltation of the modern can sometimes take on curious forms. The furniture stores carry only contemporary styles, for no one wants to decorate a new apartment with anything that is old-fashioned. Young people attach a good deal of status to owning American jazz records or a pair of blue jeans, because America stands for everything modern. They are often proud that they know the twist and do not know the traditional Yugoslav dances. One of the most popular shows making the rounds of the community cultural centers during my stay in Belgrade was a miserable copy of an American musical revue; its theme was "Down with Folklore!" Young women do not wear black, because they associate it with old crones in peasant shawls and long dresses. Many people refuse to eat corn bread because it symbolizes peasant poverty, and they are irate when the bakeries run out of white bread and they must eat rye. Once, at dinner with an old middle-class family I was served roasted new potatoes no bigger than marbles, with fresh sheep's cheese. My host remarked that this was one of Serbia's greatest dishes and a mainstay of the peasant but it could rarely be found in restaurants because people were still too close to the days when there was nothing else to be had.

Though one afternoon I heard a lecturer repeat over and over to a group of Belgrade citizens that all that was old was negative and all that was new was positive (a proposition that neither he nor his audience lived by), there is also a well-argued reaction against excessive worship of the new. One frequently hears people say that modern industrial society must be humanized by the preservation of the ancient and comfortable affections for leisurely conversation, good brandy and wine, long breaks during the day when a man sits over Turkish coffee and reflects on the world around him, late afternoon strolls along the main streets of town, group singing in the coffeehouse in the evening, the great national folk dance— the kolo—and the ways of peasant hospitality and peasant crafts. I never entered an office in Yugoslavia where I was not offered a cup of Turkish coffee; many offices employ a woman to do nothing but make coffee for employees and official and unofficial visitors. It is a full-time job because Turkish coffee is made one or two cups at a time. The coffee-maker is severely criticized if she does not learn to suit everyone's individual taste and buy a good blend freshly ground every day.

Though it is sometimes argued that these old customs must be abandoned if labor productivity is to reach the Western level, people also argue that life in Yugoslavia is only too rapidly approaching the faceless hurry of New York. Actually the tempo is still slow in comparison with America, and the old customs have not yet undergone their hardest tests. Though it has sprung up rapidly, the new has not yet replaced the old, but stands side by side with it. One day, on the third floor of one of Belgrade's most up-to-date office buildings, I saw a man emerge from the elevator with a briefcase that had a most unofficial bulge. As he squeezed through the doors of the elevator, there was a squeal and the snout of a suckling pig poked out from under the flap of the briefcase.

That was in a holiday season, when the old customs are strongest. Everyone buys a pig and then kills, dresses, and roasts it himself—even if he works in a modern office. In the evening his friends and relations come to celebrate. The guests arrive around five o'clock and take their seats at a long table laden with a huge assortment of cold meats and salads which have been perhaps three days in preparation. They begin by drinking plum brandy, the national drink. The host will have brought out his best for the occasion, and as he fills the tiny glasses he will tell his guests that this brandy is completely natural and bears no resemblance to the denatured liquor available in the stores; that because of its purity this brandy does not cause either nausea or hangovers; and that the taste is ethereal and the strength unbelievable. The guests then taste the brandy, smile with satisfaction, and ask its origin. The host will tell them not only the name of the village it came from but perhaps even the life history of the man who made it. Every Yugoslav feels he knows the one place in the country where other-worldly brandy can be found, and this knowledge is a great part of his pride and pleasure. No two hosts, of course, have the same place in mind.

After the first or second glass of brandy, large squares of a thick cheese pie are brought in hot from the kitchen. Some of the guests will leave brandy for wine or beer, while other, hardier souls will stay with the potent yellowish liquor for another half-dozen glasses. Then the roast suckling pig comes in and the conversation settles down to a calm tempo. The party may go on until two or three in the morning.

The mixture of new and old appears in the daily life of every Yugoslav. The smells of roasting peppers and coffee beans are common in city streets, and in all but the largest cities they mingle with the smoke from *chevapchichi* stands, where little sausages are cooked over an open charcoal fire. Even in the center of Belgrade one sees dress ranging from the latest Western fashions to the long full skirts and many-colored aprons of peasant girls. In restaurants it is not uncommon to see a peasant in embroidered jacket and riding breeches at one table and a group of businessmen in gray flannel suits at the next. Walking through any city street, one is likely to come upon a low Balkan house with a pigpen, chickens, and a garden squeezed in among the new buildings. I have even known people to keep chickens on the balconies of high-rise apartment buildings.

A man who lives in a new apartment decorated with abstract paintings may have a hot-water heater which is no more than a wood or coal stove attached to a tank, so that he has to light a fire to have a hot bath or wash the dishes. People who live in buildings more then five or six years old still have to take garbage down in pails and carry up coal in baskets fot the tall tile stoves which heat their apartments. In Belgrade a whole colony of Shiptars (members of the Albanian national minority in Yugoslavia) make their living by carrying coal and kindling wood for apartment dwellers.

The same incongruities can be seen in the shopping districts, where express cafeterias and modern three- and four-storied department stores selling everything from lace to refrigerators stand beside the tiny shops of myriad artisans—tailors, bookbinders, quiltmakers, coppersmiths, tinsmiths, cabinetmakers, cosmetic-makers, pastry cooks, bakers, watchmakers, repairers of fountain pens, shoemakers, shoe repair men, brushmakers, shirtmakers, brassiere-makers, coffee-mill makers, rugmakers, sausage-makers, coopers, basket-weavers, furriers, tanners, glovemakers, piecrust-makers, milliners, and men who repair runs in nylon stockings. The tailors are the most important artisans, for the budding garment industry is only beginning to build up trade. The ordinary man is more likely to go to the department store for his winter coat than for his best suit, since he can buy better material than he can find in a ready-made suit, and the tailor's work is usually better and hardly more expensive. The tailor's charge runs from a few thousand to about 25,000 dinars ($33) for a suit with vest and two pairs of trousers.

There are dry cleaners but they rub out the spots with a rag and do all the pressing by hand. The cost is therefore outrageous, and Yugoslavs are very handy at spot removal. Laundries, even those which are part of the communal organization, are utter chaos. It sometimes takes two weeks to get clothes laundered (there are no launderettes yet) and another two weeks for the laundry to find the shirts they have misplaced in their crowded quarters. The laundries also serve as an employment agency for women who do cleaning and washing by the day for private individuals.

The best organized and most modern of the social services is medicine. Socialized medicine, which until recently only covered workers in the socialized sector, is now almost universal. Enterprises pay contributions for all their employees, and self-employed persons make direct monthly payments. Free medical care for childbirth, cancer, and tuberculosis has long been available to everyone. There is a handling charge of sixty dinars (8¢) for every medical prescription. This fee was introduced recently because doctors were overprescribing and every household was accumulating a large supply of unused medicine. There is no charge for dental care except for the gold used in crowns; eye examinations and glasses are also free, though many people pay for the frames in order to choose from a wider selection of styles. Every neighborhood has an out-patient clinic and every citizen chooses his own physician from the clinic staff. If a man doesn't like his doctor he is free to switch. And if a patient is too ill to go to the clinic the doctor will come to the house after his hours at the clinic. There is also a central emergency service with doctors and ambulances ready to come at a moment's notice. When I awoke one morning with a violent stomach upset after eating some suspicious mushrooms the night before, I discovered how swift they were. Five minutes after my wife telephoned, two doctors rushed in, prepared for anything.

Many things cause the ordinary man a good deal of lost time and inconvenience: the electricity is often turned off because new and bigger cables are being installed in every city; long-distance telephoning is sometimes slower than sending a telegram; there are often shortages of imported items like good razor blades and there is a severe shortage of store space. Barbers, beauticians, automobile mechanics, taxi drivers, electricians, and handymen are usually ill equipped and often jacklegs. In spite of recent improvements, public transportation is still slow and overcrowded, especially during rush hours.

Most Yugoslavs go to work at six or seven o'clock in the morning, for the day starts early even in offices. Around nine or ten o'clock there is a half-hour break for breakfast, which may be as little as coffee and a roll or as much as beef stew or fried liver and mashed potatoes with beer. Then people work through until two or two-thirty. The main meal of the day comes after work, in the middle of the afternoon. It may be the product of a whole day's work—from six in the morning until two in the afternoon—if the woman who cooks it does not have a job. But one feature of the new middle class is that young wives and mothers do have jobs. Their professions are often surprising: they may be metal-lurgists, criminal lawyers, draftsmen, civil engineers, agronomists or bank officials. This penetration of women into new fields has gone surprisingly far, considering the traditional place occupied by women in Yugoslavia. (I have read complaints in the newspaper that women constitute *only* 30 percent of the law students.) Some women now suffer from the worst of both worlds. A woman who goes out to work like her husband may still be expected at home to help him on and off with his coat, polish his shoes, fetch his slippers, and jump when he commands.

In homes where there is an older woman, she will do the cooking if the wife works. When there is no mother-in-law living with the family, young career women often hire servants to "live in" and do the housework. Usually these are elderly women with no family of their own or very young girls who have just come to the city. Though their wages are very low, the girls are given a place to live (a great boon in crowded cities) and a chance to learn city ways before they move out on their own. Often they go to school and learn a trade while they are working as servants, and then get factory jobs. One friend of mine had hired a succession of these girls. They would come in from the country not even knowing what a telephone was, and after a year or two they would leave to work in a factory or office.

The woman who does the housework usually begins every day with shopping, for most people still do not have refrigerators. Even those who do have them find it hard to break the habit of going to the peasant market every day in summer and every two or three days in winter. Women go to market very early, for the bargains and the selection are much better at opening time—at six in the morning. The peasants' fruits and vegetables are heaped on long tables in between the vegetable stalls of the socialist farms. A traditional housewife spends at least an hour every morning tasting berries and grapes, haggling over prices with the peasants, and chatting with the neighbors she meets and those peasants who are old acquaintances. In winter and early spring the offerings are few and prices are high, and she complains bitterly. The peasants, who are no strangers to the laws of supply and demand, may raise egg prices to as much as 40 or 50 dinars apiece, the equivalent of 65¢ to 80¢ a dozen—in a country where the average wage for a skilled worker is only about $40 a month. Socialist eggs are cheaper but the socialist farms cannot yet meet the winter demand; even though eggs are imported from Israel and Denmark, there are times when the housewife is forced to buy from the peasant. Then she praises the socialist farms and is thankful that they have taken over milk sales so that the peasant can no longer raise milk prices as he used to do in winter.

In late summer the market is jammed with peppers and tomatoes and watermelons and grapes, and the housewife comes with clothesbaskets to buy her canning supplies, for even in the cities Yugoslav women still put up great quantities of tomatoes, pepper relish, and jam, and salt down barrels of cabbage for winter. Since the canning industry is still young and prices are high, the housewife saves money by doing her own canning, though of course this also means that the demand for industrial canned goods is so small that prices remain high. In the summertime there is much good feeling and laughter in the market; the peasants are glad to have customers taste and try, and they readily lower prices when a woman offers to buy all their produce. At this season the socialist stalls are not so popular, for their prices are often higher than the peasants' and they are far less willing to allow customers to pick through their wares.

Beyond the fruit and vegetable stalls, peasants in white aprons sell homemade cheese, eggs, honey, chickens and geese, shelled walnuts, and freshly ground corn meal. At one end of the market there is a cluster of stores where the housewife buys her meat, milk, butter, and bread from socialist enterprises. Here she may have to wait in line, and she may be too late. One reason for the shortages of these products is that prices have been artificially kept down to help out the industrial worker whose salary is so low. As a result, the bakers, for example, never bake a surplus; a little waste would dissipate their small profits. In turn, the retail shops never order extra bread because they cannot return the stale bread to the producer but must throw it away or sell it stale. Since calcium propionate is not added and the loaves are not wrapped, the bread goes stale quickly. Every shop calculates in order to sell out every day. Dairy stores also avoid surpluses because they do not have refrigerators and cannot keep the milk over a day. Another reason for shortages is that when shoppers fear an article is going to be scarce, they begin to hoard. One spring my landlady reported that there was a butter shortage because the Communists were trying to discourage Easter celebrations. "What a shame you didn't get any," I said. "Oh, I'll be able to make a cake. I got six pounds," she answered. On holidays there is always a battle for bread in Belgrade; although the bakers make a little extra, people buy much more than they can use. An end of these shortages is now in sight, since food prices are being allowed to rise rapidly to their natural level. When the socialized farms are stimulated to provide the city abundantly with meat, milk, and bread, as they are capable of doing, the housewife will no longer have to stand in line.

After marketing, the housewife begins the slow process of cooking, with frequent interruptions for coffee. The midday meal is large, for the country as a whole is not so far from poverty that people have ceased to think of bulk as an important aspect of good eating. This large meal begins with soup and thereafter is heavy on the side of meat and starch. The big items are ground beef and pork, boiled beef, bread, beans, and potatoes, for the tendency is to eat as cheaply as possible and spend money for clothes and durable goods. Food does not become a luxury item until everything else has been bought.

The diet is in strict rhythm with the season. In spring, when the lambs were being killed, I was often served a dish called "lamb in the handkerchief," which consists of minced lamb liver baked in the lamb's bladder. A little later there was a short period when I got my minced meat wrapped in a bitter leaf with somewhat the taste of spinach. Still later, I found it rolled in a grape leaf. As summer progressed, the hash was stuffed into a small green squash and then into a bell pepper or even a large hot peppper. In the fall it was wrapped in fresh cabbage leaves and after frost, in cabbage leaves that had been soaked in brine.

The variety of vegetables is limited to the most common fruits of the garden; there are no asparagus, yams, Brussels sprouts, broccoli, celery, or French artichokes, for the sole reason that Yugoslavs are not used to eating them. I found Yugoslavs very conservative in their eating habits. A friend of mine who was a university professor would refuse a steak if it was called by a foreign name like *châteaubriand*. Nor would he eat cheese at the end of a meal; he wanted it before his dinner, with brandy, in the Yugoslav fashion. Curiously enough, along with their conservatism, Yugoslavs are more defensive about their eating habits than about their politics or culture. I once saw an official in the government grow incensed when his English wife said there were Brussels sprouts in Poland and none in Yugoslavia. I myself once complained to a friend about the preponderance of sauerkraut in the winter diet, and though she herself was a constant critic of the backwardness and lack of sophistication of her countrymen, she grew very defensive at the thought that I was not happy with their cabbage.

After the midday meal Yugoslavs take a nap for two or three hours. By six o'clock the hairdressers and tailors are busy, the downtown streets are full of window-shoppers and promenading families, and there are lines in front of the movie theaters. A little later the *kafanas,* or coffeehouses—which are also restaurants— begin to fill up. The *kafana* is one of the great institutions of Yugoslav life, and it perpetuates the openness and outwardness of that life. It is not quiet, like an English restaurant where men surround themselves with an inviolable privacy. And yet its noise is not like that of an American restaurant where the "racket" often seems only a necessity attendant upon feeding the greatest number of people in the shortest time. It is an unwritten rule of the *kafana* that a man may order one coffee and sit undisturbed from opening time to closing time, no matter how crowded the tables become or how many people are turned away. The *kafanas* perform the function of many of our public visiting places: the bar, the restaurant, the gas station, and the drugstore; and many of our private visiting places: the porch, the back fence, the living room. They are never empty, even in midmorning. Yugoslavs who have traveled abroad often marvel that in other countries the coffeehouses and bars are deserted during working hours; in Yugoslavia they are busy even at ten in the morning. Part of the trade consists of workers who have come out for their breakfast, and many of the customers are pensioners. Since Yugoslav men retire at fifty-five or as soon thereafter as they have worked a full thirty-five years, and women retire at fifty or after thirty working years, there are a great many older people whose mornings are free. But it is still difficult to account for all the people one meets in the cafes during work hours without suspecting that some of them are supposed to be somewhere else.

Though many Yugoslavs eat no supper at all and with others it is a casual makeshift affair, people go out to the *kafanas* in the evening to drink and pass the time with their friends and relatives. The most common drinks are beer, plum brandy, and wine, often diluted with soda water. While they drink, the coffeehouse patrons may order fresh or salted sheep's cheese accompanied by a large peeled onion, or a salad of fresh cucumbers, preferably sprinkled with grated garlic. (Yugoslavs are great garlic eaters and buy it in the market not by the head but by the kilogram; in a crowded tram in the middle of the winter the effect is overwhelming.) Later in the evening they may order a meal of meat grilled over charcoal. The most common fare is *chevapchichi,* little rolled sausages made from a mixture of ground veal, beef, and pork. They are sold in orders of five or ten and eaten with mounds of chopped raw onion. This is the cheapest dish on the evening menu and even families with a small income can afford it. Every restaurant serves these little sausages in great quantities, and the price varies little. In an ordinary restaurant an order of 10 costs 140 dinars (about 18¢) and the highest price I observed was 200 dinars. Even in newer, fancier, and more expensive restaurants with a particularly pleasant setting or atmosphere, I never noticed any attempt to reduce the number of sausage eaters in favor of the steak eaters by raising the price of sausages. Too much should not be made of this: there are certainly restaurants which are exclusive in one way or another. But I was often struck to see crowds of ordinary people enjoying the terrace restaurant of the fanciest hotel in Belgrade or dining and dancing at no great expense in garden restaurants.

Though most people think of ten o'clock as bedtime, the cafes and restaurants are full until eleven or twelve. Toward the end of the evening people begin singing and drinking noisy toasts to each other, throwing the empty glasses on the floor in good Slavic style. Occasionally tempers rise and a fight erupts in the midst of all this exuberant good will. In any ordinary cafe two or three people a night get so rowdy they have to be thrown out, and most cafes have a sign on the wall reading "300 dinars charged for glasses broken deliberately" alongside the sign reading "We do not take tips" (a socialist ideal which is rarely practiced, though I did occasionally run across waiters who refused a tip). Once I saw a waiter drag a particularly obstreperous drunk by the scruff of his neck out to the sidewalk. But before returning inside to his patrons, he paused to light the drunk's cigarette, shook his hand, and wished him a pleasant goodnight. Often drunks who have been bounced move to another cafe, but there the chances for getting a drink are poor, since waiters risk a seven-day jail sentence and a stiff fine for serving drunks and are reluctant to take the risk for people who have already spent their money elsewhere. A comic drama as stereotyped as a western film takes place every night in almost any cafe. A man staggers in and orders plum brandy. He is refused and gets into a noisy argument with the waiter. The headwaiter comes over to investigate, and the drunk changes his order to beer. Another argument ensues. Eventually, he sits down meekly to a cup of strong coffee and hands are shaken all around.

By one o'clock everything is closed except for a few of the more expensive cafes which keep their gypsy orchestras and folk singers until nearly dawn. These are popular spots for the *shvaleri* (the Serbo-Croat cognate of chevalier), a word more often applied to married men who take out pretty girls from the office than to gallant young suitors. I found the Yugoslavs surprisingly free and easy about extramarital affairs. A friend of mine who was something of a *shvaler* himself (although he had a wife and daughter, was a highly respected professor, and was relatively important in the party) told me when I remarked on this freedom, "We never were much for conventional morality. We tried it during the war, but that was for political reasons. You can't afford to be loose when you're trying to make a revolution. Fortunately, we didn't stay puritanical Communists long. Perhaps now we even have a touch of *la dolce vita.*"

The transition from a six-day to a five-day work week is giving Yugoslavs more leisure. Before, they were limited to occasional two-day holidays and the summer vacation, which is the high point of the year. In his first year of employment a worker gets two weeks' vacation; and every year afterward one working day is added to his annual leave. The accumulation of time is not affected by change of jobs any more than are pension benefits. Thus it is very common for people in their thirties and forties to enjoy a month or more of freedom from their jobs. And those who are near the retirement age are already accustomed to long periods of rest.

For his vacation every worker receives certificates entitling him and all his dependents to a round trip at one-fourth fare on trains, buses, and boats and at one-half fare on airplanes. The railroad reduction can even be used in Italy, so that a man can take a trip to Rome for about $20. There are no restrictions on itinerary within Yugoslavia except that it be round in some fashion. Yugoslavs take great amusement in planning their trips so as to see as much as possible of the country in one circuit.

But with salaries as low as they are, this fare reduction would be of little benefit if Yugoslavs had to pay the same prices as foreign tourists at vacation spots. Some large factories have built their own resort hotels where their workers can get room and board at low prices.

The labor unions and various other associations have also opened hotels. Many of these specialized hotels take in ordinary

tourists when they aren't full, though the rates are considerably
higher for nonmembers. When my wife and I went to Lake Ohrid
in Macedonia we planned to stay at the union hotel since Belgrade
friends had recommended it as well run and much cheaper than
the new Hotel Palace in the center of town. But arriving after dark
we missed our turn and wound up at a hotel for disabled veterans.
It was too late to wander further so we stayed, for $3.00 a day for
room and full board. The hotel was handsome and well planned
with comfortable rooms, terraces for dining and dancing, a bar,
game rooms, and lobbies. But the interior decorator had had less
taste than the architect and the furnishings were garish. The staff
were always confused about which rooms were filled and which
were empty, the clerks did not know how to register foreigners so
that I had to fill out all the forms for them, and there were other
evidences of inefficient management. Nevertheless, the food was
solid if unimaginative, the beach was one hundred yards away, and
there was good folk music in the evening. The veterans and their
families, I discovered, were paying less than a dollar a day.

Union organizations in factories too small or poor to build their
own accommodations contract with hotels, motels, and camps to
get special rates for the factory employees. No one, of course, is
required to use the factory or union facilities, but this is the only
way many ordinary workers can afford a vacation trip. Usually the
union arranges it so that a worker has a choice of a mountain or
seaside resort at low rates. Before the war the inland spas were the
main vacation spots, but now everyone tries to get down to the sea
and the ornate watering places in the mountains are second choice.
The Adriatic is mobbed in July and August; coming from Belgrade
one is likely to meet half a dozen acquaintances on the street of
any of the coastal towns.

The summer vacation is an annual event set off from all others,
but the Yugoslav calendar also includes three important two-day
holidays. May Day is celebrated with parades in the large cities.
The one in Belgrade lasts for hours and includes military con-
tingents, floats entered by factories, marching groups of veterans,
school children, teachers, members of various social and political

organizations, and professional folk-dance groups. The streets are lined with flags, and great portraits of Marx and Lenin hang over the façade of the building which houses the Central Council of the Yugoslav Labor Unions. The Day of the Republic, on November 29, is accompanied by all of the flags and portraits of the First of May, though the parades are replaced by speeches much in the style of our Fourth of July oratory. But the biggest holiday is New Year's, which combines our Christmas and New Year festivities. People exchange cards, decorate trees, wrap up presents, revel with food and drink until the early morning hours, kiss everyone within reach at midnight, and dance in the streets next day.

Christmas is not a national holiday either on the Roman Catholic and Protestant December 25 or on the Orthodox January 6. It is celebrated only in the church. The suppression of the Christmas holiday is one of several examples of rather petty Communist antireligious attitudes. The necessity to force religion and the church out of politics is understandable in a country where religious tensions between Roman Catholic, Orthodox, and Moslem were explosive and frequently reinforced by national and geographic tensions. But the Communist substitution of new holidays for old ones is, to say the least, silly since, as in other countries, the old holidays are more traditional than actively religious. An Orthodox custom of sunrise assembly on Easter morning has been replaced by a similar assembly on Tito's birthday; many Communists refuse to attend the traditional Serbian celebrations on the family's saint day and try to emphasize birthdays instead. At one point in the 1950's these substitutions led to a centering of political opposition around the church. Men who never before cared about religion began to attend services as an expression of political discontent. This focus of opposition has now subsided and the churches go on as usual. The Catholic priests celebrate their mass, the bearded Orthodox priests celebrate theirs, and the muezzin calls the faithful to prayer from his minaret. Religious articles are sold by a socialist enterprise. The pensions and other benefits of the welfare state have been accepted by Orthodox priests, and even the Catholics are said to be coming around. The churches are open and in some sections of the country are crowded. (In Western embassies stories circulate about how the secret police take down the names of all churchgoers, but I myself have seen both Catholic and Orthodox churches so full that the idea is absurd.) The government is making a serious attempt to restore the country's monasteries and mosques and cathedrals as cultural treasures. Choirs and orchestras are not neglecting the music written for the greater glory of God, and the museums have special exhibitions of their icon collections.

But I met few people who had any serious concern for religion. It is generally regarded as a relic of the past, though there are young people among the churchgoers. My impression that religion is unimportant is partly of course the result of my long stay in Serbia, where the Orthodox Church is said to have always concerned itself more with cultural unity and uprisings against the Turks than with men's souls. One of my landladies gave me an indication of how true this must be. She told me that Christmas Day had come and she did not realize what day it was until the afternoon. "But then," she explained, "I never was a fanatic."

Perhaps the small concern Yugoslavs show for the next world can also be partly accounted for by their absorption with the things of this one. The changes taking place around them are so great that one Yugoslav novelist has called the postwar development "a jump across a ditch five centuries wide." Everyone is involved in the transition from oxcarts to jet airplanes, from wooden plows to diesel tractors, from rutted cart tracks to expressways, from peasant barter to supermarkets. Hundreds of thousands of young people and adults are attending courses in the workers' and people's universities, in their factory institutes, in community cultural centers, and in the regular educational institutions, trying to fit themselves for the complicated society which is being built. At the same time, more and more people are being drawn into the work of the boards and councils and committees which are the basis of democratic self-government. What time and energy remain are taken up by every man's attempt to acquire as much of the new as possible and shape it to his own personal life.

VI

A Place to Live

Yugoslavia lives with a severe housing shortage which will probably accompany its developing enonomy until it reaches that plateau where Yugoslavs can rest without fear of need traveling close behind them. As the country undergoes its transition from peasant agriculture to urban industry, the population which was spread out over the land is flooding to towns swelling at nodes of economic importance. New factories draw their workers from the peasant population of the villages. Capital is scarce and investments go first to build new factories; the funds for housing the workers must come from the operation of the factories themselves. Thus, new jobs open up before new apartments are built.

The war brought widespread destruction of housing both in the countryside and in cities and towns. Some rural areas are still depopulated as a result. Though these are often areas of poor soil, so that in the long run it's as well that the population has been forced out, these losses are felt most acutely in the cities, for they help to accelerate urbanization.

Belgrade itself suffered extensive bombardment from the Germans in 1941 and from the Allies in the last months of the European war. It therefore began its postwar development with much of its prewar housing in ruins. For administrative as well as economic reasons, it is also one of the fastest growing of Yugoslav cities. In

Belgrade the housing shortage has reached the point of adventure. It is not mere figures in a book that apply to other people and not to oneself. Virtually no one can escape its pressures, though some may escape its full grip.

A housing shortage means crowding in the available quarters, and crowding means lack of privacy. The housing problems of some of my acquaintances illustrate the variety of difficult situations which this crowding causes. An editor in a Belgrade publishing house, who is one of the fortunate in having received a modern two-room apartment, would like another room so that his teen-age son and daughter need not sleep in the same room. An engineer who after seven years as superintendent of a factory in Bosnia came to Belgrade to study at the university sold the house he inherited in Bosnia; with the proceeds he purchased half of a small house on the outskirts of the city. There are two rooms; his family of five— mother, wife, himself, and two small children—must sleep in one room. The other is used as the kitchen. Another friend lived in one room of the apartment of his in-laws for the first eight years of his married life. When he finally got an apartment, his two boys were five and seven years old. This man, a Communist and an executive, could have got an apartment through his large firm at any time if he had ever pressed for it. He did not press because he was active in the political life of the enterprise and did not want to give ammunition to his opponents when he criticized favoritism, bureaucracy, and irregularities. Finally, however, the crowding of his family in one room became so intolerable that he accepted a job in a new factory in the provinces, where an apartment was waiting for him. Neither the director nor the managing board of his enterprise was willing to accept his resignation, and they quickly provided him with a two-room apartment in Belgrade. (Ten percent of an enterprise's available housing is left at the disposal of the director, to be used to hold or attract people who are essential to the enterprise's operation.)

One of the principal causes of divorce in Yugoslavia is the fact that so many young married people must live with in-laws. But divorce, which provides liberation from so many unpleasant and even tragic family situations, loses its value when the divorced partners must continue their life in the same cramped quarters. Separation without divorce, one realizes, solves many more problems than divorce without separation.

Certainly the situation is improving. Many people can now laugh at the stories of the difficulties that are behind them. Couples tell of spending their evenings at the movies for years in order not to go back to a room where they could not sleep before midnight because their bed was located between the room where a large family lived and the bathroom of the apartment. Privacy was impossible; out-and-out dormitories might well have been better. One highly cultured gentleman told me how he had lost room after room of an apartment he had owned even before the war. He had released the maid's room when the medical school made an appeal on behalf of the students. Another room was taken by the commune to house a homeless family. When he was jailed during the difficult days of the break with Stalin, another room was taken and his wife and daughter were left the one last room, which was constantly traversed by the interlopers. When he was freed he had much to do to establish himself again. His financial problems were solved when he found translation work to do at home, but after a time he found it too difficult to concentrate in the midst of the noisy traffic past his desk. But then the situation began to improve. One evening he celebrated the reoccupation of one room, and there are prospects that the other family will soon move. He is translating again and he laughs as he tells of his past difficulties.

Housing construction is underway everywhere in cities and towns. More and more money is going into housing, and improved machinery is speeding the work of builders. In the center of Belgrade there is hardly a block without at least one construction site. The city is noisy and dusty, and housewives complain that it is impossible to keep things clean, but every day more people are given keys which represent a privacy and comfort they may never have known before. People joke about thin walls and tiny rooms and complain about hasty construction and mistakes, but the new apartments I saw seemed adequate and comfortable, if not luxurious.

Though some housing is built with public funds by the communes and distributed to citizens at large, most apartments are being built from the budgets of government agencies and the funds of enterprises for their own employees. Normally, then, a man gets an apartment through his job. The rents in the new apartments are generally low, between one-eighth and one-fourth of an average salary. Rents are rising, however, and in the best of the new apartments they are rising faster than incomes, so that occasionally workers with low incomes must refuse new apartments because they cannot yet afford them.

At one time enterprises and government agencies financed whole buildings for housing their employees, but now they put their money into a general housing fund and receive apartments according to the size of their contribution. This system has two important advantages. When factories were financing whole buildings for their employees, a man's neighbors were his co-workers, although the apartment house might be distant from the factory. People were dissatisfied because they could never escape their workaday problems. The openness of life in Yugoslavia—both within enterprises and within apartment houses—only aggravated the situation. The other advantage of the new system is that enterprises or institutes with funds too small for large-scale construction on their own can now use these small funds to obtain at least a few apartments for their employees. Recently it has become possible for individuals to finance apartments. Even in the past they could build individual houses, but there was no way for them to use their savings as a down payment and get credit for the construction of an apartment.

Yugoslav law allows a citizen to own his own house or the apartment he lives in and one other apartment or one-family house he does not live in. Apartments and houses are bought and sold just as in other countries. There is a difference, however, for the rights that come with ownership are limited. The right to occupy an apartment ordinarily belongs to the occupant even though he does not own it. The owner has no right to evict him even if he wants to move into the apartment himself. The price of an occupied apartment may be as little as one-twentieth the price of the same apartment unoccupied. Buying an occupied apartment is a gamble. If the occupant should move out, the new owner has obtained a very cheap apartment to move into; but if the occupant does not choose to move, the owner merely gets half the rent paid by the occupant. I recall a case when a man who had just purchased an occupied apartment telephoned the occupant to ask whether he could see the apartment he had bought. Without permission, his "property" rights were nonexistent, except in the matter of rent. Half the rent goes into a fund for maintenance of the building and for housing construction. Even if a man is living in an apartment he owns, he must pay half the established rent into this fund. Apartment buildings themselves are nationalized even though some apartments in them may be owned by individuals; thus, general repairs and improvements are paid for, not by owners, but through the rent fund. Because the right of occupancy is so important, people who want to move exchange apartments with someone else rather than sell in the hope of purchasing another. These exchanges are arranged not only within a town but from one end of the country to the other.

People who have not been lucky enough to inherit a house or apartment, or to get the low-rent housing in the socialist sector, and who lack the cash to buy an apartment must either settle in with generous friends or relations or rent on the open market. Since some private householders have more space than they need, there is a market. In the long run city residents seem to make arrangements they can afford, but transients are thrown onto this market. Students who fail to get space in the dormitories are the most hurt by this arrangement. They must often live in poor quarters for relatively high rent. Since schooling is free except for nominal fees and student restaurants are very cheap, housing has become the principal factor deterring some people from continuing their education. Probably the students' lot would be better if the presence of foreigners had not driven up the rents on the open housing market. Foreigners, it is reasoned, must have money or they would go home. Usually their expenses are being paid by some foreign company or embassy. But even if they earn their money in Yugoslavia, as I did, their native knowledge of a foreign language puts them in great demand as translators and editors. The rents they pay are apt to be higher than those in an American town for the same space with fewer conveniences. In other words, a foreigner must pay a monthly rent equivalent to twice the monthly income of an educated Yugoslav working in the socialized sector.

Because I was foreign, my experience with landlords and landladies in Belgrade was not typical, but it casts some interesting reflections on the general housing situation and in some other directions as well.

Yugoslav hotels are not expensive by Western standards and are even a bargain for the foreign tourist, but since my wife and I were planning a long stay and hoping to earn our living in Yugoslavia, we began soon after arrival to go through the want ads of the Belgrade papers. The housing situation was new to us then. (And indeed it goes beyond the limits of the American's imagination. A woman who had been working for socialism in Yugoslavia since her student days in the thirties told me once that the "For Rent" signs she saw on a trip to America seemed like something out of paradise, and she wondered whether she would ever see them displayed in Yugoslavia. Ironically and tragically, she happened to be from Skoplje; ten days after her remark over 90 percent of that city's housing was made unlivable by an earthquake.)

The want ads had little to offer, and the rare possibilities included demands for several months' rent in advance, which I could not consider until I had arranged for a job and a long-term visa. But one evening we noted an unusual offer of a two-room apartment for one month. When we went to investigate, we were met at the door by a young woman in the large-flowered kimona Yugoslav housewives wear at home to save their good clothes for the street. Conversation in Serbo-Croatian was problematical, but we reached an understanding. She and her husband were going to a mountain spa for a three weeks' vacation if they could find someone to rent their apartment for a month. When we asked what they would do for the other week, they said they would stay with her mother in the suburbs, where their son, a boy of nine or ten, would stay during their absence. Their price, 20,000 dinars, or about $27, was high by Yugoslav standards, probably ten times the rent they paid, but it was low by the international standards of our hotel, and we agreed.

We judged that little apartment to be about average for people who had neither held on to accommodations from before the war nor received a new apartment through their job. It had originally been the kitchen and maid's room of a spacious dwelling. To reach it, one had to go to the back of the apartment house and cross a small cement courtyard. The entranceway was lined with cupboards and had a door into a toilet. There was no bathtub. The main room (the former kitchen) had only a narrow passage free between the small electric stove, the wood range for heating in winter, a small sink with cold water, the cot where the boy slept, and a kitchen table with a small radio. Several of the boy's school drawings, crayon sketches of tanks and airplanes, provided some color against the gray walls. The single window looked onto the court where small boys spun around on little carts fitted with roller skate wheels. The bedroom was that and nothing more. Besides the bed there was a chiffonier, but there was no room even to stand up. Above the bed was an example of the "painting" which is sold in glass cutters' shops. It represented a huge sylvan scene where nymphs were dancing suggestively in pink raiment while satyrs, their eyes aflame, peeped at them from behind trees.

After three weeks of calling this place home and being glad to have it, we were surprised one day by our landlords, suitcases in hand. Their suggestion that we all live together in the little place for the next week set off an embarrassing discussion. They found it both strange and unfair that we should think that arrangement inconvenient, but they did not deny that we had come to a certain understanding on this very point. In the course of the conversation it came out that they had not been married very long; the boy was hers by a former marriage. This was not their only housing; they still had the room in which the husband had lived as a bachelor. Though it was located across town, they had retained it in the hope that eventually they could exchange the two places for something a little more comfortable and roomy than the apartment in which we were staying. Since they did after all have another place to go, we stuck by the terms of our original agreement but said we would find another place as soon as possible.

This time we ourselves placed an ad in the paper. At a friend's suggestion we mentioned in the ad that we were Americans and soon we had many offers. We took a room for 25,000 dinars (a little over $30) in one of the best old streets of town five minutes from the center. There were few new buildings in the street because the old ones, six and seven stories tall, had been solidly constructed. It is felt that more can be gained by removing the one-story dwellings in other streets equally near the center of town. Frequently, too, new stories were being added to these buildings, and thus more new apartments were created without first destroying the old ones. Surprisingly enough, the results were often aesthetically pleasing, as if many of the original builders had run out of money before they filled out the structures' proper proportions. Our building, we learned, had belonged to the state even before the war and had housed the executives of the state tobacco monopoly. Our landlady and her spinster daughter had lived in the building since the thirties, for the man of the family had been an official of the monopoly. Their apartment was large and comfortable, but they had previously had another, even larger one in the same building and had moved because of government regulations passed to ease the housing situation. Even in this smaller apartment, they had enough space to rent out the tiny maid's room for an additional 8,000 dinars to a Yugoslav student. In an apartment owned by the state, therefore, for which they paid 5,000 dinars in rent, they were collecting 33,000 dinars in rent for only two rooms; this is the equivalent of a very decent salary in Yugoslavia at the moment. But in that street of the old bourgeoisie with their large high-ceilinged apartments and heavy walnut furniture from the nineties, this was not an unusual case. The whole street was full of widows with rooms to let at high prices to foreigners. Many of them rented only to transients sent to them by the socialized tourist agency, which took 10 percent as a commission; others made their own arrangements with long-term foreign students and embassy personnel—these arrangements usually meant lower income but less bother and frequently the possibility of avoiding taxes. It is easy enough to criticize this makeshift unsocialist arrangement to compensate for the lack of apartments and for overcrowding of hotels in the months of good weather, when there is considerable tourist traffic through Belgrade. This capitalist arrangement is peculiarly unbridled for a socialist country. Though not all householders take advantage of the high rents available to them, particularly when they are renting to students, most rents are pressed right to the level of what the traffic will bear. Given the need for accommodations, however, it can be considered a sensible compromise, and is a good example of the Yugoslav capacity for tolerating contradictions. The extra space within private apartments must be available for housing transients; rents have to be allowed to rise to a level attractive to householders or else measures must be used like those adopted immediately after the war, when the unhoused were simply assigned to apartments where there was extra room. In those days the householder was not consulted and no rent was paid. Many of those householders are only now being freed of these assignees and are rediscovering what it means to have the privacy of their homes. Lacking the capital to solve the housing problem overnight, the Yugoslavs have decided to let time, rather than control, solve it. Every new apartment house and every new hotel is a contribution to the only real solution of the problem.

Our new room was clean and neat and pleasant. It was spacious in the way of those old apartments, and the furnishings were elegant and comfortable. There were tables for typing and easy chairs for reading. Across the hall was a bathroom with a large tub and a hot-water heater. We had the use of the kitchen, and from time to time our landlady even cooked a Serbian meal for us. It was a place of refuge from the disquieting confusion of speaking only in a language we had not yet mastered and of probing reality in a country ten times more foreign than any other we had visited, where the immense differences in culture were compounded with the products of Balkan history and the efforts of a Communist regime to make an entirely new society, one that would be new not only here but anywhere.

It is not so much the freedom of space and movement that one needs to overcome the weight of a city, but privacy, the feeling of a world the city cannot touch. City people always answer the door with more suspicion, keep their doors locked, bury themselves for several hours of the day from everything outside. But it is just that freedom of aloneness that one cannot obtain in a rented room that belongs to someone else's apartment. Some people not only use their apartments to rest from the world, to ease the strain of it, but they construct hidden worlds according to their own imagined co-ordinates. In a rented room one lives within someone else's idea of order.

We had two landladies: a mother in her sixties with a heart condition and miserly habits left from the war, who was forever coming upon some old thing, an old shirt of her husband's or a discarded pair of spectacles, which she would sell or trade to the gypsy rag dealers; and a daughter of forty, a responsible bank official with the little-girl psychology of spinsters in the old order before the war, not the independent hardness of the modern career woman who keeps her hold on the real world. They had made their invented world behind those walls and no intrusion could have disputed the coordinates which prevailed there.

They provided us with an old electric heater but stipulated that we keep it on for only an hour at a time. They thought resting it would make it last longer and were always knocking on the door to remind us to unplug it for a while. This antique finally refused to work at all (probably the constant heating and cooling wore it out faster), and they bought a new one. But this one had its special arrangements too. It was too delicate to be moved about, they said, and they proceeded to sew it to the cloth cover of a little table. This clever arrangement meant that we could live comfortably in only one spot, and that happened to be a spot we would not have chosen ourselves. We ate our meals in a restaurant nearby, and though we sometimes did not have conversation with our landladies for several days, we knew they had not forgotten us, for when we returned from these little absences we would find admonishing notes pinned neatly to the furniture. Although we had bargained that hot water would be available every day, they eventually reduced the operation of the water heater to twice a week, and even that provoked tirades. We began paying part of their electricity bill. It grew increasingly difficult and expensive to get the minimum of comfort from these ladies who were enjoying a very handsome income, what with the daughter's salary of 50,000, the old lady's pension, and the rent of 33,000 dinars, which was quite visibly going into a refrigerator and a TV set and a vacuum cleaner. Yet they heated their own quarters only when they had guests and watched TV in the evenings bundled in blankets. In winter the old lady could be seen wearing old socks which she had taken out of our wastebasket. After she bought the refrigerator, she declined to use it in winter since she could save electricity by continuing to keep milk, meat, and butter on the balcony. Her chief complaint against Communists, interestingly enough, was that they preached equality and lived well themselves while others like her suffered from the high cost of living. She used this opposition to justify the fact that she paid tax on only half the rent she collected.

The war had given the son of the family, a mining engineer who lived at mines an hour or two from Belgrade, quite a different mentality. His sister and mother told us that he was only seventeen when the war came on and he had to go to work in a bakery. There he became acquainted with workers for the first time and, as they reported it, "became one of them." He joined the Communist Party, went to school after the war, and now refuses to take special advantages for himself because of his education. His fellow workers chose him to make a trip to America to study mine operations;

in America he was offered good jobs, but he went back to the
mines in Yugoslavia. This contrast in attitudes between members
of a single family is not so very rare in a country where things have
changed so much. Now nothing could be more foreign to the son
than his mother and sister's grasping obsession with pennies.

After we had been five months with them, they added the last
straw: a demand that we buy our own linens or pay more rent.
Although we had no idea where we would go, we gave notice.

Fortunately, the publishing house where we were doing translations and editing asked us about that time to stay on for a longer
term, and we agreed to stay if they would help find us an apartment we could afford. We went about the city several mornings in
the company car with a list of addresses from the tourist agencies.
The rents were high and no complete apartments seemed to be
available. Usually a family had crowded itself into one or two
rooms and set off two or three others as an apartment. There was
no real privacy. In the end we found nothing this way and we got
our apartment through a *kombinatsiya* (the Serbian cognate of our
word "combination"). This word has a special meaning in Yugoslavia which it lacks in English. A *kombinatsiya* is a scheme, a
deal, an arrangement unforeseen by those who set up the patterns
for the orderly business of this world. Though it may be illegal, a
kombinatsiya usually only strikes into that zone covered by the
word of the law but unblessed by the spirit. More often than not a
kombinatsiya is a way of getting something for nothing by doing
things in a way that satisfies the minimum of their original intention while serving some other purpose at the same time. The
simplest and most ancient *kombinatsiya* is the use of influence to
obtain things which are being offered in any case: jobs, things to
be bought or sold, etc. Another is to build gratitude in the course
of one's ordinary business: giving out work to those who will or
might give something in return instead of to those who by some
objective standard deserve it, or instead of leaving things to
chance. Many Yugoslavs have a very penetrating eye for the "surplus value," to borrow a Marxist phrase, that lies latent in an
ordinary transaction. Their eye is deep and their mind and tongue

are quick, for it is in split seconds that one must maneuver to press these hidden advantages.

It is difficult to say what, if anything, the *kombinatsiya* has to do with the political system in Yugoslavia today. Certainly Yugoslavs did not await the arrival of socialism to discover their talent for combining. There is so much of it and so many people are so constantly and cleverly at work on it that it is a cultural characteristic. One might risk the objections of the anthropologists and say that it is a talent developed in the idleness of peasant life and simply looks more brilliant when transferred into a modern world that has been created in the course of a couple of decades. The Balkans have offered special conditions for the nourishment of this talent so akin to intrigue. Looking upon it in a socialist context, one is perplexed to choose between two alternatives. In a sense, socialism is the victim of this holdover from the past. At the same time, combining finds very fruitful grounds in the present society, for it thrives on the informal, the complex, the vague; and in Yugoslavia, where politics sometimes prevails over purely economic considerations, everything in an enterprise is complicated and to a great extent informal. Every enterprise has a party organization whose function is purely political, and though this organization cannot be said to "run" the enterprise, it can influence affairs very greatly by secret pressure on the director or by open pressure on the workers' council or collective. The very introduction of social and political complications into the running of a business so that neither production nor money-making can be pursued without other considerations opens the door to those shrewd heads who want to complicate things for their own uses.

The *kombinatsiya* through which we got our apartment was arranged by the editor under whom we worked, a man of brilliant talents for intrigue who before his decline from power for behavior unbefitting public office was head of the secret police in one of the Yugoslav republics. The apartment belonged to a member of the secret police who had continued loyal to the former minister and who came almost every morning to visit him. They had worked out many *kombinatsiyas,* no doubt to their mutual profit. I heard of one in which they arranged for someone in an art museum to make a high appraisal of a painting so that the owner of the picture obtained a higher price from another party.

Our arrangement had the pattern of a circle, a characteristic of many *kombinatsiyas*. We were to pay 60,000 dinars, or $80, a month for the furnished apartment; this was not unreasonable compared to the prices usually charged foreigners for such accommodations but it was more than we could or wanted to pay. The publishing house would contribute to our rent by overpaying us for translation and the landlord would lease to us what was a very comfortable and pleasant apartment. Everyone was getting what he wanted. We got an apartment; the enterprise ensured our continued services by advancing us a year's rent against future translations and editing; the policeman got the advance, which gave him the money he needed to get out of debt; and the editor got a slice of the rent from the policeman for his trouble and imaginative efforts in dreaming up this scheme. But if one looks at this transaction from a socialist point of view, one comes to the inevitable and eternal conclusion: the people pay. This is an expression frequently heard in Yugoslavia. It is always voiced when a blunder, waste, or extravagance is uncovered. When we were riding about looking for an apartment, a woman from the office who accompanied us asked what should be done about the gas the chauffeur wasted by wandering up one street and down another instead of asking directions. "The people pay," the chauffeur said, in a tone that included both regret and resignation. In the one little formula he expressed his guilt for wasting the gas and at the same time his understanding forgiveness, for he was clearly aware that he was one of the people who would pay.

Certainly the people were paying for the *kombinatsiya* in which we were involved. We were being paid more than the work we delivered was worth by normal standards, though perhaps the interest of the enterprise lay in keeping us at any price. But the apartment was state property and had been built with state investments to house state employees; our landlord had received it

through his job. He paid a monthly rent of 4,500 dinars and had
no right to rent it out.

Two days after we moved in with a year's lease, the rent all
paid, President Tito made a speech which electrified the whole
citizenry because it expressed everyone's gripes against the waste,
petty corruption, and self-seeking that had become commonplace.
(The speech inspired a Yugoslav joke in which a Canadian journalist is said to have asked an official what was the significance of
"Tito's speech." "Which speech?" asked the official. "There've
been several of late." "You know," replied the Canadian, "the one
against the regime.") The speech was aimed so directly at exactly
the kind of *kombinatsiya* which accounted for our pleasant new
surroundings that from the first week of our tenancy I was expecting complications. But our landlord reassured us and said we need
not fear having to move.

The signs began to appear, however, that a year's advance rent
might not be enough to assure our use of the apartment for long.
People began to come to the door looking for the landlord, and
they were very surprised to learn that he had rented out his apartment. They asked where he was and I repeated to them the only
information he had given me—that he was away in Bosnia. Then
they became interested in who I was and what I was doing. When I
told them, they invariably nodded and politely withdrew. These
people were apparently members of the landlord's family, for I
heard rumors that his family had only learned of his activities by
discovering that he had rented out the apartment; now, I heard,
they were setting about to put his affairs straight, beginning with
his returning me my money and taking back his apartment. He was
obviously not eager to do this, because his apartment was earning
him money and if he took it back he would only have transferred
his debts from his former creditors to members of his family. For
three months he kept reassuring me. But then one day he appeared
with an eviction notice. "This is just a formality," he said. "They
are pressing me in the commune administration. But it will all
blow over, believe me." From another source I heard that the

house president, a friend of the landlord and also a member of the secret police, had reported him, not for renting out state property, but for renting out his apartment to "foreigners who knew he was in the secret police." I was mystified as to why the house president should make such an odd charge, when the misuse of state property was so clear-cut. Obviously, this was an affair I would never understand. A test of influence began to develop between the commune authorities and my superiors in the publishing house, who had sanctioned the arrangement. I decided to do nothing until I got my advance rent back. When the three months' eviction notice ran out, my landlord had not appeared to enforce it or to return the money. But other people began to come to the door again. They were surprised to find me still there. Perhaps I should have been surprised myself, but I had understood that everything had been "fixed up" in the informal way things are sometimes fixed up in Yugoslavia.

Finally the landlord came, escorted by someone who appeared to be leading him by the hand to do what he had to do, whether for the party, the family, the society, the secret police, or the local authorities. I signed a receipt for the money and promised to move as soon as I could find another place to live. They told me there was no hurry. The landlord seemed anxious for me to stay now that he had fulfilled his obligations, for I would still be paying 2,000 dinars a day for the apartment. But I had had enough of *kombinatsiyas*. I found another apartment without much of a search, at the same price, under perfectly legal arrangements, with a landlady who owned what she was renting.

The apartment was in an old building. The rooms were large with high ceilings and parquet floors; and the landlady, who was new to the business of renting, had made great efforts to refurnish the apartment. We occupied the front part of the apartment and cooked on a hot plate in the bathroom while she occupied the kitchen and maid's room across the hall.

The landlady, a woman in her sixties, had left her farm in southern Serbia eight years before. She sold everything and came with her daughter to Belgrade, where they bought an apartment which was already occupied. They went to live in a furnished room and hoped the occupant would move out. It was foolhardy but luck was with her. When the occupant built himself a house in Bosnia and moved, the right of occupancy legally passed to her. But she was the victim of a *kombinatsiya*. The occupant illegally sold his right of occupancy to an army colonel who settled in before the poor woman even knew the apartment was empty. The colonel managed to take possession by bribing the house president and the house treasurer. Once he was in, she had no way but the courts open to her. As she kept repeating to me, "He had some place from which to fight; I had nothing." The colonel was ensconced and only a court order could get him out. She went to court and won her case. He appealed. She won again, and again he appealed. For every favorable decision she got, there was always a new court in which the colonel could drag out the fight and meanwhile enjoy the apartment. She, meantime, had spent up her savings and could no longer afford her furnished room. She asked the colonel to let her at least use the maid's room (the one she occupied while I rented from her), but he refused. A relative arranged for her to live in the laundry room of her building. And the legal battle lasted not weeks or months but seven years! Finally the landlady got an eviction notice for the colonel and she and her daughter were careful to push their things into the apartment the moment he started to leave so that some other interloper did not arrive and bring them another seven years of bad luck. They rented out the apartment in order to pay for repairs and redecoration (since the colonel, knowing he would eventually be forced out, had let it go to ruin) and in order to repay the debts they had accumulated in seven years of battling through the courts. One irregularity leads to another: her difficulties in obtaining her rights made the landlady feel justified in reporting for taxes only half the rent I paid.

The poor woman talked of her battle for that apartment in all sorts of disparate connections and laid to it physical ailments which were undoubtedly the result of her age. As it was, she was still quite a hardy soul; but once, she said, she had been a woman of untold strength and energy. And now, it is true, she had learned resignation. When something happened, when, for instance, the heavy snow on the roof caused leaking all over the two best rooms of her apartment and the janitor said he could do nothing, she said, "I have learned patience from my colonel. I never had it before, but now I know we shall not die from this. We can only complain afterwards and try to get the house council to pay."

The house councils are small committees elected by the tenants of every apartment house to handle the business of the house, for though most residential property (excluding individual dwellings) has been nationalized, the principle of decentralized management is applied here as in other areas. The house council has a president and a treasurer and holds regular meetings to decide on matters which under capitalism are the concern of the landlord or his agent: they contract for work to be done on the building, apply for loans, hire a janitor, and collect the rent for the apartments. The way they conduct their business is regulated by law and there are further restrictions on them at the moment, since they must rely on bank loans for most of their funds. For many years the government followed a policy of giving priority to new building, even to the point of using funds for this which should have gone to the maintenance of existing buildings. However, when the housing situation eased somewhat and the need for repairs in many cases became desperate, bank policy changed and considerable funds were made available to the house councils for repairs.

Although the house councils are organized like workers' councils or commune assemblies and are another part in the system of direct democracy, they have not come very far. The low rents which are a partial compensation for low incomes in the socialized sector of the economy do not allow the councils to accumulate much money. This holds back their development as centers of democratic action: people remain indifferent to a decision-making forum when there is no money with which to carry out their decisions. At the same time, there are signs of a lack of responsibility in using the small funds that are available. It is common to hear that the prewar landlords took better care of their buildings than the house councils now do.

There was much talk in our house about a loan to repair the roof after the snow had damaged it, and finally a woman came from the bank to inspect the damage and estimate the cost of repairs. Ten days later the news came that a loan had been granted to cover repair of the roof so that the inside of the house would not be damaged further, but there was no money to redecorate the walls and ceilings which had been blotched by the leakage. A request for money to paint the window trim had been granted, but only enough to paint the surfaces exposed to the weather. The criteria of bank policy were clear: there was money to go around for only those repairs which might lead to wasteful deterioration. The time had not yet come when the old buildings could be put in their best shape. This incident in our house made it quite clear that the house council was not acting as responsibly as a landlord might have done, for a landlord would probably not have allowed snow to stay on the roof until it caused leaking into an apartment below. He would see that it was cheaper to clear off the snow than to repair the plaster and paint the walls of the apartment. When there is only a little money, people tend to think first of their own apartments and may even neglect the building as a whole in order to paint them. Perhaps a little greater abundance will solve this entire problem.

Even now the house councils are operating, and one occasionally hears of interesting problems that they face. In one apartment house I knew of, the council even had some money. One of the tenants learned of an elevator being discarded and sold by a government agency and proposed to the council that they use their funds to replace the elevator which the building had lost during the war. Another tenant, however, proposed that the funds go toward a face-lifting job on the outside of the building. Like most other prewar buildings in Belgrade it had become a little drab and could have used a sandblasting job. What was amusing about this intramural political contest was the way in which the tenants took sides. The spokesman for the elevator, who lived on the fourth floor, had no trouble getting supporters in the upper reaches of the building. The proponent of face-lifting rallied his neighbors on the lower floors. For weeks the tenants of the third floor, wheedled from above and below, remained split. The council finally bought the elevator after its champion swayed the third-floor tenants with eloquent reminders of the two old ladies, one of them his mother, who lived above them.

One day an American student in Belgrade told me that the council in her house had been meeting every night for ten days and none of the tenants talked of anything else. It seemed that the man who built the building before the war had been a lover of the classic style and had stuck the cement heads of his favorite goddesses on the cornice of the building five stories above the pavement. Time had loosened whatever held these concrete blobs of Greek beauty in place, and some tenant had raised the question: who is responsible if one of these heavy ornaments tumbles down and kills a pedestrian? The problem could easily have been solved by removing the busts or making sure they were there to stay. But the question that had been raised was fundamental and no one knew the answer. This situation may seem strange to those who have lived their lives in the realm of the common law, but it is a frequent occurrence in Yugoslavia, where the revolution has undone the old notion of property. A surprising number of everyday technicalities become unclear when a new theory of property replaces the old one. And though there is no lack of cynics in Yugoslavia who make fun of all the talk about theory, plenty of ordinary people have discovered a new interest in the matter of society and its regulation. So while inquiries were sent in the direction of the government to learn who was legally responsible, the council entangled itself in theoretical deliberations. For a time the council members tried to pass the buck to their president, but the legal burden finally fell on them all.

The problems of the house council in a small apartment house are either routine or sporadic and can usually be solved informally. But in houses with as many as eighty apartments, like those of New Belgrade, the completely new city being built across from the capital on sand pumped from the Danube, the house council is likely to have a constant load of work. It must keep several elevators running (which is no small matter—Yugoslavia must be the only country in the world where you can see signs saying "This elevator is in order"), see that tenants are not illegally renting out rooms, settle squabbles about whose apartments need painting and repairs soonest, collect rents and keep up the building, carry on current business with stores located on the ground floor, and find more and more space for parking and playgrounds. A large building also offers greater possibilities for rendering services to the tenants. Launderette service can be set up in the basement and a recreation area on the roof; a day nursery can be organized to relieve mothers who are working or going to school; pressure can be exerted on the commune to get conveniently located schools and shopping centers. In some of the large houses the house council is like a miniature parliament and even serves as a forum on political questions outside the house. Perhaps one day it may serve as a basic political unit through which citizens will become more aware of local political events and more able to organize themselves to exert influence.

VII

On the Job

For most of my two years in Yugoslavia I worked for a Belgrade publishing house which printed English translations of Yugoslav technical works for the National Science Foundation, an agency of the U.S. Government. Although publishing is a small-scale and atypical business, much of what I saw in the firm I worked for can be taken as fairly representative of the socialist sector of the Yugoslav economy.

In the range of incomes, for example, my enterprise was quite typical. My monthly salary as an English editor was 40,000 dinars (about $53), about the average for university graduates and qualified technicians. The lowest wage—about 20,000 dinars ($26) was the general minimum in Yugoslavia for unskilled labor. The highest salary went to the director—about 81,000 dinars ($108). This was the average for directors; the maximum in most of the country was 100,000 dinars ($133). The assistant director's salary was about 70,000 dinars ($93); the senior editors, all of them well-known men of letters, got 65,000 ($86); the copy editors were paid about 45,000 ($60); the ordinary editors like myself got 40,000; and the clerks and secretaries got about 30,000 ($40). This scale was roughly that of the whole country, except for Slovenia, where the economy is stronger and the standard of living higher. In 1963 a handful of directors in that republic were even reported to be earning up to two and three hundred thousand dinars a month ($260-$400).

In theory, incomes are differentiated by the principle "to each according to his work," though in practice this usually means "payment according to qualifications and position." At this stage of their development the Yugoslavs are in no position to apply the Communist ideal "from each according to his abilities and to each according to his needs." Incomes based only on needs, regardless of differences in qualifications and effort, are perhaps feasible in a highly developed country where there is enough money to satisfy everyone's needs. They are unthinkable in a developing country which is still too short of money to meet anyone's needs completely. In such a situation there are two choices: equal incomes for all or incomes differentiated according to training and effort. A policy of equal incomes might seem more "socialist," but unfortunately it does not develop the economy. Economic development requires raising the level of work skills and general culture as quickly as possible, and this cannot be done without great individual efforts both on and off the job. If people are not to be forced to make these efforts by outright coercion—a problematical stratagem at best—they must be encouraged to do so by the offer of rewards for advancement. The Yugoslavs, who are both pragmatists and realists, have seen that when everyone is short of money, higher salaries are the most effective rewards. Though by using economic incentives they run the risk of being called "capitalist" (or at least encouraging "capitalist" traits in the citizens), this seems a small risk compared to the damage suffered by a country which coerces its workers—or even compared to the damage brought by appealing sentimentally to the worker's devotion to country, brotherhood, or socialism in order to push him to work harder.

Economic incentives are not unbridled in Yugoslavia; people cannot accumulate capital and then let their money work for them, and the generally accepted maximum and minimum salaries eliminate the possibility of vast differences in wealth. But the system is far from perfect. Some people, including the highest government officials and private artisans, such as tailors, make more money than could possibly be justified by comparing either their qualifications or the value of their work to what other people do. Unskilled workers often make less than is justified. And in many fields where it is hard to determine the relative importance of qualifications or to tell just how competent and hardworking a man is, criteria such as seniority or wartime service or even a man's political connections become too important. For example, law provides that a war veteran may be credited with higher qualifications than his actual training warrants if his experience justifies this and if he passes a special examination. In practice, however, many veterans get credited with higher qualifications without fulfilling these conditions. Thus, many people are in responsible, high-salaried jobs for which they are poorly qualified and which someone else could handle much better. This particular problem was much worse ten years ago than it is now, but it still causes a certain amount of demoralization.

In spite of the many imperfections and injustices that are evident, the system of economic incentives is working. Thousands of people are going to night school or getting scholarships from their factories to enroll full time at the university. And their salaries reflect the new skills they acquire.

Until recently all salaries were kept very low by a policy of rapid development through high investment, but this policy of low incomes is gradually changing. Salaries in my publishing house had risen greatly before I left, and several people had moved to competing firms where salaries were even higher. Since then, personal incomes have jumped nearly 40 percent.

Premiums for medical care, unemployment compensation, and social security are paid directly by the enterprise for all its employees. Ordinarily, an individual employee does not pay an income tax; rather, the enterprise pays a tax on the entire fund which it sets aside for personal incomes. There is a personal income tax, but it is paid primarily by artisans and other persons who carry on private business, since the basic exemption is well above the annual salary of most people working in the socialist sector. My salary of 40,000 dinars was thus take-home pay.

Like all workers in the socialized sector of the economy, I received free medical and dental care and two weeks' paid vacation with a 75 percent reduction on travel fares; and since the publishing house was making money, I got two bonuses a year (each equivalent to a month's salary) when the profits were divided up among the workers. But since the publishing house was too small to accumulate the large funds necessary to build apartments for its employees, no low-rent housing was available. Had I not translated for the publishing house and for various magazines on contract, I would never have been able to live on my income, for as a foreigner I had to rent on the open market, and my last apartment cost 60,000 dinars a month—20,000 more than my salary.

The Yugoslavs I worked with were all able to make cheap living arrangements. Some had obtained apartments through their wives or husbands who worked in larger enterprises, others had inherited an apartment or house, and in a few hardship cases the publishing house purchased apartments for employees.

The ordinary working day in both offices and plants begins at six or seven o'clock in the morning and ends at two or two-thirty in the afternoon. This was the schedule of most people in the publishing house. But many employees in the literary part of the enterprise enjoyed a much more flexible schedule. The senior editors made an appearance about noon for conferences and to answer the questions of the proofreaders. The ordinary editors and proofreaders worked according to norms and did most of their work at home; they also came in about noon for an hour or two. My hours were ten to one. These schedules were peculiar to the publishing business. Everywhere else people went to work for the usual eight-hour day, six days a week, since at that time the work week was forty-eight hours (it is now forty-two).

The atmosphere in my office lacked the efficiency and bustle of an American office. The pace was leisurely, with many interruptions for coffee, reading the newspaper, and chatting with friends from other departments, who liked to congregate in the translation office because of its armchairs. Eventually, however, I discovered that socialist "business" as organized in my enterprise, and in Yugoslavia generally, is not so very different from business as we know it in America.

Indeed, the best analogy for understanding the Yugoslav economic system is free enterprise. This might surprise many Americans, who have another idea of what socialism is. But the Yugoslavs have tried to introduce Western forms into their socialist context wherever they seemed to offer advantages. One of the things they have fitted to this context is precisely the free market system.

The economy is, of course, not capitalist. Capitalist enterprise is restricted to peasant farmers, who may own up to twenty-odd acres of land, and artisans, who may hire up to three helpers. All the rest of the economy has been nationalized. But businesses are not run by the state. Some loose planning is done by the central government to regulate the market and investment, but companies are basically independent. They compete on the domestic market and sometimes on the foreign market. They have trade secrets, salesmen, chains of outlets, and all the rest that goes with competition for the consumer's dinar. They adjust their prices and the quality of their products in order to make a profit. They pay taxes on their income and put what is left into the funds of the enterprise. What is done with these funds is a matter decided within the enterprise itself.

In the early postwar years the economy was run quite differently. The government administered it in detail: the national plan was in effect a command for a certain factory to produce a stated quantity of its product as a stated price. Enterprises borrowed not only investment funds but even their operating funds from the central bank. The accountants in the enterprises calculated and earmarked funds for amortizing their capital assets, but those funds were then collected by the government and reallocated where the government saw fit to invest them.

Eventually, however, the Yugoslavs rejected the idea that the greatest efficiency and rationality come from centralized economic administration and turned to the goal of creating an economy which would operate through a free market. In other words, they began to respect the idea that the essence of economic activity is independent initiative, a notion with which Americans can sympathize. In part at least, the Yugoslavs arrived at it by facing the facts of the American economic success.

As in a capitalist system, the main restriction upon enterprises is that they must operate within the framework of law. However, the laws cover a great many aspects of business operation which in capitalism are left to management or to collective bargaining. They are used, for example, to further the development of workers' management within the enterprise, for in Yugoslav theory an economic enterprise is socialist only when the workers make business policy and enjoy the profits. Although there are no owners in the economy, there are managers; and the delicate relations between the managers and the elected workers' council and managing board are regulated by law.

In addition, the laws regulate accounting procedures in detail. For instance, there exist laws to guarantee that enterprises will follow certain elementary rules of good housekeeping and at the same time not overlook the general needs of the country as a whole. Further, the laws set up a priority system: money must be used first for what the central authorities consider most essential. For instance, an enterprise may not use its profits to raise personal incomes until it has satisfied numerous requirements associated with strengthening its economic position. Among these requirements is the establishment of a reserve fund which must be filled to a certain minimum percentage of net income before the enterprise can use its money as it pleases. Enterprises are thus stimulated to do business economically and to accumulate their own funds, because in that way they can free themselves from the influence of the banks, which generally reflect government policy. So long as an enterprise must borrow its operating funds as well as investment funds, the central bank will have something important to say about its affairs. As it becomes more secure financially and builds up its own funds, the enterprise is free to use its money as it pleases; it spends and invests without asking anyone. When its economic position worsens, it is drawn into the orbit of central policy again.

Many enterprises have already achieved a wide latitude of independence because their business has been successful. When their income is consistently large enough to cover the minimum reserve funds required by law, they regularly have a surplus to spend without outside interference. In practice, they are subject to some sort of outside policy only when they need to borrow money for extraordinary projects: new construction or expensive machinery. Before a loan is approved, experts from the bank will analyze the entire project, and if they do not think it wise, or if they find it conflicts with national policy, they will not approve it. But the enterprises have come a long way since the days when they had to borrow even their petty cash funds from the bank. The expenditures they are able to make on their own are getting larger and larger. Many of them are building apartment houses for their workers, expanding into new plants, and installing new machinery without so much as a word to anyone beyond the factory walls.

This amounts to a thoroughgoing decentralization of the economy, with less and less government interference. In fact, it no longer makes sense to say that the economy is owned by the state. Ownership, as we understand it, means the right to manage economic activity and to enjoy the profits from it. Yugoslav enterprises are not managed by the government; their profits go into the government treasury only in the form of tax revenues.

Any market system has inherent problems. A promise of profit stimulates an enterprise, but it is difficult for society always to guide that enterprise in desirable directions. For example, a dozen companies in various parts of the country decided to buy licenses from foreign firms to produce transistor radios. The federal secretary for industry called all the managers and superintendents of these enterprises into his office and tried to persuade them to work together in producing transistor radios and not to persist in an inefficient plan which would squander precious foreign currency on half a dozen different Italian and German licenses. The managers and technical directors replied that their communes had lent them money to produce transistor radios and the matter was settled. They walked out of his office. This is an interesting case because the "free enterprise" managers happened to be in the wrong and the Secretary for industry in the right, but there was little he could do. Integration of enterprises through various forms of association is now being pushed in order to avoid just this kind of chaos. Manufacturers of chassis, engines, and tires may cooperate in the production of a certain model of bus. The share of each factory in the arrangement constitutes only part of its total operation. The enterprises sign contracts with each other and establish a small central office to coordinate production and to advertise and sell the finished buses. The central office has no management authority over any of the enterprises but exists only to serve the common interests of the members of the association. In this way, the economic need for central coordination is satisfied without violating the independence of the individual producers.

Because of the country's unfavorable position in relation to the more highly developed countries from which it must import machines and some consumer goods, there are still government regulations on imports and foreign currency, though everyday they are fewer.

Perhaps the greatest limitation on the independent operation of an enterprise is the fact that the director (or manager) is appointed from outside. The trend is toward giving the staff of an enterprise the right to hire and fire its director independently, but at present a new director is recommended by a joint committee on which representatives of the enterprise and officials of the commune administration sit in equal numbers. The committee's choice is then accepted or rejected by the workers' council. This committee is supposed to choose a new director from among applicants who respond to newspaper announcements, but frequently the man is chosen behind the scenes and the committee only approves an appointment from higher up. This is particularly true in the case of enterprises which are of vital importance to the national economy.

The director's position is very ambiguous. He is almost always a member of the party and is therefore obliged to abide by the general policy of the Party Program. At the same time, the local commune expects his enterprise to show a profit, because profit means tax revenues for the commune budget. Further, if the business dealings of the enterprise are not strictly legal, it is the director who is held responsible. And finally, though he is in some fashion a representative of outside power, he is at the same time legally bound by the decisions of the workers' council, which is elected from the whole collective (or work force) and sits over him like a board of directors. He is also responsible to the managing board, a smaller group elected by the workers' council to work closely with him on all current business.

In the laws on workers' management the director's duties are limited to the enterprise's day-to-day operation. He is the manager and his orders are to be obeyed in the course of business. His usual functions are sometimes difficult to distinguish from those of a hired manager in a small American company. But there are important differences. He is empowered to maintain work discipline in the course of production, but he faces restrictions an all sides. First of all, he cannot fire a man without the approval of the workers' council. Firing, moreover, is not an easy way out for the enterprise, since every employee has a contract and is well protected by law. An enterprise has to pay up to six months' salary in severance pay. Second, his day-to-day decisions must be cleared by the managing board, and his long-range policies must be approved by the workers' council. If he is highhanded or tries to ride roughshod over them, it is not impossible that the workers will get rid of him. At the very least he will find them hostile. Though the people who sit on the board and the council may not be strong enough to put him in his place, they are aware of their rights under the law and they will make trouble if things get too bad. Often they sit silent and allow the director and his colleagues on the professional management staff to railroad through their own plans for the company, but meanwhile they are learning to use democratic procedures and getting an idea of how the company is run. And since the people on the workers' council are apt to know what goes on in their own departments better than the director does, the time eventually comes when they find themselves in a position and in the mood to participate. They may participate with a vengeance.

The director, then, must be a politician on all sides. Sometimes he is too good a politician. A particularly clever director can keep the members of the workers' council uninformed about the enterprise's current business by providing them with no more than vague annual financial reports and policy statements. On this basis he can get an inexperienced or timid workers' council to approve measures that go to his personal benefit and damage the interests of the enterprise. He may persuade the workers' council to spend millions of dinars to buy him a better apartment by arguing that out of sheer self-respect the enterprise should give its director fitting accommodations. Unless they oppose him he may use the company car as if it were his own. Or he may arrange foreign travel for himself at the enterprise's expense. Since the shortage of foreign currency makes it imperative to restrict such travel to urgent business, all foreign trips must be approved by the workers' council. Presumably the workers will see that the $20 a day the director spends on trips to Western Europe could be used to import precious new machinery. But if his trip is legitimate, the cost may be returned many times over, so they do not dare simply to reject his requests. Unless they are thoroughly versed in all the enterprise's operations and prospects, they may have to take the director's word for the urgency of his business. Thus it happens that he may travel on business to Copenhagen when his business could have been handled in a letter of one paragraph, or when he had no business at all there. Directors of enterprises sometimes play a game called "You invite me, I'll invite you." I have seen two distant officials arrange implicitly to write formal letters to each other's companies stating the necessity for an exchange of visits. Those who travel abroad often live on cheese and bread in order to save their $20 a day for purchases, the most coveted of which is an automobile. (The import of automobiles was halted unconditionally in 1962 precisely in order to stop this practice.) Finally, the director can squander the company's funds in entertaining guests who have little or no business connections with the enterprise. When the workers see visiting delegations going out to nightclubs and fancy restaurants, they shrug their shoulders: "The people always pay," they say to one another.

The clever director who runs roughshod over his workers' council and manages the company as he likes, sometimes to his own benefit, is one side of a delicate situation. But though public opinion is hard on the director, all the difficulties do not lie with him. To discover some on the other side, all you have to do is imagine yourself trying to make workers' management work in a business you know and with the individuals you know there. Or ask an American businessman what would happen if the workers tried to run his factory: "They don't even know how the factory itself runs. They know nothing about business, about our markets, about quality. They wouldn't be responsible; they would put all the profits in their paychecks and let the factory vegetate. They would be shortsighted and if they made an investment in new machinery, they would think the market owed them an immediate return and they would raise prices even though the machines were designed to lower them. They would steal and take the whole factory home with them, piece by piece. They wouldn't be able to handle the complicated personnel problems in a factory; they wouldn't understand that you have to know how to deal with people; you have to be diplomatic; you have to know not only what to do but how to carry your point in a meeting. Some demagogue would lead them by the noses and get them to vote for things that were either simply crazy or which filled his pocket at the expense of the employees and the enterprise. They wouldn't work; they don't believe that managers do any work, and when they became the managers and owners they would act as they think owners and managers ought to act: by doing nothing, by taking permanent vacations. The whole thing would get too political; there would be too much red tape; a quick, unhesitating decision is what makes a successful business, and the power must be given to one man to make that decision. If he had to convince every employee that he was doing the right thing, he would spend all his time making speeches. You can't run a factory like a political convention."

This hypothetical businessman is particularly perspicacious, for his words of warning contain nothing which has not occurred and is not still occurring in the Yugoslav system of workers' management.

But if all these things are going on, how can the Yugoslav economy operate efficiently? The publishing house where I worked is a good example of how Yugoslav factories and businesses are pulling themselves up by the bootstraps to something like profitable and efficient production and to something like a functioning system of workers' management. The head of our translation department was a war hero who had fallen from a high political position and was now enjoying this soft spot as some recognition of his onetime valor and as a sign that no one knew what else to do with him. He knew no English and thus could not tell whether the translations were good or not, but he had a passion for complicating office affairs, which successfully covered up his ignorance. Having no useful work to do, he spent hours on the job demonstrating his great talent for telling stories; everyone had to listen, for he was the boss. He even drew people from other departments into our office to listen to his talk. This may seem of no importance, but such people have been a general problem in Yugoslavia.

For two years before I came to work there the department had had a Yugoslav editor with a little knowledge of English and of various scientific disciplines. This man was the only check on the translations, which were generally done by Yugoslavs. Because he was a poor judge of English and had collected a group of translators who were better at selling themselves than at constructing an English sentence, there was a two-year backlog of translations which the National Science Foundation had refused to accept.

The rest of the office staff consisted of an editorial secretary, who did most of the chief's work and tried to straighten out the complications he made; a copy editor who prepared the manuscripts for the printers; and two proofreaders who worked at home and came in once a day to get new work and clear up their questions with the copy editor. Both he and they knew a little English, but not enough.

What is interesting about the situation is that the people in the enterprise did not seem overly worried about the utter mess into which office affairs had fallen. And after all there was not very much they could do about it, so long as they could not get someone with a native knowledge of English to check the work of the translators and editor. They were doing work which they had never done before, and until they got help they could not even go about learning how to do it.

Hiring someone who spoke English as his native language gave them the touchstone they needed. The backlog was caught up; the incompetent translators were weeded out and new ones were found who worked conscientiously and knew their fields. As soon as the people in the office had some solid ground beneath them, things began to go forward and develop much as they might in an American enterprise.

They began to expand enthusiastically. First they paid to have a Yugoslav novel translated, one whose resemblance to *Lolita,* they thought, might interest Americans. As it turned out, no one wanted the novel. Then they got another idea. A book on computers by a Yugoslav professor had attracted the attention of an American publisher who was ready to negotiate either for a translation which he would print himself or for sheets printed in Yugoslavia. Though it was a risky business, the publishing house decided to print the sheets, because the job would force the enterprise to raise the quality of its work and it would bring in foreign currency. Up to then this publishing house had made more money importing office machines than publishing books, but it had recently lost its license for this handsome business. Besides, everyone was aware of the national campaign to increase exports. And perhaps the director had received some special reminder of his duty in this respect. But he had reason to be nervous about this first attempt at exporting. He had to ask himself whether his enterprise was ready to take such a jump. Might it not be better to work first with someone whose standards were not so high, and then later try the Americans? Suppose they botched this first try, wouldn't it be difficult to get another chance when they were actually ready? And they would have to push hard to meet the deadline, in order to avoid the reputation of other socialist countries for being late. Even the first steps of the project would involve large investments of the enterprise's none-too-plentiful funds; suppose they got halfway and could go no further? That would mean money down the drain, and they had already lost money on a novel no one wanted. The author of the book knew these pitfalls well enough to be nervous too. Only the copy director had no doubts—his came later.

The project was full of headaches from the very beginning. Everyone was such a novice at this kind of work that no one had even the vaguest idea how much to charge for translating and printing services. The price suggested to the American publisher was a shot in the dark, mainly intended to be low enough to attract him in spite of his doubts that Yugoslav publishers could do good work on time. The Americans wanted to see a printed sample before signing the contract. It had to be sent three times. When they saw the first attempt they commented wryly that they were willing to overlook all inessential mistakes, but it was obvious no one had even prepared the manuscript before sending it to the printer. And, to be sure, none of the spacing was consistent; the equations were not set up according to any system; letters were often broken; and the whole appearance of the sample was untidy. Not knowing what to do, the copy editor had done nothing. When the third version finally went off, he was sure it was right. I later discovered that the pages were not even in the right order—Chapter Two preceded Chapter One. But the Americans said they would sign the contract in spite of the muddle if the director would give his word that the mistakes would be cleared up in the final version. They graciously sent along a brochure describing their practice in preparing manuscripts. This at last gave the copy editor a standard by which to judge his work. It was at this point that he began to think his job was impossible, for no matter how much he improved his part of the work, he could not transform the printers for whom he prepared the manuscript. Every time they corrected errors noted by the proofreaders they seemed to introduce new mistakes. One sentence in the brochure recommended avoiding certain procedures because they involved costly hand operations. Little did our American customers suspect that the entire book was being set by hand in Yugoslavia! Nor could they have guessed why. The text required a great many Greek letters for mathematical equations and the printers had no machine font of Greek italics to match the type they were using. They had once had such a font, but someone had supposed they would never have any use for it and had thrown it away.

But the contract was eventually signed. The book was printed, the proofs were read countless times, and the final version was accepted. The publishing house had a new line of work. Negotiations were begun to translate and print a series of six Yugoslav textbooks for another American publisher of scientific books. And then the firm got a contract to translate a number of American technical books into French and print them for the new African nations which had been French colonies. This was a more ambitious undertaking, but the staff was better prepared now.

As the efficiency and dispatch of the English translation office increased, it became easier to see from a distance who was working and who was deadwood, and the director, who had hitherto allowed the head of the office complete freedom, finally saw that the freedom was used only to make muddles. He fired the chief, and along with him went an editor in Zagreb who had handled Croatian translations for the office and made the same muddle of them. There was a national campaign at the time to get rid of superfluous personnel, but at first the director had it in his head to replace the chief. Everyone who worked in the office opposed this plan, making it clear that unless he could find that rare man who knew English, knew the publishing business, and was familiar with scientific terminology in both English and Serbo-Croatian, the office staff would have to teach the new chief what they had learned only so that he could give the orders. The question in the director's mind was whether this little staff could maintain some kind of discipline, settle their occasional disputes, and do their work responsibly without the authority of a boss. His temporary solution was to take over the job himself. Whereas before he was rarely seen in the office, now he paid three or four visits a day. But this did not last long. When he was too busy elsewhere to order a letter written or a contract drawn up with a translator, the work was done anyway and then submitted for his approval. Then he ceased to give any orders at all. Though he bore the responsibility for what was done, it was clear to him that in many cases the staff was in a better position to make a decision than he was. More and more he became simply an adviser.

An informal experiment in self-management had worked. One department of the enterprise had been freed of its overseer and was handling its work better than before. No new chief was hired; the enterprise paid out fewer salaries for more work; and the little unit enjoyed a very real independence.

On one occasion it looked as though that independence would be lost. The proofreaders were doing sloppy work and were lax about learning the Greek alphabet and the syllabification of English words. The copy editor and the English editor were having to take up the slack. Rather than call in the director, the staff held a meeting and the editors made their criticisms. The proofreaders rose to defend themselves, complaining that their norms were too high and the editors had no right to criticize them. Tempers grew hot and they threatened to complain to the director. But they calmed down when they were reminded that if the staff could not be jointly responsible for the quality of their work, the director would hire someone to tell them what to do. Their feelings had been hurt—it is apparently more difficult to bear criticism from one's colleagues and equals than from a superior. But after three or four days of chilly relations, they agreed to take their share of the work. The director was never told of the difficulties.

Of course, this was only one office in a publishing house which was itself small compared to a textile mill or machine tool factory. Getting responsibility and decision-making down to individual workers cannot be done in this informal way in a big factory. But it is to achieve much this same independence and self-management that the Yugoslavs have instituted the "economic unit," a concept taken from the highly organized corporations of the industrial countries. In the capitalist corporation the executives divide the operation into economic units so that they can follow the work of individual departments and intervene if costs go too high or other problems arise. In this system, department heads are made responsible for the work done under them and are stimulated to keep it on a certain level of efficiency. In Yugoslavia the basic concept has been completely refurbished: there it is designed to make it possible for workers to participate directly in management and decision-making and to enable the enterprises to follow the principle of payment according to work. In some factories miniature workers' councils have been established in each of the economic units and the foreman's or superintendent's position is like that of the general director in relation to the factory workers' council. In other factories the whole working force of the economic unit constitutes the decision-making body.

Part of the annual profits of an enterprise are divided among the economic units according to their performance in making those profits. Within the unit itself, this income is divided up by the workers as they see fit. They may divide it in equal shares; they may share it proportionally, according to their normal salaries; or they may apply the principle of "payment according to work" by setting up production norms for individual workers or groups of workers engaged in a particular operation. In my economic unit of the publishing house there were norms for editors and proofreaders, but the profits were divided up, not according to whether those norms were fulfilled, but according to monthly salaries. This was the practice in most enterprises at the time, for it is much simpler (if less fair) than trying to pay people according to the work they actually do.

The economic unit is a way of decentralizing power within the enterprise itself; it is the last step in the process of bringing economic decision-making down to the individual worker. The worker thus takes on the responsibility and receives the rewards for cutting costs and raising labor productivity. But raising labor productivity does not depend simply on the efforts and efficiency of the workers; new and more efficient equipment must continually be installed. Some factories have begun to decentralize a part of their investment funds so that decisions about new machinery are made as much as possible by those workers who know the spot into which the new machine is to fit, who know their own department and know which machine will make the most difference. Hiring and firing is another function being transferred to these units, on the theory that the people in the department know best the kind of man they need and are best able to say who is not working or is unqualified.

As one might suspect, troubles can arise with this system. In one factory the unit which provided the raw material began to pile it up before the doors of the unit that performed the first phase of manufacture. They had taken the new system to heart. They speeded up their operation and raised their production figures in order to get a larger slice of the total profits. But they worked too fast and the quality of the raw material declined. This made trouble in the first phase of manufacture. Moreover, the raw material, standing in piles out of doors, began to deteriorate. It became clear that this unit would contribute more to the overall manufacturing process if it worked according to the needs of the first phase of manufacture. In other words, there should always be enough raw material but never too much, and the quality of the raw material should make it easy to work with in later stages. So the incomes of the two units were integrated, and the supply unit's share of the profits was subordinated to the production of the first phase of manufacture.

Another problem is how to include nonproduction departments like personnel or accounting or the repair shop in the system of "payment according to work." One way is to reward them for cutting down the costs of their own operations. But in many cases a better solution has been found through integration. For instance, in one factory the accounting department signed a contract with the main production unit; they were to deliver accounts and other data within a specified time in order to get a share of the income of the production unit, which was able to cut costs by seeing where it was making unnecessary expenditures.

In another factory the repair shop was first set up as an independent economic unit, and its efficiency was judged by how much the mechanics were able to pare their costs. But it soon became evident that the unit made a greater contribution to the total level of production if it took an interest in the condition of the machines before they arrived in the repair shop. The income of the repair shop was then made dependent on the efficiency of the production unit, and the mechanics began to visit the production unit and ask the workers how the machines were running. They were able to make small repairs on the spot and to see the larger faults in time to cut costs and lost operating time.

My enterprise was one of many in which the concept of the economic unit was applied halfheartedly. Partly this was a reflection of the director's ambiguous attitudes. Though he was exceptionally willing to let people work without interference from him, he seemed inherently incapable of letting the formal system of workers' management develop. He had built up a clique to support his policies and he used the party and union organizations to get his own way and keep power in his hands. No more than a minimum attempt was made to keep the workers acquainted with the current financial situation of the enterprise. Although the staff numbered only two hundred people, the details of business were put in the opaque language of tax manuals. There was rarely any "meat" in the meetings of the workers' council or in those to which the entire staff was summoned. The people elected to the workers' council and managing board were either members of the director's clique or people who were too pusillanimous to object to his wishes. The function of these elected bodies was to agree with the director, and the function of the rest of the workers was to sit and squirm during the occasional meeting at which they heard long, dull reports on what their bodies of self-management had agreed to.

At one meeting I attended, for the election of the new workers' council, there was some open political struggle, but it indicated nothing so much as the peculiar conception of democracy held by those who were running the enterprise. The morning of the meeting I heard rumors of a move to change the list of candidates which had been drawn up by the union officials and the director, i.e., by the powers-that-be in the enterprise. A young woman who was an editor and translator and a long-time Communist was behind the move. The original list contained thirty names, of which twenty-five persons were to be elected to the council. This meant that in fact the electorate had to choose at least twenty people nominated by the powers-that-be. But the discussion never turned on this point of principle. The point which the young woman raised was that there were people on the list who had been serving term after term—ever since the beginning of workers' management. She pointed them out in the meeting and asked them one by one how long they had served. She insisted that it was time that other, younger people be put on the list and mentioned several names. The head of the union organization, an essayist and philosopher and one of the senior editors, replied that it was a good list, and he saw no reason why it sould be changed or in fact why it should contain more names than the places on the council. But the young woman stuck to her point. Then the question arose of whether the collective should add new candidates to the list—as was its legal right—or whether an old-timer should be taken off the list for every new man put on. The director made a soulful speech expressing his sympathy for those who had to be rejected when there were more candidates than seats. He begged the collective to make replacements rather than additions so that the rejections would be kept to a minimum. In line with this, five of the long-term members—some of them with evident reluctance—stood up and withdrew their names. The workers, without discussion and with the hesitation of people unused to democratic procedures, voted to put five new people on the list to replace them. Since these five received more votes than anyone else in the next day's balloting, the end result was that the collective improved its position by rejecting ten of the original list instead of only five. But the essential question of democracy was approached obliquely, to say the least.

Most people in the enterprise blamed the director for the stagnation of workers' management, and certainly he was in part responsible. A man in his early forties, he had been a Communist since the war, which he spent in a Nazi concentration camp in Belgrade. He had important connections, was generally respected outside the publishing house, and was a good businessman. Under his management the enterprise had come out of the red and prospered financially, partly because he was willing to try new things and partly because he knew how to delegate responsibility. But he was not a literary man. Though he made admirable efforts to improve his literary culture and knowledge of foreign languages, he was ill at ease as director of an enterprise in which many of the workers were writers and intellectuals. Fearing their contempt, he gathered around him the worst party hacks in the enterprise and behaved autocratically in the meetings of the workers' council and managing board. Any attempt to oppose his policy decisions he regarded as a personal insult. One day at a meeting of the managing board a member asked whether the European literary journals to which the enterprise subscribed could be made available to other interested people after the director had read them. He denounced the question as an insinuation that he was spending enterprise funds for his own uses, and walked out of the meeting. His cohorts then pushed through a motion to reject this innocuous proposal. When he was not threatened, the director could be very egalitarian. On business trips he rode in front with the chauffeur and they talked as equals. He attended his meetings while the chauffeur attended to the car, but afterward they lunched together, drank together, and stayed in the same hotels. Though it is true that he had demoralized the staff to such a point that the assistant director left the company saying that he could no longer stand the humiliation of dealing with the director's hacks, it is also no doubt true that the director meant what he said when one day he told me, "The director's position is so confused and his job is so thankless that I would never do it except out of party duty. A director is caught in the middle; he is the only man who's never right."

It is a disappointing truth that people like this director, who have an official responsibility to push the democratic revolution forward, are often actually blocking it. But it is also true that democracy can only be fostered to a certain point. A government can set up democratic institutions which make it possible for more people to participate in political life and influence political decisions, but whether or not a democratic spirit springs up in these institutions is in the last analysis the responsibility of the people. Many people in Yugoslavia are less than willing to assume this responsibility. These are the antiheroes of Yugoslav socialism—the "little citizens," as they are called in Serbo-Croatian.

The man who takes no interest in the social world around him and who works away methodically like an ant, arranging the elements of his private life, securing and furnishing his apartment, maneuvering himself into a comfortable job, weaving himself a nest, is a little citizen. But he is no littler a citizen than the man who applauds everything being done in Yugoslavia but has no wish to get involved because he is bent on making his mark in some specialized field. A professor of electrical engineering at the University of Belgrade told me once that many of his students were little citizens. "They think mathematics is the beginning and end of life and care about nothing else," he said. "I have a hard time convincing them that one can be a mathematician without being a man, that although mathematics is a very fine thing, it is still a rather small part of human civilization, human philosophy, and human life."

Those who criticize the way others conduct public business but refuse to take part themselves or even to make their objections openly are also little citizens. The favorite topic of conversation of one of my landladies was the house council in our apartment building. She gave me daily accounts of the inefficiency, stupidity, and dishonesty of those who were serving on the council. One day

I asked her why she didn't attend the meetings or become a member herself. "Surely," she replied, "you don't think I'd get involved with those scoundrels!" I asked another woman one day how well the system of workers' management functioned in the factory where she worked. She shrugged her shoulders. "I never stay for the meetings," she said. "Why not?" I asked. "Oh, let the others run it," she replied. "They don't care what I think."

In my enterprise the six senior editors were called little citizens. Five of them were Communists; all of them had some reputation as men of letters; and they included a poet and a novelist among the best in Yugoslavia. They had no reason to fear the director and did not; if anything, he was afraid of them. These were obviously the people to start a move to put teeth into the managing board and the workers' council, for their position was unassailable. But the editors showed complete indifference toward workers' management. The explanation was fairly simple. They were all involved in their own projects, their poems and plays and essays and novels. They came to work for only a couple of hours a day—from noon to two or two-thirty—while most other employees worked a full eight hours. For those two hours they sat in comfortable armchairs in a newly decorated office, drinking coffee and chatting with prospective authors, arranging for the books they would edit. They had little contact with other workers, never leaving their private world except to confer occasionally with the copy editors who saw to the printing of the books they edited or with the ordinary editors, who did the detailed work on the books (the senior editors did not do such trivial things—their job was to decide which books to publish, arrange for authors or translators, and see to the big problems). Though each of them edited only a half dozen or a dozen books a year, they were very well paid. In short, they had a soft spot, and though their literary work might be important to society, they were not accepting their responsibilities as ordinary employees and ordinary men to act in the political situation before them. They were complacent about a situation which was discouragingly far from the ideal set forth in the program of the League of Communists and in their own novels and essays.

The other workers—the ordinary editors and copy editors and secretaries and accountants and proofreaders and chauffeurs and cleaning women, etc.—resented the senior editors' indifference toward them and their cause, and with some justification. Their positions were not so secure. Many of them were not Communists; if they tried to fight the director, they might be accused of not understanding the aims of the society or of acting out of selfishness. Some excuse might be found to fire a man if he tried to fight alone, and if he tried to organize a group to fight with him, he might be accused of forming a clique. The clique which ran things now watched their critics carefully and were always happy to report opposition to the director in order to win more favor themselves. True, the assistant director, a non-Communist, had quit because of this clique and had had no difficulty getting a similar job in a government publishing house, but he was a highly trained financial expert. It was not so easy to get other jobs in Belgrade if you were a secretary or clerk, for the schools were pouring out people with equal qualifications, and many enterprises were laying off people in the push to raise labor productivity.

Nevertheless, the workers in my enterprise had behind them the force of law, the authority of the government leadership, and the public opinion of the country. If more information was necessary for them to understand the business of the enterprise and participate in the discussion, they could have begun their efforts modestly with a demand that they be given mimeographed copies of all materials before the meetings, in time for them to study carefully what could not be grasped from a mere hearing. If they were afraid to fight openly, they could have fought cautiously. They did not have to attack; they could simply pose innocent questions. "Why, comrade director, is this money necessary?" "Why do we need three company cars?" "Why must this trip be made to Bulgaria or Germany?" Instead they sat silent in the meetings. Afterward each criticized the others for being too timid or indifferent to speak out.

Everyone found a reason for waiting until someone else began: "I
have a wife and family to support; I have to be careful" or "I'll be
on a pension soon, no need to cause trouble" or "I couldn't get
such a good job anywhere else." And so here in the publishing
house, where the high cultural level of the workers would lead one
to believe that the system of workers' management would function
smoothly, it was at a disappointingly low stage of development,
and demoralization lay over the whole collective.

Even so, the process of development had not come to a complete standstill, and, as I saw at the last meeting I attended, a
single incident could change the atmosphere greatly.

The reason for the meeting was a report to the entire staff on the
work of the managing board for the previous year. The reading of
the report took at least an hour, and at the end we were no more
enlightened and a good deal less ready to take an active part in any
discussion. We were bored and looking at our watches. We had
heard a description of the business of the enterprise during the past
year without recognizing any connections with what we had actually been doing, but no one had the energy left to try to pry further
information out of the managers.

Then a member of the managing board spoke up. "Comrades,"
he said, "this report was fine for those of us on the managing
board who have already heard reports from the heads of the various departments, but I am not sure how much it means to those
who have not heard those reports. Therefore I think it would be in
order for the department heads to give us those reports again
before the whole collective, so that everyone can know what I have
learned about our current business."

The director frowned, but there was no refusing. When the
workers make a justified demand, the resistance falls away with
remarkable ease. For the principles of the system are in black-and-
white in the Party Program and a director cannot afford to be
accused of openly violating these principles. So then we heard
detailed reports from the heads of the commercial and export
departments and even from the director himself. Here was what
the workers should have heard in the first place. Our activity was

put into terms of real prospects, real negotiations, and real contracts. It suddenly appeared that the publishing house was doing something an ordinary man could understand: exporting books to America, importing foreign language records from Russia, printing translations of Yugoslav scientific books in English, arranging book sales on the installment plan so that the ordinary worker could buy books, printing art books for the Bulgarians, and so on. I felt that the whole system of workers' management in my enterprise took an enormous step forward in that hour and a half in which the professional staff told us not abstractly but exactly what they were doing, in terms that made sense. For once I felt that these men were acting as if they were responsible to the workers, and not the workers to them. It was a good feeling.

VIII

Looking Further

at Self-Management

WHAT I saw in my own enterprise was not encouraging about the present state of workers' management, but neither was it discouraging about the future. The forms of the system were a reality, and the importance of forms should not be underestimated. If there was only an occasional burst of spirit in the meetings I attended, the lively dissatisfaction expressed outside the meetings indicated that people expected something of the system. If my observations gave me confidence that workers' management would come alive even where it had been stillborn, I shared the widespread belief that its rate of development was slower than necessary. The most important question was whether I could expect to find the same situation in every Yugoslav enterprise, or whether my publishing house was unique. I decided to look further, not to study workers' management in any systematic way, but only to answer that one question. I told the people at the Ministry of Information that I should like to see enterprises where the operation of workers' management might be more lively.

The first place they sent me was a machine tool factory at Zheleznik, just outside of Belgrade. The psychologist there happened to be a close friend, and I had had many long talks with him about the difficulty of introducing the sophisticated and demanding ideas of self-government in a country where the general cultural level was still very low. From his attitudes, from his respect for the trained personnel and his pessimism because of the primitivism of people both in sandals and in city shoes, I thought I might already know something which would guide me in the questions I put to the presidents of the workers' council and the managing board and to the director of information (whose chief task in Yugoslavia is to inform the workers inside the factory but who also handles public relations).

I was met by the young information director, who led me into a large, paneled office where we sat at a little table. He began at once to tell me the history of the factory, which was built in record time in 1947 by youth brigades. I heard not only how much cement was poured and how much floor space the factory covered, but also that 1,800 of these young people had learned to read and write during the construction of the factory and 1,608 of them had become skilled workers. (These are extremely important matters in a country where one-third of the population ten years of age and older has not finished four grades of school, and almost 82 percent of the population has not finished the eight grades of elementary school!) The machine tool factory had not had an easy time of it. When the 1948 split with the Soviet bloc made it necessary for the country to build its own equipment, this factory was put into service. It made everything from lathes to brickmaking equipment, from railroad switches to tank cars. Such versatility was costly. Much of the work had to be done by hand. The machines had been obtained mostly from Germany as reparations—in the late forties they were not new and now they were long past their time. There had been no chance to modernize production because of the great variety of jobs the factory had had to perform.

Now, I was told, the factory was beginning a vast program of reconstruction and modernization which was to be accompanied by specialization so that they could profit from efficient and modern operation. They were working hard to build up their investment fund, which the government would match three-to-one for the costs of the reconstruction. They would swing more toward assembly-line production of medium and heavy machine tools; they would continue to equip entire factories, but would limit themselves to factories for the production of building materials. I got the impression that the factory had been sacrificed to build up Yugoslav industry generally. Whereas many of the factories equipped with machines made here were fully adapted to present economic conditions and well on their way to independence, this factory, like the older brother who goes to work first and puts his younger brothers and sisters through college, had to catch up with a world which thanks to its efforts was now ahead of it. With all this in my mind, I was not surprised later on in the conversation when the president of the workers' council used the word *zavod* to describe the factory. This word is usually used for establishments which are part of the government, like our executive agencies. There was good reason why the people at Zheleznik should feel themselves more a part of the government than a part of the economy.

Two men entered. The president of the managing board, a man of fifty, in a deep green sport jacket, could have passed for a commuter from an American suburb. I asked him about the factory's line of machines, and he talked with what seemed to me great competence about the technical details of their lathes, drills, and milling machines. He did such a thorough job of cataloguing their machine tools that at the end of the list he was forced to leave for another appointment. Not one word had been said about workers' management.

I was left with the president of the workers' council, a tall man of nearly fifty who was dressed in shop clothes, and with the young public relations man, who seemed to be all over himself—too much the disciple to teach and too much the apostle to learn. The high-pressure salesmanship of this nervous fellow made me wonder about his product. He blandly stated that the present system in Yugoslavia made it possible for ordinary people to influence foreign policy. His logic was that a Communist regime was the true representative of the people and therefore the people could be said to be making the foreign policy, because the means of production had been nationalized. Democratic theoreticians are very wary of the problem of setting up a democratic apparatus for making foreign policy, and with good reason. Why did this young man try to convince me of something so fantastic, of something which no political leader would dream of claiming?

What bothered me most about his fanaticism was that he was so young. He was not old enough to have fought in the war and revolution, even as a child. One reason I had heard cited for the political indifference of the younger generation was that the party was encouraging the overzealous, the pious, and the unimaginative rather than the clearheaded, the independent, and the clever. If this man was typical, the policy which thrust him forward was a blundering one. While the ideas of the Communists were getting through to many of the bourgeois of the older generation, young people with ideas were being alienated by just such parrots as this salesman from a society which would soon be theirs and which would badly need their work and criticism.

The president of the workers' council was a man of a different stamp altogether. Since his hands were covered with grease, he offered me his wrist when he came in, a custom I knew from printers' shops. He was kind about my Serbian, pretending that my accent was like that of Shumadiya, a district in central Serbia. But it was not just his flattery that made me more comfortable with him. Here was a man who did not feel he needed to convince me of anything. He knew what he knew; he knew what had been gained; he knew where his country was going. He would be happy if an American journalist who chanced by could understand and write about Yugoslavia, but he knew too that his country's development depended very little on random words and very much on his own actions. He was solidly rooted in the whole process of the prewar party, the war and revolution, postwar industrial development and now development of a new kind of democracy. When he used the Marxist phrases "democratic centralism," "social consciousness," they were not empty; they were filled with years of

patient work, in which he had lived those ideas. He could think
with them and explain things to himself, as he might work with
various cutters on his lathe. When he worked a piece of metal on
the lathe, the cutting was not always smooth. The finished piece
was not always polished on all its sides, but the dimensions necessary for the job at hand were all exact. This unpretty piece of
metal would do the job demanded of it and would hold up for a
long time. That was the way he thought.

When I told him that I was disappointed by the workers' council
at the publishing house, and that no one had anything to say in
meetings, he remarked that perhaps they should change the
name from "workers'," to "nonworkers'" council. Then he made a
remark which I was to hear frequently: "Intellectuals are that way,
you know. Maybe they have it too easy. If you want to see workers' management, you have to see how the production workers do
it." If anything, he said, his problem was too much discussion: the
meetings lasted too long, too many different points of view were
expressed, the arguments got too violent. "In our factory," he told
me, "we are really workers, and the revolution means something
very real to us. When our men are given the right to express
themselves and make decisions, they feel they have gained something important, and you could never take it away from them."

I brought out the list of questions which I had painstakingly
written out in Serbian. He leaned over them with me, and suggested that he and his colleague would answer them one by one as
they appeared. *Are some workers reluctant to serve on the workers' council and uninterested in workers' management?* His answer
to this question was immediate. "We have no such workers," he
said. "Our workers consider it an honor to be a member of the
workers' council. Members of the workers' council are respected
by the others." I had no reason to think that the workers in this
particular factory were uninterested, but I knew how hard it was to
set workers' management into operation, particularly in a country
where industrial workers were recruited from an unmechanized
agriculture. And he had not told me how they had managed to get

all the workers interested, only that they were so, as if it were only natural that they should be.

The second question went to the information director. *How do you inform your workers of the proceedings of the workers' council and of the current business activities of the enterprise?* The young man seemed a little surprised at the question, as if he thought it trivial and pointless. He had no difficulty in rattling off the various means of information used within the factory: all resolutions of the bodies of workers' management were immediately mimeographed and posted on bulletin boards throughout the factory; meetings were held from time to time of the whole collective to inform the workers about certain important problems; finally, the factory had a monthly house organ. Again I could not say that these means were insufficient, but I suspected that they were, and I knew they had been found so in other factories. Few workers will stand at a bulletin board long enough to work their way through fifteen or twenty pages of parliamentary jargon. Meetings of the whole collective probably meant canned speeches, not questions and answers or discussions. The monthly newspaper was a notoriously feeble instrument for keeping a work force interested in a factory's current business activity. I was beginning to foresee disappointment in my visit.

My other questions were written from various critical points of view. *Doesn't the self-management system lead to too much politics in the operation of the factory; don't the meetings and discussions detract from the real business of production?* They looked at each other and answered a simple "No." This answer made the pattern of their reticence clear. Since they intended to speak of no specific problems, I would never know even of their successes in overcoming them. I went on: *Does the delicate division of responsibilities between the professional staff (or management) and the various bodies of workers' management lead to unnecessary conflicts?* I was pretty sure of the answer beforehand: "We have no conflicts at all; the authority is divided clearly and no one goes beyond the area of his competence. The system works very efficiently." They wanted me to believe, in sum, that the whole system of workers' management in their factory worked exactly as foreseen in theory. But the theory was familiar to me; I had come there to find out how it looked from a concrete local situation with its own specific problems. And yet my visit had yielded not one single thing that was peculiar to this factory. I went on to my last question mechanically, since the interview had become a mere formality. *Doesn't the system of economic units, which in fact decentralizes the factory itself and brings self-management down to the level of the individual departments of the factory, lead to a sort of anarchy, in which each department pulls against all the others instead of with them; what is the glue that holds the whole system together?* The question was long, and yet I knew that the answer would be short. It was short all right, but it was not the answer I expected. "The system is not anarchical," said the president of the workers' council. "The League of Communists still has the last word here, and that is the glue which holds everything together." And that was that.

Then we went through the factory. I was astonished at the clutter and confusion in which they turned out very respectable lathes and milling machines. There were too many people and not enough machinery. The lighting was desperately poor. In the paneled office we had talked of the continuing high proportion of manual labor in their operation; out in the factory I saw the manual labor: half a dozen men kneeling over a single large casting, rubbing it with hand tools. The shortage of machines multiplied the number of men on a job and increased the time of every operation. I wished them well on their reconstruction, for clearly they were in need of it. It was helpful to see this factory and keep it as a reminder of the primitive beginnings from which the country was trying to advance. It was perhaps too easy for a foreigner to forget these difficulties as he asked his questions about the operation of workers' management. I could well imagine that in a factory so badly in need of machinery a good many responsible men might look upon democratic management as a luxury.

My guides also showed me the factory's recreation facilities: the large restaurant where workers could get an inexpensive hot meal and the gymnasium where young boys and girls were playing basketball and volleyball. We saw the factory school only from a distance. I had already heard from my psychologist friend about its remarkable activities: everything from reading and writing to mechanical drawing and English was taught here, and the worker-students had the benefit not only of teachers from within the factory but lecturers brought in from outside.

Finally I went to the new "hotel" which the factory had built for its unmarried people: eighty-five young men and fifteen young women. It was a fine modern building up on the hill where the factory had been steadily building apartment houses for its workers. The settlement was already a small town with curving streets shaded by plane trees and many grass lawns and gardens. The landscaping had not yet caught up with the newer buildings, and the recently built shopping center was reportedly still disorganized and providing only halfhearted competition to the nearby peasant market. But a supermarket chain was building a new store and every year the number of those waiting for apartments was declining. The shape of the future factory village was promising. To those who remembered the bare heath of fifteen years before, it must have seemed almost miraculous.

The manager of the hotel met us at the door and led us upstairs to look at the rooms. This embarrassed me a little—I did not want to be put in the position of some kind of international inspector. But a pleasant thing happened which made me glad I had come. When we reached the second floor, the manager led the way down the hall and suggested we go into Number 42, which the occupants had fixed up nicely. But when we were still three or four doors away a very neatly dressed young man in his early twenties came out of Number 42, blushing to his ears. He suggested that we go into Number 45, since the occupants of that room had just taken consumer-credit to buy a radio-phonograph and they had many pictures on the wall. The young man accompanied us through Number 45 and several other rooms. In our fifteen minutes on the second floor his face remained a bright red.

Later, out in front, the director confirmed my assumption that
the young man had a female visitor in his room. I commended
such liberality, saying that in America we would always find some
old maid to regulate the social activities of young men and women
in accordance with our Puritan traditions. Behind the forms, of
course, we would behave as human beings have always behaved
about such things, but I was happy to see that here no such artificial restrictions were put on the young people.

Back at the Ministry of Information I mentioned my dissatisfaction with the visit. The official who had arranged it said, "You
should have made a fuss. Of course they have problems. There are
problems everywhere. The next time I will go with you, and we
will uncover all their difficulties." I also talked with my friend, the
psychologist, who forwarded my complaints to his superior, the
personnel director. They invited me to come back to the factory
for another conversation, this time with the personnel director.

Before my return visit my friend suggested that I concentrate
my questions toward the problem of people. I was aware of his
own special concerns, but he had also given me hints of the factory's personnel problems and the personnel director's resolution
to solve them with decisive measures. The factory had too many
people, some of whom were doing nothing and hindering the activity of their colleagues. Because of an earlier shortage many trained
people were holding jobs at a level justified by their schooling but
in a department for which they had not been trained; others had
risen into jobs whose responsibilities were beyond their qualifications. The first problem, which meant a waste not only in having a
man in a job for which he had not been trained but in losing the
advantage of his training in some other department, was easy to
solve. But how were they to solve the political problem of demot-
ing those who had risen too high in order to replace them from the
now ample supply of trained people?

During the general campaign to get rid of excess personnel my
friend and his director had made a detailed analysis which served
as a guide for deciding who should be laid off or moved to another
position. But during the three hours of our remarkable talk these

things were mentioned only in the most general terms. Again I did not get what I went after: a detailed description of how problems were solved or not solved in the system of workers' management. Nevertheless, I passed a very stimulating three hours, listening to what one might call a historical brief for the existence of present-day Yugoslavia.

It was also an explanation for the existence of the man before me, a man nearing fifty, extremely thin, nervous and tired, perhaps tubercular. He smoked furiously, lighting a fresh cigarette every few minutes. He coughed badly. His fingers trembled. His speech wavered. He stuttered. He strained to get the right word, to fit the various threads of his thought into a single whole.

The threads began far back: with the settlement of the South Slavs in the Balkans in the seventh century, with the Turkish defeat of the Serbs at the Battle of Kosovo in 1389, the Serbian uprising in the early nineteenth century, the Austro-Hungarian colonization of Bosnia, Croatia, and Slovenia, the French Revolution, the work of Karl Marx in the British Museum, the October Revolution, the dictatorship declared in Yugoslavia in 1929. Even the history and evolving significance of America, from Columbus on, was one of the threads caught up by the shuttle of his nervous mind. Upon this historical and ideological foundation he built up an impressionistic history of the past thirty years in Yugoslavia. This was his own direct experience, what he had lived through, seen, and fought for. He described the war, concentrating on the discipline of the Partisans, how they did not loot and mistreat the population, how they released captured peasants who had been impressed to fight against them, how they sacrificed themselves to carry the wounded and to protect hordes of civilians from the German offensives, how they fought for unity and brotherhood among the peoples of Yugoslavia, and how they stifled their desire for revenge. At the end of the war, he said, his unit happened to go up into Austria as the Germans retreated. And he described the bitterness of the Yugoslavs when they saw farm families who had lived in relative peace during the war with their children still safe and at home, with their stock unslaughtered, with their houses unburned. From the direction of Austria had come the invader who left Yugoslav houses in ashes, Yugoslav cattle slaughtered, and Yugoslavia itself torn to pieces. Yet the Yugoslavs did not return inhumanity with inhumanity. After the war came the digging out of the ruins, the distribution of food, the fight against rampant disease, and the dramatic attempt to study and learn something about making a peaceful, developing society. In 1948 there was the break with the Cominform and the political rift in the country.

For this man, nothing seemed to have become any easier since then. He was still sacrificing himself desperately as if the country were still occupied, as if no food were available, as if typhus were raging. No man takes Yugoslavia's present problems lightly, for the country has set itself great tasks and built up great hopes. But there was more than seriousness in this man. He was still living in crisis. I thought about my conversations with other people who were responsibly involved in taking this country forward: the professor of agriculture, for instance, who told me with a sigh of relief that he was an optimist, that farm problems were getting easier, that at the beginning they had had to create their possibilities, but now they were faced with the less painful and agonizing problem of learning to make use of these possibilities. I also recalled those who were putting pressure from their various positions to move the political system toward a new juncture of revolutionary with democratic socialism. These men were giving a great deal, forcing the country forward faster and faster, and yet they lived rather easily with their problems. Was it that the others were more concerned with the long run and the broad view and that this man dealt only with trying to fit the splendid ideas into a difficult concrete situation, or that they had begun to feel the relief of easier times with their easier problems and he still had not got over the old habits? Perhaps his anxiousness contained something of both. But in a country that is changing so profoundly and so rapidly, some phases of the development are apt to be spotty. In some places Stalinism might never have existed; in others, the heavy atmo-

sphere of dogmatism still lingers. The direction is the same everywhere, but the development is uneven.

At the end of three hours this almost cosmological disquisition
narrowed down to that present moment and to that factory in
which we had been served half a dozen rounds of cognac and
coffee. The man stopped speaking, but he was clearly still struggling with his thoughts. A slight change in his tense face suggested
that he was going over what he had said, trying to see what he had
left out, wondering whether he had really said what he intended.
Then his face lost that deeply pensive expression and his eyes
shifted to me. "I am not sure," he said, "that I have satisfied you."
I did not need to lie in order to say that I was completely satisfied;
I had witnessed a very rare performance, and if I should come to
understand what I had seen and heard, I would have learned something far more valuable than what three hours before I had stated
as the purpose of my visit. But though I was exhausted by the
mere effort of listening to his tense sentences, he was tireless. He
began to recall out loud the phrases I had used in explaining my
mission. "Yes," he said, "I believe we have not talked about the
problems here in our factory. Let me assure you that we have had
them all. It is not easy to build socialism, and we know it as well
from our experience here in this factory as people in other places
know it." He insisted that we deal with problems in the factory,
but when I asked him about difficulties in introducing the system
of economic units, his answers were not specific. I felt sure he was
ready to tell me anything I wanted to know, but some difference in
our way of thinking made certain connections impossible. After
three hours in which one of the energetic streams of Western civilization had been spread out before me, the details of relations in
this factory seemed too trifling for me to press him. I said that my
questions had been answered and pleaded another engagement.

I left discouraged, but I still felt that workers' management
could and would work. I believed that these men would struggle
through every possible situation, no matter how difficult, and
would always direct their efforts toward making it work. Fortu-

nately, I had an opportunity to look further. In other places I was able to find a less restrained atmosphere, one in which people could talk more easily about how self-management had already progressed in their institutions.

One of these places was the Children's Hospital for Tuberculosis and Lung Diseases in Dedinye, a very pleasant suburb on a hill at the edge of Belgrade. The hospital had been the mansion of two middle-aged sisters who before the war made of it a kind of tourist home. It had broad, wooded grounds and great bushy borders of roses along gravel paths. During the occupation it had served the Germans as a Gestapo headquarters.

When I came through the gate, I found two sturdy prefabricated buildings set among the trees just inside the fence. One, I read from the signs, was the reception ward and the other the outpatient clinic and laboratory. The roses were in bloom and there were cots lined along the gravel paths in the shade where the children lay very still under their light covers. In a grove of elms further away from the main house (from the outside there were no signs that the mansion had been turned into a hospital), several teenage boys were standing around in their pajamas and robes near a tent containing more cots.

The façade of the mansion had the usual classical embellishments, now reduced to harmony by thick ivy which reached clear to the third-story eaves. The gracious crown of the architecture, however, was the roofed porch before the main entrance and the long stairs which curved down around from each side to the drive.

I went up these stairs and entered. There was no one at the door to whom I might explain my presence. I stood there for a moment to enjoy the bright simplicity of the interior, which was bathed in the spring sunshine, thanks to a glassed-in stairwell at the end of the short entranceway. The house had not completely made the transition to a hospital. No doubt this fact was an exasperation to the doctors, but it was good to be spared the mechanical and antiseptic appearance of the modern medical institution. On one side of the narrow hall were a round table and two low chairs painted with the ivory enamel which gives nurseries their special brightness. On the other side a glassed-in bookcase, painted with the same bright enamel, contained frilly little dolls and crude dogs which the children had made. A young father was there to fetch his four-year-old daughter, who was holding up her arms for him to put on the new pink dress he had brought for her homecoming. A nurse brought along her things in a paper bag. Before she went, the little girl had to go back to show her wardmates her new dress and to say goodbye to them.

When father and daughter left, I told the nurse my name and she showed me to the office of the director. After I explained my general interests, he suggested that he fill me in on the situation of the hospital. When members of the managing board came, I could put my questions about self-management to them.

The hospital, he told me, had nearly three hundred beds and they had recently added the two prefabricated buildings I had seen on the grounds. One of them was for out-patient examinations and inoculations and the other was for quarantine and diagnosis of new arrivals. They had just completed a steam heating system for those two outbuildings and they would get a tunnel through to both of them before the next winter.

Until recently they had intended to build an additional children's hospital for tuberculosis, and the money had already been appropriated, but their campaign of preventive medicine, using BCG vaccine from Sweden, had been so successful that the new hospital would not be necessary and they were even taking a few cases of other diseases into their hospital. Now, for instance, they had a case of meningitis which had been sent to them from southern Serbia.

(Although Yugoslavia has long been heavily infected with tuberculosis, the centers of the disease are now mainly limited to run-down areas on the outskirts of the cities where newly arrived city dwellers, including many gypsies, are crowded together. In the more stable parts of the city all children receive inoculations. There is much less TB in the countryside in spite of the poor living conditions, because there is more fresh air and food and less personal contact to spread the disease.)

Soon we were joined by several members of the managing board of the hospital, mostly doctors and nurses in their late thirties or early forties. Their seriousness was not the tense seriousness of my previous hosts. I asked them to explain to me how the hospital was run, and they outlined the whole system. Since a hospital has special responsibilities toward the community, hospitals have councils responsible for long-term policy which are made up partly of members of the hospital managing board and partly of people from outside the hospital who represent various social interests. Among these outside members are representatives of the social security agency, which pays all hospital bills, the Socialist Alliance of Working People, which conveys the complaints of citizens, and the local commune, which is concerned about medical care provided in its territory. Medical questions are decided by the professional collegium of the medical staff. The managing board, which is responsible for the actual running of the hospital and for short-term policy, is elected by all those who work in the hospital from among themselves, with care that all the various staffs—medical, dietary, maintenance, office, and nursing—be represented.

The board members gave me a long list of matters on which they decided, and then I asked what was the most serious thing which faced them at that moment. Two or three of them replied in unison: "the distribution of personal incomes!" Surprised and amused at their own enthusiastic response, they began to explain. Like many other hospitals, they said, they were struggling with the problem of devising criteria for setting their salaries according to the principle of "to each according to his work," and trying to work out a system for dividing up their periodic surpluses which would stimulate them to be more conscientious and economical without diminishing the quality of the care given to patients. Institutions in the nonproductive activities had been much slower than factories in trying to apply these principles, they said, and thus they were still at something of a loss. Criteria used in factories were difficult to apply because medical care could not be measured as simply as manufactured goods. There was some question whether any quantitative standard for evaluating medical care could serve as an equitable criterion for remuneration. Yet doctors had to be paid like everyone else, and conscious effort to evaluate their work and reward them accordingly was perhaps better than reliance on mere tradition or on the law of supply and demand.

In describing this problem to me, they gave no signs of the lines of division between them on this important issue. I was sure, however, that they had had long and bitter arguments on the ins and outs of the problem, for they all spoke with candor and excitement. But they had reached agreement upon one thing: the point system they had set up on the basis of effort, qualifications, position, and experience was imperfect, but it was the best they could do. They would try it for a time, and perhaps living with it would give them a new slant that would enable them to improve upon it later. No one pretended he had all the answers. The sheer difficulty of the problem had taken them beyond their differences into a common effort to solve the insoluble. One woman said they had gone in desperation to every hospital in Belgrade asking other managing boards for advice, and everywhere they had been told that no one had licked the problem, that their own efforts were as good as anyone's. They all nodded in agreement. Another woman sighed: "Perhaps with enough time and experience we will see our way."

Our talk ended with this, except that I asked whether I could attend one of their meetings, and they said they would be delighted, though it was a shame they had already drawn up their point system, because their discussion would have been interesting for me to hear. The director remarked that perhaps they would give me a more realistic view of the system if they simply invited me to the next meeting, whether they were expecting an important discussion or not. We agreed on this.

The most striking thing about that short conversation was how readily these people had talked to me about the problems they faced. Whereas in the machine tool factory I would have been quite satisfied to hear the details of a problem which had been solved, these doctors and nurses had unhesitatingly talked about a problem that had stymied them and even said their discussions had led them to the point of wondering whether the principle of payment according to work could ever be solved satisfactorily in a hospital.

After a week or two I received notice of a meeting of the hospital managing board. This time I was met by the president of the board, a man who had said little on my previous visit until the time came for them to ask me questions. Then he had complained, sharply, that his respect for America and admiration for our achievements was being severely damaged by newspaper reports of the injustice suffered by the American Negro. Taken slightly aback by his fierceness, I assured him that I felt the same way.

Now we greeted each other warmly. He explained that the meeting would begin a little late. They would wait a few more minutes for the director and another colleague to return from a village fifty miles away where they had spent the morning on hospital business. If they did not arrive soon, the meeting would begin without them.

The meeting, he said, would be pretty much routine except for one matter. This was included in the agenda under two headings: *the financial report of the hospital's business for the first five months of the year* and *the awarding of points for the second fiscal quarter*. The financial report, he said, would show a surplus at the end of June, and the discussion over points would turn on how much of that surplus would be applied toward personal incomes and how they would use their point system in dividing the money.

The president left for a moment to make some last-minute preparations, and meantime the director arrived and changed into his hospital smock. We went into the small room which housed the hospital's scanty library. A small square table occupied the center of the room, and the members of the board were squeezed in two rows between the table and the wall, all the way around the room. The director and I stepped over the legs and knees of the others to reach our chairs. He introduced me briefly as a guest from America. I had some misgivings about being known as a foreigner, thinking that the participants might smooth things over for my benefit. More than once I had noticed that people I interviewed wanted me to think that conflicts did not occur in the system, when I wanted to hear about conflicts as the very proof that the system had some "teeth" in it.

My fears were not justified. Even the reading of the minutes from the previous meeting did not pass without objection. One doctor, a woman of about forty, spoke up immediately.

"Neither I nor anyone from my department was here when the commission for job classification presented its report. That report says our department needs a medical assistant, but it isn't true. We need a lab technician. And I'd like to know why no one from our department was consulted when they were making the job analysis."

An immediate wrangle began over the parliamentary propriety of her objection. Someone pointed out that she was not correcting the minutes, which were accurate, but the report, which was not under discussion at the moment.

"But how could you adopt the report with such a mistake in it and not give us a chance to discuss it?" she said angrily.

Now the director, speaking as an ordinary member of the board, calmly explained that the report had been accepted from committee but did not yet constitute the decisions of the board. At a later meeting the board would discuss the report in detail and reach its own conclusions. Then she and her colleagues could present their case for a change.

The woman grudgingly nodded her understanding of the procedure and sat back.

The director added for the benefit of those not present last time that in order to expedite the meetings, which had grown too long and too time-consuming, the board had adopted a rule that all corrections to the minutes must be presented in writing so that meetings need not be halted while the secretary wrote out the correction.

The minutes were then adopted and the president introduced the hospital accountant, a newly elected board member, who gave the financial report through May. This meticulous fellow not only gave the usual opaque column of figures, but he had also calculated some more readily indicative averages, percentages, and unit costs. Finally, he compared the "actual cost" per bed-day with the amount paid per bed-day by the social security agency, since the difference between them constituted the surplus the hospital now enjoyed. He ended his report with an appraisal of the hospital's position, anticipating the discussion which was to follow. No doubt aware that the majority of the members were disposed to vote for an immediate dividend to supplement their ordinary income, he began earnestly: "Our position is not what one would call bad, but neither is the surplus too large a sum to be kept in reserve." He went on to enumerate several extraordinary expenses which would be necessary before the year was out and would have to be covered from the surplus.

When the accountant finished his little lecture on good steward-ship, the president recognized three or four people in turn who made the case for the majority. They found the accountant's position rather conservative. They did not intend, they said, to drain away the surplus at the expense of the hospital and the care of the patients, but they felt that he exaggerated the outstanding expenses. There was every reason to think they would operate in the forthcoming months with the same efficiency as in the first months of the year. Hence the surplus for the whole year would be twice as large as the present one. They were willing to debate the size of the takeout and the level at which the point system would be honored, but since their work and efficiency had created the surplus, they did not consider themselves irresponsible in wanting to take a modest part of the fruits.

But the accountant was not alone in his conservative view of the surplus. The head nurse spoke up, a woman of about forty, the predominant generation at this meeting and practically, if not statistically, in Yugoslavia as a whole. She spoke very carefully and earnestly, apologizing for not having all the words at her command to say what she meant, though she explained in good simple language what might have taken some of the other members of the board longer.

"I object," she said, "to the accountant's calculation of the 'real cost' per bed-day. His figures are for actual costs based on what we've spent. But they wouldn't represent the actual costs if we had spent everything our plan called for. We're mistaken to think we have 'earned' this surplus; if we had bought what we said we would, there wouldn't be any surplus at all."

The president called a vote, and the majority stood together unshaken.

Then discussion began on how high a percentage should be set aside for incomes. Here the majority, having once won its point, showed itself responsible. They were satisfied with a modest quarter of the sum, and they had their own calculations of forthcoming expenses to prove they were not acting recklessly.

The accountant stuck with his original cautious policy and spoke for a smaller percentage, but the head nurse was now on the other side from him. Again she apologized but again she spoke with great forcefulness. Her point was that the system of payment according to work was supposed to give people an economic stimulus to work more responsibly and efficiently. "The efficacy of that stimulus," she said, "depends on our showing our respect for it by putting money into it. The hospital has been short a nurse for the last three months, and the other nurses have had to take up the slack. But not everybody has worked equally hard. Some of the girls have just done their own jobs and others have given much more time and energy than is normally expected of them. These girls expect their extra work to be rewarded. And now that we've officially introduced the point system, we ought to put some teeth in it by setting aside as much money as possible to be divided up according to points."

Someone else added that even though the amounts distributed through the point system would not be very large, they would be a sign that the system had been introduced in good faith and was being respected.

A woman doctor said that perhaps a good moment had come to mention the problem of an overtime system. "We are behind other hospitals," she said, "in recognizing and paying for overtime work. We cannot go on forever letting our doctors and nurses, however gladly, give their one day of rest to the hospital without proper remuneration." She excused herself for making this interpolation, but perhaps, she said, the problem of overtime pay, which would be the next big task before the managing board, was not unrelated to the matter under discussion.

The discussion had apparently come to an end and the president was preparing to ask for a vote when a doctor behind me, a man who had said very little in the discussion, said he wanted to raise a general point before the vote was taken. "I foresee some difficulty," he said, "when we announce that there is a surplus and that we voted only twenty-seven percent of it for personal incomes. Perhaps we should not make all the figures known. I don't think people will understand."

A wave of discomfort passed over the members of the board, but the director turned and made short shrift of the proposal. This suggestion, he explained, utterly violated the principles by which the board was trying to conduct its business; the other employees should not be kept ignorant of the surplus. At the same time the board should not vote a high percentage of the surplus to personal incomes just because it feared a reaction. So long as the board made a responsible decision and knew its reasons, he saw no reason to doubt that the other workers would understand those reasons just as readily as the members of the board had understood them.

The doctor did not reply.

The vote was taken and was nearly unanimous in favor of the twenty-seven percent dividend to be applied to personal incomes through the point system. Another fifteen minutes was spent on routine matters: the hospital would send delegates to a half dozen conferences; payment of school fees had to be approved for several girls going to nursing school at night; a suggestion by the head nurse that the hospital pay tuition for a young girl who had recently come to work as a cleaning woman and who had shown intelligence and industry and a desire to become a practical nurse had to be approved.

During that fifteen minutes I reflected on the director's answer to the doctor in the back row. I had guessed that the openness and liveliness of self-management in this hospital must depend in great part on his confidence that he could maintain his own authority as director without encroaching upon the board's jurisdiction and on his belief that the workers and their representatives on the managing board would hold up their end. The system of workers' management assumes, in common with most democratic thinking, that people, given a chance, will understand reality and act responsibly. The director's confidence in his workers gave me a feeling of optimism about the future of democracy. It is not a feeling which journalists have occasion to report very often, whatever their beat.

Still, I left wondering whether my optimism was not merely the result of an exceptional place run by exceptional people.

IX

Workers' Management
on Its Feet

THOUGH YUGOSLAVIA BEGAN to develop after the war from a very
low base, it is rapidly becoming an industrialized country. Between
1956 and 1960 industry grew at an average rate of 14 percent a
year. By 1960 industrial production was more than three times as
great as in 1939. After a brief slump in 1961 and early 1962 the
economy began to boom again. In 1963 the industrial growth rate
was 15.5 percent, and in 1964 it was 16 percent.

The development remains uneven in spite of efforts to equalize
it: certain regions in the South are still very backward and Slovenia in the North is far ahead of the other republics. But econo-
mists now consider Yugoslavia as a whole to be in the middle stage
of development, and ambitious Yugoslavs are speaking of reaching
the level of Italy in the next decade or so.

Already the economy has developed to a point where it must
export heavily if it is to continue expanding. Population growth
and further rises in the standard of living will expand the domestic
market, but there are certain inherent limits to this growth; the
population will never be large enough to consume mass production
of very many industrial goods. At the same time, a developing

economy requires more and more imports—machines for modern industrial processes, certain essential raw materials, and increasingly varied consumer goods. These must be paid for with exports, or the country's balance of payments will show a greater and greater deficit.

If it is to export, the Yugoslav economy must specialize in products which can compete with other nations in the world economy. But the Yugoslavs do not want to specialize in exporting grain and ores, as before the war. The director of the Institute for Foreign Trade explained their goal this way: "The Swedes," he said, "don't produce much steel but it is of a very high quality, and it is exported all over the world. The Swedes couldn't compete with Japan, Russia, or the United States in producing cheap steel. But they'll always have a market for their steel and they can charge a very high price for it because everyone needs some of that quality. It's at this level that we want to specialize—below it the inequities are obvious. For example, we now export a lot of primary forest products—pulpwood and rough lumber. We would be better off exporting finished products like paper and furniture. But to do this on a large scale, we must first develop other things, like waterways and river barges to bring raw materials to the factories, skilled cabinetmakers, and so on. Our idea has been to develop the whole economy up to the point where we can see what it is best for us to specialize in. When we discover that, we intend to dig in and work very hard at trying to do it better than anyone else. But in order to find out what we are good at, we have to turn outwards now and start competing on the world market. In other words, we have to test the economy to see which industrial branches and which enterprises can hold their own with world competition and which cannot."

Until recently, production was so low the Yugoslavs could concentrate entirely on turning out more goods. But the rapid advances of the economy are bringing ever greater complexity, not only in technology, but in every aspect of business and economic life: organization, finance, communication, trade, distribution, and transportation. The financial aspects became so complicated in the

1964 boom that one Yugoslav economist said economic trends had not only burst the framework of economic policy but had left behind the real material possibilities of the country. Investments rose 40 percent instead of an expected 10 percent—and investments by banks rose 109 percent. Imports increased greatly, prices went up, and the cost of living jumped. Though personal incomes rose nearly 50 percent between 1962 and 1964, the real standard of living of some workers in lagging industries actually dropped.

What is most interesting is the Yugoslav idea that these problems arise largely because workers' management is still limited by government restrictions and bureaucratic interference from directors, the party, and the local communes. Their theory is that when workers' management means real control in every enterprise, the economy will get on a more even keel. This contrasts sharply with the Russian idea of how to make an economy run smoothly. In the last few years they too have taken steps to free enterprises from overrigid government control. But in Russia this trend has only made the director more powerful within the enterprise. It has not meant any greater power for the ordinary worker. Yugoslavia is still the only socialist country which believes in workers' management and acts on that belief. The test of workers' management is whether it can justify this confidence: can it function economically and efficiently in a highly developed industry and deal with the complicated problems of a modern economy? It is not enough that this new system of management meet the tests of hospital and school administration or of management in small enterprises that are not subject to keen competition.

Those who have seen workers' management function in their enterprises are optimistic. They feel that the workers' councils and managing boards can make sound business policy and see that it is carried out without destroying the professional manager's authority to make specific decisions in good time. They do not doubt that the system will not only prove as efficient as other systems of management but will be more sensitive to community needs and more responsible. The mere existence of the system, they say, is stimulating workers to see their own work in the context of the factory's overall operation and to understand the factory's place in the context of business, finance, and the community. Already it is becoming an important way for talented people outside the party to influence economic decisions and challenge lingering bureaucracy in enterprises.

One man told me about a bright young engineer in his enterprise who had advanced up through the workers' council to become president of the managing board. This young man, he said, was not a member of the party, but workers' management had given him the opportunity to show his managerial ability and develop it to a point where he was already regarded as the logical person to succeed the director of the enterprise.

One whimsical theory I heard was that workers' management will be defeated by its very success in helping talented workers to develop themselves, for it is becoming a source of personnel for the managerial staff. The flow of competent people from the labor force into management, the reasoning goes, will eventually downgrade the quality of the workers' council and managing board. Though the managerial staff will be bursting with talent, the factory's long-range policy will be left in the hands of incompetents.

In enterprises where workers' management is not functioning well, people are often so pessimistic as to doubt that it can work anywhere. A number of people in my publishing house felt that as long as the director's policies were making money for the enterprise the workers would never be able to put a stop to his autocratic control. "Then," they said, "if he slips up and the business starts losing money, the workers' council won't discover why in time to do something about it. But when the commune officials see that we aren't making enough money to pay a nice chunk of taxes, they'll blame the workers' council as much as the director." I heard scores of anecdotes about the failures of self-management in other enterprises. Directors were living high on expense accounts by deceiving the workers' council about where the money was going; incompetent directors and superintendents were discouraging trained people from taking an active part in workers' management; workers' councils and managing boards were ill-informed and lackadaisical or they were working with the director for their own interests and against the rest of the labor force. I even heard of one enterprise in a small town where the director and all the members of the workers' council belonged to the same family.

The contrasting views of workers' management make it clear that the system is developing unevenly: in one place it may be well established; next door it may be a mere form. Much depends on the immediate situation in a particular enterprise. In order to see the details of how the system was functioning, I decided to look closely at one enterprise where it was already on its feet. I chose the Galenika Pharmaceutical Company in Zemun, a suburb of Belgrade, after seeing for myself that it had progressed well beyond the first stage of giving power to the workers' council and managing board. With its two thousand employees and its involvement with the problems of high-pressure business, Galenika seemed a good place to see what the problems were and how well they were being solved in modern industries. I attended meetings of the workers' council, managing board, and most of the other factory organizations, read a great deal of material on the history and present situation of the factory, kept up with all the current information bulletins and reports on factory work over several months, and talked on many occasions with the director of information and with other people in the factory.

Like many other branches of the Yugoslav economy, the drug industry must now turn largely to the export market in order to continue its expansion. The necessity of turning outward came upon drug producers rather suddenly in 1962, when a handling fee was introduced for filling prescriptions in pharmacies. Doctors had been overprescribing and patients were accumulating enormous stocks of free pills in their medicine cabinets. The handling fee (about 8¢ per item) was enough to cut down on this waste; patients took home only what they needed. As a result the national health service cut its purchases sharply.

Galenika was suddenly faced with the problem of competing on the world market with the highly automated drug manufacturers of the West. The workers' council and managing board, the director and his managerial staff, and the factory's political organizations (the League of Communists, the Socialist Alliance, and the union) held a conference to assess the situation. The report they issued to the labor force was like an analysis of the problems of the whole Yugoslav economy. Their past successes, they found, had resulted from preferential business conditions and unusual efforts by individuals rather than from satisfactory long-range policy, efficient internal organization, or hard work by the labor force as a whole. Their machinery was old and their capital scanty. Work procedures, they said, dated back to the medieval guild. No self-operating mechanism coordinated one department with another. Bureaucratic habits stifled individual initiative; informalty clouded over authority and responsibility; no one seemed to know where socialist self-management left off and day-to-day professional decisions began. If they did not maintain maximum production, tighten up their organization, and start operating at a profit, they would go bankrupt.

Galenika merged with two other Belgrade drug companies that found themselves in a similar situation. The merger had immediate advantages: they could unite three maintenance, accounting, personnel, sales, and shipping departments, pool investments for construction of a new factory to house the scattered operations, and streamline production. There was only one problem. After the merger the managerial staff found that the factory could maintain current production with 10 percent fewer employees and save itself 95 billion dinars ($127,000) a year in salaries.

In a capitalist enterprise there is no essential difficulty in such a situation. The management applies all necessary pressure to make the company's operation efficient and to increase profits for the owners. If this means layoffs, the workers resist through their own solidarity and organization. But the problem is delicate indeed in an enterprise where the workers themselves are the stockholders, so to speak, and where their representatives are responsible both for formulating sound business policy and for safeguarding the personal interests of the individual workers. A poll taken by the Institute of Social Sciences in Belgrade showed that when confronted with a need for layoffs in their enterprise, 40 percent of Yugoslav workers wanted the extra workers shifted to other departments, another 40 percent wanted to expand the factory to create jobs for everyone, and only 11 percent supported an attempt to increase efficiency and raise labor productivity by firing surplus workers. In other words, traditional labor solidarity still outweighs the interest of owners and managers in making a realistic accommodation to the demands of efficiency. In many factories, the poll discovered, workers were opposed to firing a fellow worker even when they saw that the dismissal would directly improve their own incomes. I was told by a leading Yugoslav political scientist that socialist theorists had not foreseen this problem when they worked out the idea of self-management, and they had therefore provided no guidelines for a practical solution.

The efforts to solve the problem are thus still in the stage of experimentation. Since streamlining the economy cannot wait upon the formulation of theory, factories have had to work out the problem as best they can, with whatever ideas and organization they have at hand.

At Galenika it was a long and difficult process involving the combined participation of the professional management, the workers' council and managing board, the political organizations in the factory, and the whole labor force meeting in their departments.

The managerial staff suggested firing 160 people. Their proposal was based entirely on the fact that the organization could be streamlined by eliminating that many jobs. The political organizations suggested other criteria to be considered before the actual layoffs were made: Is a worker going to be thrown out on the streets? Is he married? Does he have another source of income? How much sick leave has he taken in the last year? Is he politically active? Does he take part in workers' management? Is he a veteran? Is he a good worker? Has he been fined by the factory disciplinary committee for tardiness, negligence, or insubordination? The party recommended in particular that good workers doing unnecessary jobs should not be fired but shifted to other departments where inefficient workers could be fired to make room for them.

The workers in each economic unit discussed the recommendations of the management and those of the party and voted on whether their co-workers on the management's list should be fired or not.

One economic unit had thirteen people on the list to be fired. The decisions of their fellow workers were typical of what happened all over the factory:

M.C.   Superfluous but good clerk. We will find a place for her.

O.P.   Messenger. Good discipline. Should be kept.

R.V.   Charwoman. Has something to fall back on. Should be laid off.

J.M.   Messenger. Allergic to drugs. Has chance of another job. Should be laid off.

D.B.   Janitor. Has other income. Should be retired on his pension.

L.T., G.S., R.M., and A.O.   Should go because they were only hired for three months.

T.V.   Janitor. Veteran with two children and no apartment. Should be kept on as a hardship case.

T.J.   Janitor, ailing, veteran, no one to take care of him. Should be kept on as a hardship case.

E.F.   Janitor. Vote on his case split. Should stay.

I.K.   Watchman. Tends his farm and comes to work tired. But is wounded veteran with four children. Should be transferred to another unit.

Another department had no surplus workers, but the unit agreed to lay off six unsatisfactory workers in order to take up a surplus from other economic units. Of those 6, 4 had taken from 48 to 212 days of sick leave the year before. The fifth had twice been penalized for infractions of discipline. The sixth was eligible for a pension.

After the workers in the economic units evaluated each case, their decisions were reviewed by the political organizations, to be sure that friendship and enmity played no part in the decisions.

The final decision on each case was made by a 5-man commission from the workers' council; they gave notice to 97 of the 160 people on the original list.

These ninety-seven were then given a chance to appeal to the managing board, and the union arranged to get enterprise lawyers to assist them in preparing their appeals. One woman said her economic unit had not classified her as superfluous but had simply said she should be transferred to another department; they had agreed to retain her if no other job could be found, since her poor health made it impossible for her to find other employment. The managing board agreed to keep her on. Another woman claimed she had been brought into the enterprise from another job and it was highly improper to lay off someone who had been deliberately attracted from another firm. The managing board kept her. One man said it was true he had frequently taken sick leave, but it was because he caught cold where he worked. Since his economic unit said he was a good worker, he was transferred to another department. A lathe operator said he was the best machinist in the company and had even been recommended for promotion to supervisor. He was certain he had been fired because he had refused to make his foreman a household gadget out of factory material on company time and because he had criticized the behavior of some of his superiors. The man was promoted to supervisor.

Many unsatisfactory workers were retained because of their personal difficulties, although every one of them would mean a less profitable operation for the factory as a whole and for his particular economic unit. Faced with the problem of balancing efficiency and individual needs, the workers' council suggested setting up a special economic unit for the hardship cases. Would it not be possible for these people to produce some drug whose production had been abandoned as marginal? Obviously such a unit could not contribute to the factory's earnings, but perhaps it could at least meet costs. It could be exempted from the demands for efficiency and profitability put upon the other units. But the managerial staff said this was not a good idea: a department composed entirely of poor workers could certainly not cover its costs in an operation that a regular unit had already given up. The workers' council decided then to distribute the hardship cases throughout the plant so that every economic unit would bear an equal share of the common burden.

In the end eighty-five workers were given notice. But the factory made an organized effort to soften the blow: here, too, efficiency was not the only thought. The workers' council gave 20 million dinars to the director to help them find jobs through negotiations with other firms. The local employment security office, oddly enough, had a department which manufactured cardboard cartons. They said they could employ thirty workers if they had the money to buy new machinery. Galenika lent them the money, and the number of jobless was reduced to fifty-five. When a local distillery asked to lease one of the buildings Galenika had vacated at its merger, the director offered to lease the space if the distillery would hire twenty of Galenika's laid-off workers. The distillery agreed. Other jobs were found with various firms in Belgrade. At the end of the month only eighteen people, all highly qualified office workers, were left without jobs. The job market for such people was already flooded in Belgrade, but since the country as a whole was short of people with their qualifications, the enterprise felt these people could take care of themselves. Nevertheless they were told that if they had not found jobs before their severance pay ran out, the factory would help to find them something.

The party played an important part in these layoffs. As an organization it supported them as economically necessary and its individual members helped to explain to other workers how they would benefit the factory. In addition, the party offered social and political criteria for firing people, and party members pushed these criteria in discussing the cases in their economic units. The party then reviewed each case before the final decisions were made. This role of the party raises many questions about how workers' management is developing. I spent several hours discussing them with the information director at Galenika, who was very much a party man himself. Sasha was a trim little fellow who talked rapidly and accompanied his words with abrupt gestures of his hands. "The work involved in making the layoffs cost me nineteen pounds," he once told me, "and you can see I can't spare it." I could believe him just from seeing how much energy he expended in normal conversation. He had little time and much business. Though often I could not see eye to eye with him about the role of the party, I could not doubt his good faith, for he had clearly made the development of workers' management not only his job and political duty but his passion as well.

I had heard that in some enterprises the party organization played the role of a discussion club which treated only general ideological questions, but when I mentioned this to Sasha, he responded sharply: "You've been misinformed. I can't imagine the party organization as a club. True, we discuss ideological questions at our meetings, but then we vote and take a position to which we all adhere regardless of our personal objections to the resolution."

At the same time, he insisted that the party did not give orders. When I asked him about its role at Galenika, his answer was tortuous: "We try to apply party principles to conditions here in the factory. We're guided by the general policy statements of the Party Program and by current resolutions of the Central Committee published in the daily press, but we don't get detailed directives from above. We discuss the large questions of factory policy and take positions for which we fight as individuals in whatever job we hold in the factory and in the various factory organizations. We argue about the stand we're going to take, but once we've taken a vote we all stand by the decision and argue in favor of it. All our party meetings are open except those where we treat organizational questions like admission and exclusion of members. Everyone in the factory knows who is a Communist and who is not."

"But," I commented, "people must feel that when a Communist speaks, they are being told what to do."

"That might be the case if we stood up in meetings of the workers' council and managing board and said, 'The party has decided thus and so,' for that naturally repels people and hurts instead of helping workers' management. This is done in some places, but it only means that the party is weak; they are not able to lead the people, they have cut themselves off. If they had built up respect through the wisdom of their decisions and through their efforts to strengthen workers' management, then they would not have to issue commands in the name of some authority outside the factory. It is only natural that when the party acts in an authoritarian fashion people will want to oppose it whether it is right or wrong. A party which faces that kind of resentment can never be strong. Sometimes the workers' council here at Galenika chooses to reject our proposals, but when the chips are down we can usually get everyone behind us. That's because we try to lead through persuasion. My idea of the Communist is a man who after talking ten minutes with fifty strangers can start down the street with them behind him."

"But isn't it sometimes stifling to have party leadership in every area of social life—even if its leadership is good?"

"We feel it's necessary because we still don't have enough competent people to go around. We can't let the workers' council fail to make a good decision because its members are ignorant or lack imagination. But we're constantly educating people, and we are trying to bring along the young people—those who were born during the war, who have grown up under socialism—so they can take over from some of the older people who have not been able to keep up with the country's development. Meanwhile, one of our aims is to engage as many people as possible in the work of society in general and in workers' management in particular."

"And how does the party get nonmembers to act with intitiative and responsibility in workers' management?" I asked.

"There are many ways of doing this. I will tell you how I myself do it. If I have an idea about something that might be done in the factory, I call into my office a group of perhaps ten people, some of them Communists, but most of them not. I tell them about the problem and ask for their opinions about what could be done. Each one in turn has his say. And then they say, 'You must have some plan of your own or you wouldn't have called us,' and I say, 'Well, here is my plan, but I'm not sure how good it is.' And after I have told them my plan, I say that we are not ready to make a decision and suggest that we meet the next day to decide. Then they leave, but I know that they'll think about the problem in the meantime. In other words, I have already got them interested. The next day they will adopt either my plan or a better one they have worked out themselves. Then comes the question of how we are to carry it out. We'll decide informally who should take on what part of the job, and then we'll go to work. When the project is finished we'll get together again to go over it. I won't praise the Communists, for they are expected to take on these burdens, but I'll praise the work of the nonmembers and encourage them. Later we'll ask them to do other things. For instance, I might suggest that a nonmember make a speech in his department on some issue. I will say that it is best that he make it because these people are his buddies on the job and besides he knows the details of his department. He may never have spoken in public before and may be frightened. I will encourage him, help with his speech, and even tell him that I read my speeches, though it isn't true. He'll tremble when he gets up, and stutter and even get things all mixed up. In the discussion after his speech we will discreetly correct some of the mistaken impressions he has given; later we will praise him for his speech and encourage him. He is becoming engaged in social business without even realizing it. Perhaps after a year or two, when we are sitting over a bottle of beer somewhere, I will ask him if he remembers when he took that first step out of his private life, and then for the first time he will realize that he is not the same man he was: he is engaged in the business of society. And thereafter he will work consciously and deliberately.

"Let me give another example. Since I am active in the union I was once called to go to a socialized farm where there was trouble among vegetable pickers. The workers were from all over Yugoslavia and had been brought there for seasonal work. Naturally I did not know any of them. The vegetables had to be picked immediately. But the workers were too discontented to work, and the union was trying to straighten out the trouble. As soon as I arrived I called all the workers together, maybe two hundred of them. I began to ask them what was the trouble, but I could see

Tito during the war

Tito and Moša Pijade in jail

YUGOSLAV INFORMATION CENTER

The bombing of Belgrade in April 1941

YUGOSLAV INFORMATION CENTER

Partisans, 1943

A Partisan hero, about to be hanged, raises his arms in defiance

Open-air market in Belgrade

Peasant market in Ohrid

Cattle sheds on the Belje Socialist Farm

Workers' houses on the Belje Socialist Farm

Picking hops in Slovenia

New Belgrade, being built on sand pumped from the Danube

The Turkish Bridge at Mostar

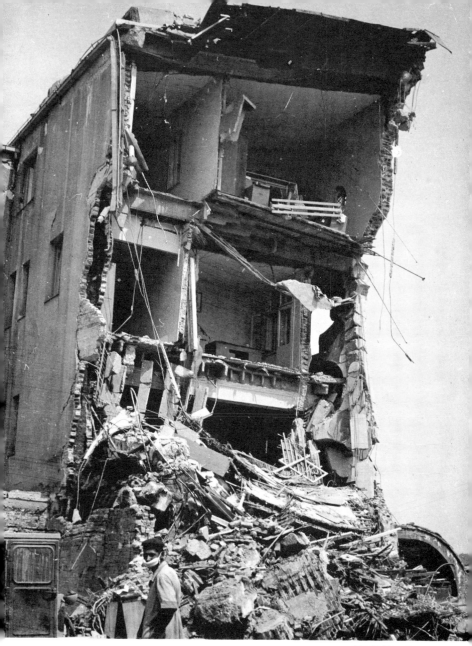

Rescue workers dig in the rubble of Skoplje

A workers' council meeting

Workers' council meeting at a garment factory in the Voivodina

that I wasn't getting through. Then I requested that all the members of the party stand up. There were about fourteen of them. As soon as they stood up, an old man in the audience pointed to one of them and said, 'Why, he's no Communist; he stays drunk all the time and has been in two fights.' After the old man finished his accusations of this member of the party, I called a closed meeting of the party organization. I asked the Communists if what the old man had said was true. They agreed that it was; the man was a troublemaker and had broken the morale of the other workers. I proposed that we exclude him from the party; a vote was taken, and he was excluded. The result was that the old man became the chief organizer of the picking operation, and the vegetables were picked on time. The old man was not a member of the party, and it gave him heart to be listened to and to see that something was done on the basis of his charges."

Something in the way Sasha described his efforts to get people to participate in workers' management struck me as smacking of manipulation. I suspected he was really making all the decisions himself and merely pretending to give the workers some say in their affairs. And he did not voice the liberal views on the party I was accustomed to hear. He put too much emphasis on the party's role as initiator of all things and too little on the initiative frequently stifled by party domination. It is intriguing to think of the party as "weak" when it is autocratic, and "strong" when it functions only as a leader and persuader. But this view assumes that the party is ideal, in that it builds its authority through leadership and persuasion; my own skeptical view is that the real party is more likely to manifest the weakness of autocracy. What I saw and heard in Yugoslavia confirmed my view, and the 1964 Congress of the League of Communists adopted a new statute for party organization precisely because the party as theretofore organized was contradicting and stifling the democratic developments described in the Party Program.

I understood Sasha's thinking better, however, after I had sat in on my first meeting in his factory—a session of the managing board. It was quite obvious that workers' management at Galenika was functioning at a high level of competence. Clearly the party did encourage workers' management in this factory, and clearly Sasha had done a good job of drawing in competent people. All the people who sat on the board had already served on the councils of their economic units and had attended the factory's seminars on workers' management. As one executive told me, "We're an up-and-coming enterprise with great ambitions, and we can't let these people learn on the job when that job is making the policy of the enterprise. They already know what they're about." When I went to their meeting, they were still new, but the dispatch and clarity with which they handled the business of the day was extraordinary. (Interestingly enough, it was impossible to pick out the Communists in the discussion. This is a common difficulty in Yugoslavia, and I learned early that guesses were as often wrong as right if one assumed that anyone supporting government policies was a party member. It was also unreliable to assume that people opposing government policies were not members.)

In a meeting that lasted nearly three hours, those twelve men and women on the board, only one of whom was a university graduate, decided on the status of the factory restaurant, the sale of a piece of land, the purchase of a new machine, a bank loan to cover payments to a Hungarian firm installing new chemical apparatus in the factory, the sale of wood scraps, the dissolution of a lease on a building on Belgrade, a loan for the development laboratory, decisions from the economic units to open up new jobs, formation of a commission to oversee the stockroom and warehouse, requests for aid to two workers attending school, a report from the housing commission on several cases of alleged hardship, a mistake in a shipment of pills to Tunis, and half a dozen other matters.

The shipment to Tunis was curious because it touched on factory discipline, a delicate problem in Yugoslav enterprises. In this case, a Tunisian firm had ordered 10,000 pills and only 5,000 had been shipped. The managerial staff now proposed to send the other 5,000 free to make up for the mistake; the managing board was

agreeable but wanted to know why the mistake occurred and resolved to penalize the person responsible. The threat of firing as
the ultimate penalty is avoided as much as possible in Yugoslav
enterprises, both because workers do not like to fire their fellows
and because this type of penalty is associated with capitalism. At
the same time, however, workers must be held responsible for the
quality of their work. This is not easy in a country where workers
have few traditions of discipline and responsibility. Every enterprise has a disciplinary commission which investigates complaints
of insubordination and negligence and imposes penalties which
usually consist of a 5 or 10 percent cut in pay for a period com-
mensurate with the violation. This is not always an attractive solution. The disciplinary commission sometimes seems childish and
pompous, and it involves complicated procedures with the possibility of misuse. But it is one way the Yugoslavs have found to
hold people to greater responsibility without threatening them with
dismissal.

The greatest excitement in the meeting came over one of the
alleged hardship cases reported by the housing commission. A
young man who had just received the key to a room which he was
to share with another man wanted to give it up and resume his
position at the head of the waiting list for housing. He complained
that the room did not have its own toilet, had no separate closet
where he could hang his contaminated work clothes, etc. The
members of the board rose up in arms. Why was this man wearing
his contaminated work clothes outside the factory? This was
a menace to public health. And how could he complain when so
many others were just as badly off: men with families, men who
had fought in the revolution, men who had worked longer in the
factory, and men who gave more time to the burdens of unpaid
political work?

A man sitting across from me rose to explain what had been in
the young man's mind. A false rumor had gone round that one-
room apartments would soon be available for unmarried men and
women. His idea was to refuse the double room and then be first to
get one of the new apartments.

The board took back the key to the room but angrily resolved to put the young man's name at the bottom of the waiting list.

Then an associate director of the enterprise, who was representing the director at the board meeting, rose to give a survey of the housing situation. The prospects, he said, were that the enterprise would house everyone eligible for an apartment within three years. By that time all hardship cases would be eliminated and the factory could think of keeping up with current housing demands. Until then it would be impossible to think of separate apartments for unmarried persons, except for those suffering from tuberculosis. He closed with a rousing condemnation: "For this man to present his case as one of hardship is an act of inexcusable selfishness." Everyone in the room applauded.

From this meeting it was obvious that the managing board at Galenika was deciding primarily on specific matters. From what Sasha had told me about the party, it seemed pretty clear that the Communists on the board must play a leading role; but this was not apparent to an outside observer. When I checked the reports of their decisions over the last year, I found that the board almost always accepted management proposals, except in the matter of opening up new jobs. It looked as if the management was largely having its way. This is not necessarily a bad thing. There is nothing wrong with giving the director and his staff their head so long as an enterprise is doing well. But when it begins to founder or when the managerial staff begin to abuse this liberty, the managing board and workers' council must be ready and able to take things in hand—and the Yugoslav theory is that they will do so, partly because their own pockets are affected and partly because they will feel some social responsibility for ill effects suffered by the community.

In looking over the work of Galenika's managing board, I found just such an occurrence. Every month the management submits its production plan for the following month, to be approved by the managing board. No plan was submitted in July because the factory was going to be shut down in August for vacations and repairs. But some workers had less than a full month's vacation and were to return to work during August. At its last July meeting the board instructed the management to include the production done by these workers in the September plan. This the management neglected to do. The managing board refused their plan and returned it for correction. Sasha was delighted by the action of the board, for he figured the management had probably not been guilty of an oversight but had hoped those extra working hours would be forgotten so the enterprise's production would show a particularly good record in the following month. This would of course have gone to their credit.

The workers' council at Galenika functioned as a broad policy-making body. Their proposals to the management and managing board were general recommendations: the production superintendent should propose ways to increase labor productivity and prevent increases in the labor force; the managing board should draw up a more effective sales program and increase the advertising staff; unnecessary property, equipment, and materials should be liquidated, and so on.

But the workers' council was not as quick or sharp about management as the managing board. This was quite evident at one meeting I attended. The main business was approval of a statute on the parliamentary procedures of the council and the managing board. Everyone in the room had a copy before him and the president began to call out the page numbers. "Page one." "Approved." "Page two." "Approved." From time to time someone would point out a need for correction, and after a short pause the booming voice of the president would resound again and the weaker voice of the assembly would answer "Approved."

It was a hot day, the statute went on for twenty pages, with minor corrections, neither very vital nor exciting, and I was already disappointed at the fact that everything was so routine, when they reached the last matter on the agenda: approval of some appropriations requested by the management. As everyone waited for the silent approval which would liberate us, a member of the council raised his hand and then lowered it, no doubt having reminded himself of the general discomfort. But the president, a forceful man, insisted gruffly that he speak his mind.

"Well," said the man, "I have a question about the appropriation for those new warehouse shelves. As I understand it, they would have to be imported, and that seems a lot of money in foreign currency when we need other things so badly. Besides, we already have the shelves from the old warehouse. Why don't we use those?"

The director spoke out sharply; he did not ask for the floor. "I suggest that the workers' council approve this appropriation exactly as we presented it."

The suggestion fell like a command. But a man sitting next to me spoke up in support of the workers' council.

Then the associate director stood up. "It seems to me," he said, "that both sides are taking an extreme position in this matter. We need not leave it at all or nothing. I've been told that the old shelves will not finish out the new warehouse because they must be altered to fit. But the resolution could be worded so as to require the management to use up the old shelves first."

Sasha sat on the edge of his seat and beamed with delight. The man who had initiated the discussion presented the reworded resolution. Sasha whispered to himself as the man presented it: "And now cut off the money until it is needed." But the resolution was passed without mention of stopping the money. The workers' council had made a mistake and given the staff money it had not wanted to give it.

Sasha was disappointed. The development of independent workers' management might depend in part on people like himself, but there was only so much he could do. It was his job as information director to teach people enough about factory affairs so that they would know when to put a brake on the professional staff. It was not his job to tell them what to do when the staff caught them off guard. He was not a member of the workers' council and he attended their meetings as an observer—as any other worker in the factory. He could sit on the edge of his seat and hope the board made no mistakes, but that was all. I saw him itching to speak, but I never saw him try to horn in on what was not his affair.

In the union organization, where he held an official position, it was a different matter. At one meeting of the union's executive committee, a group of about twenty men and women, I saw him win one battle after another. The first one had to do with the ever present problem of housing. Several apartments had recently been distributed, and appeals were about to be heard from those who felt they had been overlooked. The complaints were to be reviewed first by the union committees in the economic units and then passed on to the executive committee for a final decision. Sasha suggested that each member of the executive committee attend the meeting of one economic unit. In this way they could discover the content of the complaints twenty-four hours before they formally received them.

A stout man on the other side of the table grew red in the face at the very idea. "Look here," he said, "you want to take us back five years in the development of the economic units. It's that long since we went down to run their meetings. Let them have their say on the complaints; we'll get them in good time."

"I'm not suggesting," Sasha replied, "that we go down to run their meetings or even participate. They should handle their business and we should handle ours. I'm suggesting we go down there on our own business, to save time in disposing of the complaints."

Sasha was clearly concerned about the efficiency of democratic procedures. The right to appeal about apartments insured greater justice and minimized hidden resentment. But every new elaboration of the democratic process demanded greater efficiency, since Galenika was not a political club but a drug producer engaged in competitive business. The distribution of apartments was vital; it could not be allowed to drag on.

The stout man was opposed to Sasha's method of expediting the matter. He knew of the long efforts necessary to create independence in a body formed from above. Those at the upper level—the founders—want the lower body to act independently and responsibly, but they naturally tend to equate responsibility with decisions that suit their own opinions. At the lower level there is long-lingering respect for the old discontinued authority. The combined effect of these two things can delay independence indefinitely. This man feared that the presence of members of the executive committee would disquiet the members of the economic unit councils and destroy their independence.

No meeting of minds was possible. Sasha formally presented his motion and a young man who was the factory secretary of the League of Communists seconded it. The motion carried by a narrow margin.

Sasha was the key figure in the next argument too. The factory youth organization had formed a soccer team to play in an industrial league. They had asked the union to sponsor them and had been promised financial support. The matter seemed routine enough as the secretary read out the team's request for 100,000 dinars to cover equipment and organization. But then the council members began to ask, "Now why 10,000 dinars for a rubber stamp?" "And where does this particular sum go?"

No one, however, thought of rejecting the budget until Sasha suddenly said: "No, we absolutely cannot go on this way. The sports committee of the youth organization was informed of this meeting; the chairman was supposed to be here to explain this request. If they want our money, they can damn well come and explain the things we don't understand. I don't question the estimate itself—and there is certainly no question of our willingness to give them the money—but they can't do business in this sloppy way, and I propose we reject their request until they come here to justify those expenditures. It's a simple matter of principle."

A man across the table jumped up. "This is absurd. If we reject the request they won't be ready for the soccer season that's about to open."

"That would seem a good reason for them to have come when they were invited," Sasha replied.

"But Sasha," the man retorted, "you're a member of that sports committee. Why don't you explain to us what the figures mean?"

"Sure," Sasha said, "I'm a member of the committee, and I

could probably explain some of those items, but I'm not going to do it because the young man who is chairman of that committee didn't even take the trouble to authorize me to do so."

The argument went back and forth for a few minutes but nothing new was said. Finally Sasha crossed his arms and smiled at his exasperated opponent. I was sure he had organized his support for his first motion, but clearly this problem had arisen unexpectedly, when the young people failed to show up. Yet he was certain he would win the vote, and he held his ground without saying anything more. At length the president repeated the proposals for and against approval, and Sasha won again. In the argument about going down to the economic units I had hoped his opponent would win, for a little loss of time seemed a small price to pay for making the economic units feel independent. But here I felt that Sasha was right. Workers' management is meaningless unless people accept the responsibilities that go with it. It is often inconvenient and downright unpleasant to attend meetings, but when people fail to show up, they are in effect abandoning their power to those who do come. The best way to avoid this is to refuse to take the power. The sports committee of the youth organization did not fail to send its representative to the next meeting.

The last piece of business was merely technical: every worker in the factory had been considered a union member, whether he paid his dues or not, but Sasha was now leading a movement for check-off, the system of taking the full dues out of the workers' paychecks.

"But then people will drop out of the union," someone said.

And another man added, "We should stick to the principle of 'let every man pay what he will' if we want to keep people in."

But Sasha objected. "I see no reason to worry about people dropping out. Even now a few people refuse to be members. We'll get more money if we take the full dues. Let a certain percentage of the workers drop out and then we'll know where we really stand and try to discover why they wanted to get out."

The disagreement touched off a discussion of the union's role in a factory with workers' management. When the forms have been set up for the workers to run their factory, there is no one for a militant union to militate against. Then what should the union do? In Yugoslavia it has become a pillar of the establishment, supporting rather than opposing the decisions of the party and the government—which in theory always represent the working people. The union implements those decisions in its sphere: fringe benefits, housing, vacation facilities, and so forth. The difficulty with this is that the interests of the real working people are not always, at least in the short run, those which determine policies in a factory or the party or the government. This might be expected when the majority of party members are not production workers but white collar workers and professional people. The work stoppages which have occurred in some Yugoslav factories in the last couple of years are evidence enough that the union's present role is not entirely satisfactory—or even clear. There is a general malaise about its function on the local scene, but it is too big a problem for one factory to solve; and the discussion at Galenika finally petered out. Sasha's desire for clarity about where they stood was not enough, though he managed to get checkoff at Galenika.

Where Sasha's push toward clarity was really effective was in bringing workers' management up to an extraordinary level of competence. He wanted everything to be open and clear. The one thing he could not tolerate was criticism spoken in a whisper, but he understood that if people are going to criticize openly, they must have all the facts in hand so that they feel secure from accusation and counterattacks. Sasha's great passion was getting the facts out to everyone. He had begun with bulletin boards where he posted copies of every decision made by the workers' council and managing board. That wasn't enough. So he began to use a loudspeaker system for reporting factory news. Then he began to publish a monthly magazine with articles by staff members on plans for the enterprise and on specific problems inside the factory. Next he added a weekly newspaper. But he was still dissatisfied.

"Now," he told me, "I think we are doing a good information job with the managing board and pretty well with the workers' council. But I'm still not satisfied with my work in the factory as a whole. When it comes to informing two thousand workers about the enterprise's business and the proceedings of workers' management, there are real problems. I've gone on now to a factory information bulletin. It has no definite schedule of publication, but we've put out forty numbers in the last five months. They run from three to ten mimeographed pages. No one in the enterprise can leave the premises without passing within two feet of piles of these bulletins. They have things in them which ought to interest everybody. Here is one, for example, devoted entirely to individual workers' questions to the managerial staff and the answers put by the staff. 'Why does our packing arrive so late? How do the production departments stand with raw materials? How are our products selling and what is the position of the customers who owe us money? Can we reduce overtime work in the transport department? Can anything be done about freight containing glass which is often poorly marked?' No worker can reproach us for not making the material available to him. He needs only to reach out his hand.

"But some people are still out of it all. The other day I asked a worker the name of the head of his sector. He didn't know, though he'd been working under the man for seven years. I see this as a very serious problem. It may be that this worker cares about nothing beyond his nose, or it may be that the sector head is so high-hat that he's lost all contact with those who do the work under him. In the first case, I'll know that one individual is deadwood. But if the sector head is at fault, then I've stumbled onto something important.

"So, in spite of all our publications and the information conveyed by word of mouth in the meetings of the economic units, the union, and the whole collective, there are still people who don't know about the business of their own factory. At the moment I'm pushing a project to organize round-table discussions in which we'll provide a panel of experts and our people will be able to ask questions and speak their own minds. We'll treat subjects important only to us at Galenika and also subjects of general interest. I expect to bring in speakers from outside: professors, public officials, and the like. But when that project is underway and has become an accustomed feature in the life of the enterprise, there'll always have to be something else to take us one step further. I'll think of something."

This was Sasha's view of workers' management, and the view of most Yugoslavs I met: we'll always need to go one step further; but we'll think of something. The things they thought of often seemed to me ambiguous—the party, for example, is in many ways a questionable means. But I never found any ambiguity in the desire to develop the system. I was much impressed by the effort made in this one factory not to allow economic realities to be the only principles by which they organized the everyday task of making medicines. Whether democratic self-management by workers' councils and managing boards can prove economically advantageous is still a question. But there is no question that workers' management allows a man to get more than money out of his job. It offers him something very important: a chance to move out of his atomic existence as a worker on number so-and-so machine; it allows him to begin to comprehend the important workings of the society he lives in. It is here that the social adventure begins.

X

Toward a Socialist Agriculture

For various reasons, beginning with certain attitudes of Karl Marx and ending with the specific conditions in which revolutionaries have tried to apply Marx' teachings, agriculture has been the thornier side of socialist economy. Yugoslav agriculture is no exception to the rule. The Yugoslav Communists made a revolution under conditions which had very little to do with Marx' predictions and prognoses. At the time of the war Yugoslavia was not a highly developed industrial country "ripe" for socialism but an underdeveloped country with 75 percent of its population living on the land. It was the peasants, whose very agricultural methods and implements were centuries out of date, who made up the bulk of the revolutionary army.

Peasant life represents much that a Communist wants to get away from: the low and undynamic living standard of subsistence farming; the low cultural level with its illiteracy, illogic, superstition, and prejudice; the waste of human energy and talents in an out-dated economy that lags further and further behind the modern industrial world.

In a peasant agriculture crisscrossed property lines divide even small holdings of a few acres into a dozen or more tiny patches, which may be several miles apart. Valuable forests necessary to prevent erosion are cleared to make new plowland because the soil of old fields is exhausted and no fertilizers have been added. The peasant plows with slow draft animals, frequently with wooden plowshares. He relies upon traditional plant varieties in an age when scientific selection has produced varieties of amazing capacities, and plant seed which was not grown under certified conditions and whose percentage of germination has not been tested. He slaughters his suckling pigs on holidays because there is not enough grain to fatten the sow's entire litter. He grows corn and wheat on slopes up to 45 degrees, raises livestock breeds which eat too much feed for the amount and quality of the meat they produce, and devotes good orchard land to fruit varieties that bear at the wrong time and produce poor fruit which is often rotten because insects and diseases are not controlled.

One can feel the futility of all these things and struggle against them without being a socialist. American agriculture is the most advanced in the world, and yet it has progressed without abandoning the conception that the land is a private not a social resource. The Yugoslavs want all the advantages of the modern economy, but they want to organize production on socialist principles. The peasant, however, clings to his little private holding as the basis of his existence. He wants to own the land he works and work it in his traditional way even though his standard of living, his contribution to the national economy, the productivity of his labor, or the advance of his culture may suffer.

The Yugoslav socialists who led a peasant revolutionary army faced a very difficult political problem. They considered the peasant's title to the land a relic of the past and no part of the future socialist society. Yet one of their revolutionary slogans was "Land to the peasants," and after the war they had to keep their promises. The small plots given to landless peasants further reinforced the predominance of holdings too small for modern agriculture and increased the problems with peasant landowners.

Yugoslavia is not poor in good farm land, but it must use what it has in a modern way that produces large market surpluses to feed an urban and industrial population. That modern way means large farms which make mechanization possible and efficient; stock raising with good breeds, scientifically prepared feeds, and mass fattening in sheds built for that purpose; certified seed; chemical fertilizers and insecticides; modern methods of cultivation; good farm-to-market roads; and above all, technical skill and knowledge on the part of agricultural producers. Since we have all these things in America, we take them for granted. To understand the Yugoslav situation right after the war we must imagine not only an agriculture without them, but the absence of an industry to provide them and the absence of capital to procure them from abroad.

The Yugoslavs were fortunate in at least having the mineral and energy resources upon which to build an industrial base. In the first fifteen years after the war they developed that base to a point where Yugoslav industry was faced with the problem, not of furnishing the domestic market with industrial goods, but of finding its place in the world market. Agriculture, however, had to suffer a certain lag behind industrial development. As industry was being built, ceilings were set on agricultural prices so that industrial workers could feed their families on earnings low enough to allow accumulation of capital in industry. In other words, the accumulation of investment funds in industry came partly from agriculture through price ceilings on farm produce. In the early years it was wiser policy for the country to import grain and pour investments into industry rather than to try to bring up agricultural production before industry was ready to supply it with the necessary machinery, chemicals, and capital. Agriculture, then, was not only neglected but even drained. Only in 1957 and 1958 did massive farm investments begin to correct agriculture's unfavorable position in the economy.

Agriculture lagged behind industry in economic and technological development, but it lagged even further behind in the establishment of socialist forms of organization. In the late fifties investments began to shift from heavy industry, and agriculture began to enjoy larger investments. But even in 1963 only about 10 percent of Yugoslavia's arable land had passed into the hands of socialist agricultural enterprises, though on that 10 percent the socialist sector was producing 30 percent of all market commodities.

Yugoslav agriculture thus experienced many years of waiting. Many observers both inside and outside the country feel that the wait was too long. Those waiting years included the mistakes of hard-line policies which almost lost the Communists the support of the peasants. This was the period of the compulsory cooperatives. The peasants were dissatisfied with the arrangement, which did not stimulate them to produce at full capacity. The expected rise in farm production did not materialize. The inefficiency of the cooperatives themselves also contributed to this failure. The meager tools and resources which were pooled from private holdings could not be used efficiently in common: fifteen plows could not be transformed into one tractor or a dozen scattered pig pens into one modern hog house. Eventually the leaders came to recognize not only the political but also the economic and technical unfeasibility of these early cooperatives. They allowed the peasants to withdraw, and most of them did. (This retreat is an example of the style of the Yugoslav leaders, who are inclined to regard popular discontent as a sign of their own failure in designing policy. Sometimes this recognition of failure seems a little tardy, but generally popular acceptance is a *sine qua non* of Yugoslav policies. Sensitive to the fact that "Stalinism" can arise out of the intoxication of leaders with their own vision, they are more likely to suspect their policies than the people when the two come into conflict.)

Now, after years of painful development because of great physical, economic, and organizational difficulties, Yugoslav agriculture is beginning to see brighter days. The way is finally open toward a modern agriculture which will be socialist.

I began my own look into Yugoslav agriculture by asking the advice of a friend who translated an agricultural journal from Serbo-Croatian into English and taught English to students at the Agricultural School of the University of Belgrade. He promised to arrange meetings for me with the professors of agriculture at the university. Within twenty-four hours I was called to a meeting with the dean of the School of Agriculture, a dynamic young man with much of the energy and ambition which Yugoslavs often call "American." The dean began our conversation by telling me of the reorganization taking place in the School of Agriculture.

"We give three degrees in our school," he said, "and each gives training for specific positions in our farm organization. The first comes after two years of study and qualifies a man for one of the lower technical positions on a large farm. He might, for instance, take charge of broiler production or hog raising. He needs another two years of study, or the second degree, to fill higher technical positions, such as supervisor of all livestock production or field crops or orchards and vineyards. The third degree, which requires yet another two years and a dissertation, is designed to train men who will teach and do research. The dissertation must be relevant to the problems and needs of Yugoslav agriculture.

"But what I wanted to tell you is that our reorganization is intended to greatly increase the number of graduates with the first degree. Registration for this degree will be unlimited this fall, though our facilities are already overburdened. The reason is that we've realized the importance of people in making the agricultural revolution. We now know that we can't make all the changes we want in agriculture simply by manufacturing more farm machinery and stepping up agricultural investments. Very often the real changes in the countryside are made by farm boys who've come here and then returned with some training. So we're going to give some sort of training to everyone who wants it, even though this old building was designed for a few hundred students and is already being used by some thousands. We are building new facilities out near our experimental fields, but we'll be even more crowed here before we can move."

"There've been tales," I said, "in the newspapers of agronomists working as waiters or muscians in Belgrade because they couldn't find other jobs."

"That's in spite of the shortage of agricultural technicians in the provinces," he replied. "As you probably know, one of our country's problems is that young people who leave the provinces to get their training in the city are sometimes reluctant to go back where their training is needed most. Many become so attached to urban life that they prolong their studies by delaying their examinations, and then some who have graduated will even change professions to stay in the city. I can tell you of a case or two the newspapers haven't hit upon yet. One fellow very cleverly became a specialist in grass seed and by working one day a week at the soccer stadium he earns a salary equal to mine. Otherwise he does nothing with himself but study the soccer pools. Another fellow plays saxophone in a dance band. He makes more than three times what I do. In all, I know of perhaps half a dozen of our graduate agronomists who've stayed in the city rather than take the jobs for which they were trained. I doubt if our share is greater than any other field. There are factories in the provinces which need engineers just as there are farms which need agronomists. Probably the newspapers cite the agronomists because it does seem absurd that a man should specialize in farming if he doesn't like rural life. I don't understand these people myself, but it's better to have a few waste their training than to tell everyone where he must go.

"Another curious thing is that there are some places where no one will go. I've had great trouble filling a position near Mostar. You would think young men would be challenged by the difficulties of developing agriculture in that region where the peasants live so poorly. Perhaps they think it is hopeless to farm in a terrain where all the water disappears into the limestone, but I don't think we should give up so easily."

There was a short pause and then the dean sat forward abruptly. "I have a proposal which I hope will suit you. This evening an American professor of viticulture and fruit selection is arriving for a three-day tour of vineyards and orchards around Belgrade. Viticulture is also my field, and I've visited this professor in California. Now he's to be my guest. I understand English better than I speak it. If you come along with us, you'll perhaps see things that will interest you, and you can interpret for us."

I accepted his proposal, which explained why this meeting had been arranged so suddenly, and we met next morning to have a look at Radmilovats, the experimental station where the school's research in grapes and fruit was concentrated.

The station was about fifteen miles from Belgrade. As we drove out—the dean, the American professor, and I—the dean sat silent while Dr. Peterson asked me general questions about the Yugoslav economy. I explained decentralization, the independence of Yugoslav enterprises from government control, the market economy, and workers' management. I tried to use American analogies and references, but I soon felt I was not getting across. He had been to Russia and he wanted to use the Russian system as the base from which to understand the Yugoslav system. Since I had not been to Russia, I could not make that detour with him, and in any case I felt it was a sign of a general national weakness if two Americans should be impeded in a discussion of Yugoslavia by the idea that all Communist countries were the same as Russia.

When the orchards and vineyards of the experimental station came into view, spread over the rounded slopes of a little pocket of hills behind the bluff that guards the Danube, the dean sat up in his seat and began to talk in Serbian. I followed him in English for the professor's benefit.

"The original station," he began, "was established before the war with a bequest to the university for the practical training of agriculture students. More land was added after the war with the Agrarian Reform Law, and now adjacent fields are for sale and we are buying." He pointed to a narrow field of wheat stretching up one of the knolls. It had been plowed vertically, a practice all too common in Yugoslavia, which has great erosion problems. "You can see how that farmer has let the land run down." True, the young wheat had a pale, almost whitish cast. "He has gone off to the factory to make his living like many others," the dean said. "Now we are buying his field at the going price in these parts. That piece of ground will do much more good under our vineyards than under his stunted wheat."

The car stopped beside one of the buildings in the center of the little valley, and the dean was first out of the car. He was radiant, like a country gentleman back on his estate after protracted city affairs. Perhaps his election to a term as dean of the faculty had kept him in town more than he would have liked. He had visited the professor's domain at the university in far-off California and now it was his pleasure to show the work he had organized over many years to a man who would understand and appreciate.

We set off through an orchard. The professor stopped to inspect some cold damage on an apple tree and began to ask about climatic conditions. He too was in his element now, within sight and touch of these plants which were familiar even though he had never seen them before.

We arrived at the viticulture laboratory, which was housed in a building just completed. I judged by the professor's sincere admiration that the dean's pride in it was justified by any standards. In the laboratories we saw many instruments bearing the red-white-and-blue plaque with clasped hands that indicated they were obtained through American aid programs.

It took us three hours to cover the plantations of grapes. The dean was in his glory, for what we saw was an international collection of methods for pruning and training grapevines. He said proudly: "You can see here the history of my travels. Whenever I came home from a new wine region I set up a model of the method used there in order to test it under our conditions." The professor was amused at this mammoth project and would exclaim as we approached a new plot: "Ah, I see you've been through northern Italy!" or "And there is what you saw in the Concord region of New York." "Yes," the dean would say, "we Yugoslavs like to take from all sides; we improve on what we take if we can." I appreciated this remark, a commonplace in Yugoslavia today, more than perhaps the professor did. He had not had the chance to see how much the Yugoslavs had "taken" from America.

When I asked the dean how the work of his station had affected commercial grapegrowing, he said that here they had worked out the optimum space of vines for the region and that current experiments on supports and pruning would eventually lead to replacing the traditional and still common method of tying vines to stakes like tomato plants. "But," he went on, "the station's function is

research, not enlightenment. Our close contacts are with the socialist farms and the cooperatives, though from time to time we do
give demonstrations to which private farmers come. But it's the
cooperative here which performs the function of your county
agent. The cooperatives transmit what they learn from the station
to the individual farmer and encourage him to introduce the new,
more profitable methods."

Our visit to the station ended with an elaborate ceremony of
degustation, for the station produces its own wine, sells it to Belgrade's finest hotel, and is planning a new modern wine cellar. We
were a sizable group around the conference table in the library and
the wine was good and plentiful, but we were neither gay nor
relaxed. The three of us were already late for a luncheon with the
mayor of the commune, and though I exerted myself I could not
translate fast enough to bring Dr. Peterson into close informal
contact with the young and serious staff of the station, who wanted
very much to know his views on their common field of science, on
agriculture and science in general, and finally on those human
questions of politics and society which Yugoslavs find particularly
compelling.

The dean made two remarks which must be stock on such occasions, but the professor's responses were curiously cold. When the
dean said there were no national or ideological barriers between
scientists, the professor said, "Yes, but only in scientific matters."
To the dean's later remark that wine specialists were the most
convivial scientists and political differences disappeared in their
conviviality, the professor said, "Yes, but only after the first five
bottles."

I was not sure how I felt about the professor's refusal to join in
the spirit of the dean's remarks. I liked his honesty. Too much is
sometimes claimed for the power of scientific and cultural exchanges to break down barriers. Chemists and violinists have their
political views like other citizens. If the political barriers are real,
why should they not feel them like anyone else? On the other
hand, any exchange which presupposes some common ground

must help to humanize the image which each side has of the other, replacing caricatures of propaganda with the faces of real men.

Neither the political nor the scientific questions were settled, and we rushed away to have lunch with the mayor of this fruit-growing commune. He turned out to be another of these energetic young men, but he did not have the dean's smooth control. He greeted the professor with such an enthusiastic welcome that his impatience for our arrival seemed to have built up not in a few hours but over a lifetime.

The mayor led the way up to one of the most beautiful restaurants in Yugoslavia, set on a high bluff covered with vineyards. The terrace of the restaurant is surrounded with grapevines, supported in the traditional fashion on stakes stuck in the ground, whence the name of the restaurant, "Vinogradi"—vineyards; and it commands an unsurpassed view of the Danube, which spreads open in a wide curve at just this point. A long island thickly overgrown with willows stretches around the bend. Across the river the vast plain of the Voivodina stretches without a roll or wrinkle until it is lost from view in the haze at the horizon. The interior of the restaurant is magnificent, with its rustic wooden beams and authentic decorations from Serbian folk art.

During the meal the mayor put ceaseless questions to Dr. Peterson on general trends in American agriculture. He seemed to be checking out a sweeping analysis he had made through various articles he had read, and the professor's answers pleased him immensely. But we ran into difficulties when he moved on to the relations between American industry and agriculture. For the professor insisted that agriculture included the whole of the economy since all economic activity was ultimately based on the land and its resources. The mayor and the dean stared at me in perplexity as I translated the professor's perverse concept. They asked me to put it another way, thinking there might be some linguistic misunderstanding. The mayor finally shrugged his shoulders and dived enthusiastically into a new subject: the local canning factory in this commune, which was rich because of its fruit, wanted to produce fruit cocktail. The professor wrote down the names of several new fruit varieties and told the mayor how he could keep up with the rapid development of new hybrids.

Then it was the professor's turn to ask questions. There were many things he wanted to know about Yugoslavia. His questions were just as pointed as those the mayor had put to him a while before. He listened with interest to an explanation of the ambitions these two young Communists had for their country: rapid economic development, workers' management in the economy, and decentralized self-government in political administration. He admitted that all these things sounded very fine, and he was impressed by the enthusiasm of the two men before him. But then he suddenly led us afield. What basis, he asked, could atheists have for distinguishing between good and evil? If there was no God, then how could one justify a good act? For himself, he found the concept of God more and more necessary in his scientific work. I found I could no longer take a neutral view of my position as interpreter. I decided not to collaborate in a "dialogue between deaf men," as the French say, and engaged the professor in a discussion of religion on my own. Why should I allow the understanding which had been reached with fruit cocktail to be undone with a futile discussion of God? The dean understood the difficulty, and he and the mayor left the table for a few minutes.

When they returned, we went out onto the stone terrace to view the Danube. The dean took the professor to the edge and pointed into the distance at the little village of his origins. I turned to the mayor. How had this luxurious restaurant come into being in a socialist country? Who put up the money to build it?

"Why, we did!" he said, with that same excess of energy with which he had greeted the professor. "We had money in our communal investment fund and we looked around for some way to put it to work. We wanted a quick return because we knew we would eventually need the money for other things. We decided to build a restaurant which would attract people with money to spend. After all, you can't squeeze water from a stone, can you?"

Although I had long since become hardened to the reality of differences of wealth in a developing country, something in the

man's cold calculation reawakened my egalitarian spirit. I asked
him how much the restaurant charged for an order of the broiled
sausages which are the most constant fare of the ordinary Yugoslav who takes his family out to a restaurant in the evening. The
mayor relayed the question across the terrace to the headwaiter.
"Two hundred dinars," came the reply from this dignified figure—
the universal type of the headwaiter—who was no doubt amazed
that men who had just enjoyed the restaurant's most elegant cooking should already be hungry for its simplest. The price was not
unreasonable, though it was about sixty dinars more than that of
ordinary restaurants.

The mayor was telling me of the half-dozen other tourist
projects the commune had already built or was planning to build
when our companions joined us for the ride back to Belgrade. I was
exhausted and could see that the professor was, but our hosts were
still alive with energy. They seemed dissatisfied with the progress
that had been made in introducing the professor's inquiring understanding to the Yugoslav way of thinking. They kept telling me to
translate to him the phrase "Socialism is the standard of living."
Leaning far back in his seat, thinking no doubt of the blessings of
sleep, the professor only nodded. And again they had me repeat
the phrase to him, but what had been missed with the professor
had been missed. Not even their combined energies could convey
over a lunch table all the national history and personal experience
which had culminated in their present enthusiasm—particularly to
a man who had come the evening before from one country foreign
to him and in two days would travel to another, continuing a trek
which had already gone on for six months. There was something
pathetic in that vain expense of energy at the end of a hard day in
the hope of breaking down barriers which were neither slight nor
pointless. They were right to think that those barriers can and
must be broken down, but they abandoned their usual realism in
thinking a frantic thrust at those barriers would be enough. I felt I
knew this better than they did. As for the professor, he seemed
resigned to the fact that there would be barriers between him and
Communists, and his stay in Yugoslavia was not long enough for

him to realize how easily he might have explored with these men areas of common ground that stretched far beyond the realm of grapes and wine. I knew these things better than any of them. As a guest in their country for two years I had been a constant attendant at those barriers. I had tried to break some of them down myself and had found Yugoslavs were willing and able to come halfway to break them down from their side. But breaking them down is neither easy work nor quick work. The barriers are real and they have their point. No American can understand Yugoslavia without first bringing much of America and much of his Americanism to consciousness; likewise no Yugoslav will ever be able to explain Yugoslavia to an American without first understanding America and the Americanism of the man he is talking to. It is not enough to be sure of his own rightness and humanity and the rightness and humanity of his system any more than it has ever been enough for Americans to put over American thinking through the sheer strength of their native convictions. I understood how the two men felt, but they understood neither me nor the professor. And if I had not talked long with other Yugoslavs who had understood me and America, I would have been as far from understanding them as the professor had been. These ideological fences have been built from both sides and they come down only when both sides are working at it and when both sides have furnished themselves with the right tools.

When the American professor had departed for the next country on his arduous itinerary, the dean suggested that I continue my look at Yugoslav agriculture through talking with a professor of farm organization at the School of Agriculture.

After we had compared notes on Piedmont, North Carolina, where he had spent five months, the professor said, "Our ultimate aim is to establish the industrial farm, or combine, as the socialist form for rural areas. "This is a farm so large that it can efficiently supply its own industry, that is, processing facilities—a dairy, a slaughterhouse with cold storage lockers, a cannery, and mills to make feed, to press oil from soybeans or sunflower seeds or to make sugar from sugar beets. It has its own staffs for administration and research, a great pool of equipment which can fill the granaries with the speed sometimes demanded by the weather; it may even have its own chain of butcher shops, dairy stores, and produce markets in the city. Its workers are trained specialists whether they drive tractors or do biochemical research, and they live in a community of apartment houses, a school, shopping center, etc., which makes it easier to eliminate the endemic cultural lag of rural areas. The management of these farms is organized on the same principles of self-government as industry. A hired professional staff of managers and technicians works with the elected workers' council and managing board. The operation is divided into economic units, which are given a certain independence in management decisions, distribution of income, accumulation of funds, investments, and the making of contracts outside the enterprise.

"The concept of the industrial farm brings us close to the big socialist farms of the Russians and other Communist countries, but we differ from them very much in the route we have chosen for arriving there. We have rejected the use of coercion, and we feel we're justified not only for the obvious humanistic reasons but also because our way is more effective and efficient."

"How far would you say you've gone," I asked, "on the route from small fragmented private farms to a socialist agriculture based on the industrial farm?"

"At present," he replied, "we have only a few of these farms. New ones will be formed out of the present socialized farms and voluntary cooperatives, which are transitional farms. The socialized farms were organized right after the war with land the state acquired through expropriating the property of wartime collaborators and through an agricultural reform law which set a maximum for individual private holdings. These farms now operate on their own, much like industrial enterprises. The voluntary cooperatives, which are altogether different from the old compulsory cooperatives, are the cornerstone of present agricultural policy. They vary greatly in size, form, and function. We invented this flexible institution to help increase production of badly needed market commodities on private land, and to facilitate the transition from small private holdings to large modern socialist farms.

"Our project now is to increase the socialist landholdings from ten to thirty percent; on that basis the socialists sector can produce ninety percent of the farm products sold on the market."

"How do you propose to obtain that land?" I asked.

"We'll buy it. There's no longer any problem with finding land to buy, particularly in the best farming regions. The exodus of young people away from peasant life has been greatest in the areas where farming has progressed furthest. The reason is that more industry is being located in the flat country and the young people are going into the factories or into specialized farming occupations in the socialist sector and selling their land or leaving their parents—who are really too old for it—to tend the farm. But the availability of land doesn't solve all our problems. We have to have the money to buy the land, so the rate at which we buy is limited by the capacity of the cooperatives and large farming enterprises to accumulate capital. Another problem is that the plots up for sale are so scattered that it's very difficult to farm them efficiently in a modern way even after we've bought them. And finally, we are after all a socialist country, and we must think about the fate of these old people whose land we buy. Even when we pay the going market price for the land, we aren't giving them enough to live on for the rest of their lives. What's going to happen to them when that little sum of cash has been spent? We can't go any further until we answer that question. But we might be coming to an answer. The Slovenians have begun to try a system of giving these people pensions in exchange for their land. The first attempt didn't work well because there wasn't enough money to carry through properly. But probably this is our solution and we'll eventually go about it more methodically and with greater resources."

The farm experts at the university suggested that I visit an industrial farm and a general cooperative. The first would give me an idea of where they wanted to go and the second would reveal something of how they intended to get there. Early one morning I took a bus from Belgrade out to a 75,000-acre industrial farming complex called the Belgrade Industrial Farm. This farm had been created not through expropriation but by reclamation. What was a marsh between the Danube and Tamish rivers and the Karash Canal has become a fertile island, although its surface is twelve feet below the spring water table.

The farm went into operation immediately after the war and began to supply a hungry Belgrade with milk, vegetables, and meat. Since then there have been many improvements: poor domestic breeds of hogs, dairy cows, and beef cattle have been replaced by select foreign breeds (the farm is now exporting high-grade beef to England and Italy); the number of tractors and combines has greatly increased (though the last draft animals were replaced by machines only in 1960); and facilities have been tremendously expanded.

The farm's industrial center—including an administration building, apartment houses, a dairy, garages, and a feed mill—can be seen from a distance of several miles, for the buildings rise high above the flat savannahs stretching out of sight in every direction. The impression is one of order and efficiency, but I liked it out of pure prejudice. Having grown up in the flat country of South Carolina, I am in favor of any project that strikes up out of the plane stretching the low line of the horizon, and raises a man's eyes off dead level. I am excited by a conception of agriculture which makes it possible for a farmer to live in a fifth-story apartment and look out over wheat fields with a martini in his hand. Of course I had heard that this farm was one of the country's luxuries—government investments, not its own profits, had built it up. But was it necessarily wasteful, I wondered, to build an example of what one wanted for the future? Besides, in time this type of comprehensive farm—engaged in every phase from planting the seed to merchandising the packaged harvest—would presumably justify itself financially.

My guide took me first into the dairy, which looked like the completely modern plant it was supposed to be. No disorder marred the spotless white tile of the walls and floor and the shining stainless steel of the pipes. Nothing was left of the primitive way in which dairying was done until very recently in this country. The dairy had progressed far beyond the shops and the consumers— very few of either had refrigerators. All the city's milk had to be dispatched from the farm every evening, and householders still boiled their milk so it would keep.

When the guide showed me the room in which butter and cheese were packaged, I noticed the labels for some Gorgonzola cheese which had appeared sporadically in the Belgrade supermarkets. "I'm responsible for that," the man said. "Every now and then I make up a little, but you know Serbs are very set in their ways when it comes to food." I told him that my wife's trips to the supermarket had finally convinced her she was the only Gorgon- zola buyer in the city, since she always found the same lot of cheese, until finally it grew too moldy to eat. "True enough, there are not many consumers, but perhaps one day we'll break through," he said.

The slaughterhouse was as ready-made and modern as the dairy. On the ground floor we saw lines of Italian motors driving the cooling system. As we were climbing the stairs I glanced out the window at the farm land which stretched for miles in every direction and for the first time I grasped the full meaning of the term "industrial farm," for the sounds that reached this staircase were unmistakably those of a factory, if a fairly quiet one, and yet outside there was no pressing city but only wide acreage spreading to the horizon.

Upstairs we saw thousands of frankfurters being wheeled into ovens. These I had seen sold on the streets of Belgrade by the farm's own chain of little white kiosks. Beside the ovens great red mixers held hundreds of pounds of the smooth hash of veal, beef, and pork for the grilled sausages eaten in restaurants. Young broil- ing chickens came on a hook conveyor into a narrow room where three women in white smocks, with the help of whirling modern devices, bled them, scalded them, plucked them, and dressed them. I asked my guide where all these chickens were sold, since I had seen relatively few in Belgrade supermarkets. He explained that the farm had just begun broiler production and this department worked only a few hours a week. Here was an indication that the industrial part of the farm was not yet operating efficiently. This expensive foreign machinery was being used at a fraction of its capacity.

We entered a chilly passage between the thick oak doors of the refrigerator lockers. A man dressed like an aviator came toward us pushing a side of beef and disappeared into a locker. Beyond the passageway was a large room where four men and women on a raised platform were plying long knives about a steaming beef carcass. They stepped about heavily in hip boots. When I asked my guide how many shifts were now working in the slaughter-house, he replied that this expensive plant was working only one shift and was supplied by that single team of four people I had just seen slaughtering the cattle. This confirmed my impression that the farm was still more a "model" than an efficient plant.

If my impression of the industrial farm was that its day had not quite arrived, my visit to a general cooperative in Ruma indicated that this institution was flourishing. Ruma lies in the flat and fertile region north and west of Belgrade, and its cooperative is one of the more successful. The director, a man in his early forties, and his three assistants, none of whom could have been over thirty, did not pretend that all cooperatives were as successful as theirs. But they said the cooperative was so appropriate in the present state of Yugoslav agriculture that its failure anywhere must be the fault of the technical personnel and the managers.

I asked them to explain how the cooperative worked. "The primary purpose," the director said, "is to popularize modern farming methods, to teach the peasants to use fertilizer, insecticides, and certified seed of good varieties. The director noticed my smile and stopped. I explained that his words had brought to mind a joke I had read in a Belgrade newspaper. An agronomist came to a village meeting to explain to the peasants the advantages of modern farming. He talked with great patience and went into great detail. Near the end of his lecture a man who had come late asked his neighbor what it was all about. "Well," said the neighbor, "he's talked about fertilization, mechanization, and agricultural aviation, and it looks mighty like there's going to be another war."

"Yes," the director replied, "the first steps in introducing modern technology and rational organization are the most difficult. In our particular case we've already largely succeeded in this. Only about fifteen to twenty percent of the farmers in our area still refuse to work with us, and they are mainly obstinate old people who'd rather farm in their old way than grow a good crop in a new way. They aren't the best farmers. We've been so successful with our lectures and films and recommendations that now most farmers come to us for help. We're no longer begging them to use fertilizer; they're begging us to sell it to them. And last year, much to our embarrassment, our supply gave out. Imagine, after all these years of preaching, we were so successful we couldn't even satisfy the demand. When they saw the success they had with fertilizer, it went easier with insecticides. More and more of them are coming to us for recommendations. When a disease hits their crop, they pull up a plant and come to ask us what they should do. Sometimes they don't understand why we can't cure everything."

The cooperatives have more than an educational role; they own heavy machinery and make a variety of arrangements with individual peasants and groups of peasants. They lease the land and farm it themselves, or enter into contract to do the heavy work at planting and harvest while the farmer tends the crop in midseason. At harvest time the farmer and the cooperative divide the yield, which means that they share the risks. Or the farmer can pay the cooperative to do part of his work for him. These arrangements spare the farmer the upkeep of draft animals beyond the horse he uses for transportation and light farm work. In many cases the cooperatives have been so anxious to extend cooperation among private farmers that they have rendered their services at cost. Sometimes the peasants take unfair advantage. A common practice is to lease a run-down piece of land to the cooperative for a short term. When the lease runs out the farmer either takes the land, which the cooperative has improved with deep plowing and mineral fertilizers, and farms it himself, or he rents it as improved land to someone else.

The director of the Ruma cooperative had had his problems

with the peasants too, but he was enthusiastic about the progress he saw around him.

"Working with us," he said, "has improved the peasants' economic position tremendously. Now they're buying furniture and radios and television sets, and a few are even buying automobiles. They no longer get up at three o'clock in the morning, but at six. They no longer work themselves to death doing the heavy work, since that's done with our machinery. They're better off than ever before."

"But," I asked, "isn't it possible that you've made private farming so easy and profitable that your efforts to bring land into the socialist sector will be slowed down?"

"It isn't working out that way," the director said. "Although the land in our area is some of the best in the country, the price is very low and we've been building up our landholdings rather rapidly. The fact is that the young people here don't want to live a peasant life, even though it's easier than it once was. They want to go to school and learn a trade or a profession, or a least get a job in the socialist sector of agriculture where the future holds good wages, a modern apartment, social security, and so forth. Young girls are turning away from boys who stick to the old peasant ways. They want to marry a tractor driver or an agronomist. And their parents encourage this. One of our problems is that here where the farming is good it is the best farmers who go into industry. The factories tend to hire the same men who've been receptive to our efforts to introduce modern agriculture and are less interested in peasants from more backward areas. Therefore, we find ourselves in a half-way position. Our best farmers, the ones we've invested most of our time in, are going off to industry and selling their land to farmers from, say, the hills of Bosnia, where the farming is poor but land prices are high because of population pressure and the scarcity of jobs. These men from Bosnia come into our area determined to make a better life for their children and to see that they get an education. But their determination to work hard is combined with great ignorance about modern farming. So then we have to do the whole job over again: from breaking down the farmer's resistance and building up good will and trust to putting across our message about the superiority of modern scientific methods over traditional methods."

"I've been told," I said, "that land purchases are a problem because the land up for sale usually consists of tiny scattered plots. Is this your experience?"

"Yes, of course, this situation is inevitable when the land in the private sector is so split up. But sometimes the fact that the holdings of private farmers usually consist of little scattered plots is a help to us in consolidating our own holdings. First of all, the law allows us to exchange land we've bought for land that is next to some other holding we already have. The farmer next to us can't refuse the exchange so long as we offer him a better piece of land that's closer to his house. He does, of course, have the right to appeal against our decision, but we have so far had only nine appeals against the several hundred exchanges we've requested. So we're building up our landholdings and becoming an efficient modern producer in our own right. Our main concern at the moment, as a matter of fact, is constructing our own fattening sheds and feed mill. We're going into the stock raising business on a large scale."

Not all cooperatives have advanced as far as the one at Ruma. Progress depends, as the director said, on the cooperative's organization and efficiency. It also depends on the region and on the peasants' level of education. There are big differences between the prosperous plains and the poor backward mountains.

The success of the cooperative in penetrating the backward countryside with modern ideas about farming has made farm production less of a problem, but distribution of farm produce remains inadequate and sometimes affects the cooperatives' efforts. For example, a Macedonian cooperative persuaded the farmers of its district to give up growing wheat and to concentrate on rice, a more suitable crop for the locale. But when the farmers found they had to travel long distances to get the wheat they needed, they switched back.

The principal distribution problems are not with grains or industrial crops, where organization is simpler and has gone further, but with fruits and vegetables intended for retail sale. In 1963 a fruit-growing area near Belgrade had a bumper crop. Since contracts for distribution had not foreseen this abundance, much of the fruit rotted. Most retail produce is sold in the open-air market, where the socialist farms and cooperatives compete with the private peasants, who bring in their own produce and rent a booth for the day to sell their vegetables, fruit, flowers, eggs, homemade cheese, poultry, walnuts, corn meal (ground by hand), and the products of their handicraft: wooden spoons, brooms, rugs, and lacework. These peasants could sell their produce to a cooperative with trucks and a permanent stall at the market, but many still have time to make the day's trek to the market, often a great distance away, and they do very well in the competition with more modern methods of distribution. They take more care with their vegetables, often shell the peas and beans, and either pick out the spoilage or allow the customer to pick for himself. The enterprises with perma-nant stalls that represent socialism in the open-air market are reluctant to do either of these things, and yet their prices are at least as high as those of the peasants. The peasants' stalls occupy four or five times as much space as the permanent stalls dealing in fruit and vegetables.

The reasons behind this situation are numerous. First, the large socialized farms cannot derive the same advantage from large-scale plantations of tomatoes, lettuce, and peppers as from wheat and corn. Second, the socialist farms concentrate on those crops which give them the best return and which fit into their plans for future development, whereas the private farm holding represents a family which can afford to convert time into cash at a rather low rate. The children and old people around a small farm can all pitch in to help in the vegetable garden. Since the peasant's idea of success is to turn his great reserve of time into money even at very uneconomic rates of exchange, the prices of peasant produce would probably stay even with the socialist produce no matter what the level was.

But the influence of peasant economics on the distribution system is probably temporary. The declining farm population is relying less and less on private farming for its income. Distribution is poor not because of the peasant but because a system to replace the peasant market has not yet been built up except for bread, meat, and milk, which are handled predominantly by enterprises in the socialist sector.

One reason for the delay in solving general distribution problems is the concentration upon supermarkets as the foundation of the marketing system. They take considerable capital investment, and accumulation of capital takes time. Yugoslavia's first supermarket was originally a U.S. exhibit at a Belgrade trade fair. After President Tito was shown the exhibit, so the story goes, he asked whether it was for sale and arranged to buy it. To this day the shelves in the supermarket bear a tiny notice that they are on loan from a company in the Midwest. This original supermarket now has many copies and counterparts. The big cities have improved on the original. Several chains of supermarkets are gradually building up networks over the whole country. Chains of small stores, formed largely from shops privately owned before the war and later nationalized, are moving toward the supermarket form of merchandising. The supermarkets are already competing with the open-air market. The steadiest customers are those city people who try to save some of their time for leisure. They buy refrigerators to save them from the daily round of purchases. They buy canned and frozen goods. They shop in the late morning or the afternoon and not at six in the morning, the hour of the open-air market. They have a taste for delicacies like caviar and pheasant, which are not offered in the open-air market.

But the supermarkets have not yet come into their own. In part their development must wait upon changing habits and tastes, but at the same time the peasant market in summer offers much better vegetables and fruit than the supermarket, at better prices. The supermarket does not yet have behind it the efficient distribution and warehouse system which makes it the most efficient and cheapest form of merchandising. Distribution problems are the same as those of the large socialist farms with their permanent stalls in the peasant market. Perhaps the present concentration on this problem will give significant results in the next few years. But even then the private peasant will not be thoroughly displaced. Large-scale cultivation and distribution will make the competition much stiffer for him as time goes on, but one thing is clear: the best peasants will be able to survive as private landholders indefinitely if they concentrate on crops which are suitable for hand labor. The land limit established by the agrarian reform law is about twenty acres—sufficient to support a family if the land is used rationally for fruit and vegetable crops which require much handling or for which the demand is steady but too small to make large-scale production possible. The number of private peasants living solely off their land is dwindling rapidly and will continue to do so, but some of the survivors may well make a very good thing out of their little plots. The consumer will benefit, for the ever present competition of the peasant will put continual pressure on the large-scale farms and supermarkets to improve their quality.

When one day I asked a professor of agricultural economics what the problems were in agriculture now that it had come this far, he sat back in his chair and put a finger to his temple. Then he smiled. "Well," he said, "I'll tell you. In America you have a very important and effective institution, one that performs a vital economic function for your society. In one way or another that function must be performed in every economy, whether it is capitalist or socialist. And we socialists have not really discovered a mechanism which will effectively perform that function in our economy."

Having deliberately built up my expectations and curiosity, he paused. I tried to guess the American institution he was referring to, but my face showed my bewilderment.

"I'll tell you," he said, "the institution I'm thinking of. It's your stock market."

At hearing a Communist praise that sturdy capitalist institution, I blinked.

"Let me explain myself," he went on. "In every economy, no matter who owns the means of production, there is at the end of every year a certain amount of surplus money which will be reinvested. In Yugoslavia, for example, we have kept our economy growing by maintaining an extremely high investment rate. But we neglected something else. We thought it was enough to reinvest a big sum of money every year and failed to invent a mechanism to guide that money to the right places. In agriculture, for instance, a big investment will go to waste on some farms and on others a small investment will produce a comparatively large return. Like most socialists, we've tried to direct investments through a central body—the Agricultural Bank. But we realize now that our investments haven't been effective. The money has gone too often to the inefficient farms while the profitable farms have gone begging. This doesn't happen with your stock market. All the investors want is a high return on their investment; so a company offering a high return will attract investment and one that promises a low return will not. Our problem is to give our socialist economy a mechanism which will do the work of your stock market.

"We haven't gone very far. The only point we've agreed on so far is that we should give the power of investment to the direct producer who created the surplus money through his own work. This means that we want to decentralize agricultural investments. We want investments to be economically efficient, to be made by the people who made the money, and to be guided by certain criteria which respect the needs of the country as a whole and provide coordination and harmony in our agricultural development."

That harmony has not been achieved yet, certainly. One sees vast differences between one farming region and another. But though hay is sometimes still pitched with forked branches, the theoreticians and agricultural experts are breathing a little easier; they feel themselves at the end of the first stage, *the creation of possibilities*. The stage which stands before them, in which they must learn *to make use of those possibilities,* will be easier even though its problems will be extremely complicated. They now have something to work with, and when they find the right solutions to their problems, the results will be more or less immediate and evident.

XI

Traveling in the East

BELGRADE SITS ON a bluff overlooking the confluence of the Sava and Danube rivers. From Kalemegdan Park, which occupies the tip of the Belgrade promontory, one has an open view of the Pannonian Plain stretching from the northern shore of the Danube up into Hungary. Except for the thin ridge of the Frushka Gora hills to the northwest, the plain is perfectly flat, and only its vastness and the haze lying over it prevent one from taking it all in at a glance.

This great stretch of northern Serbia—which is officially the Autonomous Province of Voivodina—produces the bulk of the country's grain crops and sugar beets, and much of its finest pork and beef. "This land is so rich," the peasants sometimes joke wryly, "it can stand socialism for another hundred years."

After months of watching buses depart for towns in that plain, I boarded one. We left the city by a new bridge over the Danube and then traversed broad savannahs crisscrossed with deep drainage and irrigation canals. The soil was black and corn grew thick on both sides of the road. A few miles beyond where the road turned off for the Belgrade Industrial Farm, we crossed a little river fringed with willows and were in Panchevo.

In the center of town a pleasant park shaded with horse chestnuts bordered on the cathedral square. The surrounding buildings were in an unimaginative Austro-Hungarian style of the last century—solid reminders that until 1918 the Dual Empire stretched down to the Danube at Belgrade. Today there continues to be a sizable Hungarian minority in the Voivodina and the province has schools, newspapers, radio programs, and even street signs in both Serbian and Hungarian.

New department stores and office buildings were going up around the central square. Beyond the center I saw only a half-dozen tall apartment buildings scattered among the one-story houses. The new structures were too few to dominate the drab and out-of-date, and I felt no sense of the move toward the vertical which is so common today in most Yugoslav towns, even where there is room for sprawl. At the end of the bus line, far on the other side of town, everything was one-story high and the brewery opposite the station presented long and aimless blank walls to the dusty street.

I went into the beer hall opposite the station to taste the local brew. This drinking establishment had apparently been converted from an old factory shop, but the "conversion" amounted to little more than removal of the machinery. Nothing had been done to brighten up the social life of the large numbers of people crowding the place on the weekend. The room was immense and poorly lighted, with perhaps two hundred crude wooden tables jammed into it. At one end a large bandstand had been pushed out of the way after the revels of Saturday and Sunday, but it was characteristic of this squalid place that only one of its back corners had been pushed to the wall. It looked as though it had been thrown and left where it landed. In a sociological study a witness of the weekend mayhem at a similar tavern in a mining town reported: "The music is so loud that conversation is hopeless. You are surrounded by a nightmare of drunken confusion. You have to keep your hand over your drink to keep out the flying glass." Such places do more than provide a space for drunkenness; they justify it. They are being replaced by civilized and attractive coffeehouses and restaurants as fast as money can be found and energy generated in the gloomy backwaters of the country. But where they still exist, they make it easier to understand the extremism of the lecturer I once heard exhorting a group of citizens: "Everything that is old is negative and everything that is new is positive."

Every Yugoslav over forty can remember when such places were typical. Now they serve as a reminder of one reason why Yugoslavia had a revolution and why the energy of that revolution is not yet spent after twenty years of postwar development. The rebellion against stagnation and stupor seized the entire young generation of the thirties in Yugoslavia. Their protest was not necessarily Marxist or even political; rather, it began with the activities and discussions of thousands of physical culture societies, philosophy clubs, and cultural organizations. Their aspirations were broad; they wanted fresh air, light, cleanliness, order, education, and, above all, the promise of a future in which they could invest their energy. Now, twenty years after the Liberation, one can still say that the idealism of the Yugoslavs is largely derived from that original reaction against the torpor and stagnation of the prewar Balkans. Their attempt to draw every man into the making of society—so that he can consciously and competently change his situation—is aimed at dealing the final blow to social stagnation and despair.

While drinking my beer I fell into conversation with a middle-aged couple at the table next to mine. The man told me that he was on his last day of vacation from the Panchevo glass factory and that he and his wife had just taken the greatest journey of their lives. Using the reduced travel fare, they had bought first-class tickets from Belgrade through the heart of the country via Sarajevo in Bosnia down to the coast at Dubrovnik. Then they had used their reduction again for tickets on one of the coastal steamers up to Split, where they had been welcomed royally by some of his long-unseen relatives.

"I never expected to see the sea, and I never dreamed it was so beautiful," his wife said. "I was very frightened to go so far, but now we will go every year. We are nothing, you know, only peasants, and we have never traveled."

We treated each other to beer and moved on to things economic. The man began by saying that if he were not tied down he could make a good living as a traveling watch pedlar. He knew ways to smuggle them in, he said, and he would pin them to the inside of his coat so that in a flash he could display his wares to a customer or hide them from the authorities. I threw a little cold water on this plan by mentioning the competition he would have from the excellent Soviet watches sold in Yugoslav department stores at a price of six to eight dollars.

"Oh well," he said. "I'm tied down anyway and have a good job." Then he began to tell me about his job in the glass factory. I asked him about workers' management there.

"There's not much to it," he said. "One sign is that our director is appointed behind the scenes by the high-ups in Belgrade.

"But," he went on, "we do have the system of economic units in our factory. We keep our own accounts in our unit and we build up our own funds, depending on how well we work. If we get some money together we can vote a little extra salary for ourselves and decide who'll get how much; or we can invest the money in a new machine and pick out the one that suits us best. I think that's important. The only catch is that we have to decide ourselves who is to be laid off. Six of us worked on the old glass cutter, but then we got a new cutter which needed only five men. We were all comrades, but one of us had to go, and we had to decide among us who would be the one. Our agony lasted for weeks, but finally one man went off to work for a while in West Germany and that solved our problem."

Here was a man who in one breath could contemplate easy fortune as a smuggling watch pedlar—certainly one of the more unsavory capitalist professions—and in the next show enthusiasm for the economic unit, one of the most important but difficult socialist forms produced by Yugoslav theory. In this, of course, he was not exceptional. However consistent theory tries to be, reality is inevitably a tangle of contradictions, and these are naturally reflected in men's thinking. Perhaps the most remarkable thing is that sophisticated ideas like the economic unit have caught on as much as they have, since they have by no means become a way of life as yet.

Probably this man entertained the get-rich-quick myth out of pride in his own ability. He was an intelligent fellow and had not received his fill of education. He knew he was capable of more than his job demanded. Perhaps one day he will feel courageous and take up his schooling again. People all around him are doing so, and the opportunities are there. He had the courage to take his wife to the coast they had never expected to see. No doubt he said to her: "Everyone else is going to the coast. Why don't we go?" One day he might say to himself: "Everyone else is going back to school. Why don't I go?" And the country will then be minus one would-be watch pedlar.

I left the beer hall and walked down a wide street toward the outskirts, hoping to get a look at the factories which are making Panchevo into an important industrial center. (There is a new nitrogen fertilizer plant built with American money, the glass factory where my friend in the beer hall worked, and a light bulb factory. Nearby oil fields and natural gas sources promise other industrial additions.) But after twenty minutes, when I came around a bend and saw that the houses continued out of sight, I decided to turn back.

Panchevo is a typical Voivodina town. Nothing rounds it off— the streets drift on endlessly into the emptiness of the prairie, presenting interminable vistas of low one-story houses. Except for their color and minute details, the houses are all alike. They are long and narrow, with one end facing the street. The living quarters are at that end, and toward the back the building serves as barn, chicken house, and stable. The family strip of plowland is merely an extension of the narrow house lot into the prairie. Everything is arranged to keep each household to itself. The houses are all turned in the same direction so that the porch side of one faces the blank side of the next. The window over the sidewalk juts out so that one can peer both ways up the street from behind lace curtains without being seen.

Towns like these give a very different impression from the rest of Yugoslavia, where life is open and always flowing out into the social. Here the rich farm land has always meant a high standard of living; people are solidly housed, clothed, and fed; disease and illiteracy rates are low, and one finds few evidences of Balkan primitivism. But there is torpor in the air which even revolutionary energies find it hard to shake loose. The streets are empty and monotonous; the houses are stodgy; and the food is heavy and stultifying. It is said that peasants going out to the fields to work carry a pound of bacon and a pound of bread for lunch. When my wife and I asked for the specialty of the house in a Novi Sad hotel, enough goose and roast pork and beef and rich gravy and mashed potatoes for a dozen people was set before us. A Voivodina recipe for pork goulash calls for two pounds of pork, one pound of sauerkraut, one and a fourth cups of lard, half a pound of onions, and half a pint of cream. Yugoslav jokes about the Voivodina always turn on the dimwittedness which results from just such dinners as this.

Novi Sad, the capital of the Voivodina, contrasts sharply with the smaller towns of the province. Set on a broad sandy bend in the Danube, the city looks across the river to the green hills of the Frushka Gora. Along the Danube sparkling white apartment houses break the monotony of the flat prairie, and in the center new government buildings rise above the old-fashioned Voivodina houses. An old city with a long tradition of culture and sophistication, Novi Sad now has a flourishing theater, a rapidly expanding university, and a lively publishing business. One of the most outspoken literary and political journals in the country is published here. As the center of a wealthy agricultural district, the city is acquiring new factories, apartment houses, bridges, and highways, which are giving it the look of a modern city. Elsewhere in the plain the new forces its way in only gradually and the traditions seem to include only scorching summers, snowy winters, and muddy springs. The level fields stretch as far as the eye can see, the people sit heavy and well fed behind the blank faces of their houses, and flocks of fat geese pick in the mud of their wide streets.

The geographers disagree about whether the Danube is a natural regional boundary or not. This dispute seems strange to anyone who has looked down upon the Danube from Belgrade or from any of the bluffs which accompany the river along its right bank south of Belgrade. Such abrupt and vivid changes in landscape must be rare. The left bank, fringed with willows, is low and there are no rises behind it; the Voivodina stretches flat to the horizon. The right bank rises rapidly to a high bluff and behind the bluff are rolling hills covered with vineyards and orchards. Directly behind Belgrade, only a dozen miles to the south, stands Mount Avala, from which one glimpses the tops of real mountains further south. Though people say that Shumadiya, the name given to the green hills of central Serbia, begins only at Mladenovats, thirty miles south of Belgrade, the hills and forests stretch right into the city itself and are only really stopped by the Danube.

Shumadiya is the heart of Serbia. The nineteenth-century rebellions against the Turks began here, and all the modern Serbian and Yugoslav kings stemmed from two rough-and-ready leaders of those rebellions. The region is also supposed to have given Serbia its characteristic cookery, and its plum brandy and sheep's cheese are famous all over Yugoslavia. Today Shumadiya is making its way toward modernity. With the growth of socialized farms and progress in cooperative arrangements, the peasants are shifting from small plots of corn and wheat for household consumption to vineyards, orchards, and livestock raising. Many of them are moving to the growing industrial towns to take jobs in automobile and machine tool factories. The towns are taking on the look of urban centers with imposing squares and new hotels, restaurants, and housing projects. On the outskirts dozens of small private houses are being built by workers with credit, by self-employed artisans prospering from the rapid urbanization, and by peasants who work in the factories and in their spare time grow fruits and vegetables for the expanding local market.

One of the trips I took down into Shumadiya was to visit a peasant, Miladin, but the word "peasant" perhaps gives the wrong impression of a man who had toured America and talked with

Mayor LaGuardia, who had published two or three little books of short stories and memoirs, and who had a library of several hundred books. He did no heavy farm work because the cooperative paid him more rent on his land than he could make by tending it himself. Instead, he used his time to write a bit and visit his friends and prospective publishers in Belgrade—so often, in fact, that he kept up his contacts there better than most of us who lived in the city. Nevertheless, he was a peasant: he had lived all his life in the same village, and he wore the Shumadiya peasant costume—a short brown wool jacket trimmed with black braid, a collarless white shirt, and leggings like riding breeches, worn with sandals made of one piece of leather turned up into a "nose" at the toe and strapped to the feet by thongs crisscrossing up the ankles over heavy woolen stockings. Most important of all, he considered himself a peasant, though an enlightened one. One of his short stories was about a self-taught young man with ambitions who decided to stay in his village and use his knowledge to help the ignorant people around him. The story was clearly autobiographical.

Miladin had invited the entire staff of a Belgrade magazine to come and celebrate the village Saint's Day. Over a dozen of us set out from Belgrade in several cars. Our car had brake trouble, so we stopped in the town of Kraguyevats for repairs. I spent the time standing at a junction on the edge of a park listening to a group of young men talking about the soccer results and giving directions to tourists without even a pause in their conversation. Only once in their talk did they mention the stream of Austrian and German cars going to Greece; one boy remarked that the day before he had sent some Germans up a cart path into the hills. Doubtless this is an often repeated joke during the tourist season. On October 21, 1941, the Germans gathered up seven thousand people from this town and shot them in reprisal for Partisan attacks on German patrols in two nearby villages. For some years after the war Germans were advised to take another route south, for one day a local butcher recognized a German from that massacre and killed him with his cleaver.

The road out of Kraguyevats, once the main highway to Greece, had obviously had no maintenance work for years, and now the paving was so full of potholes they could not be avoided. This is an example of the neglect many Yugoslav roads have suffered because all the available highway machines are concentrated on new construction. Until recently the same policy of deliberate neglect was applied to housing. The old buildings were allowed to run down while the available funds were used to put up new apartments. The policy has now changed in housing; and doubtless when there is more money for graders and other machinery the older roads will get more than occasional stopgap repairs. Another interesting difficulty stems from the attempt to take highway maintenance out of the hands of the state. The highway networks are being turned over to highway enterprises which will maintain the roads out of their income from service stations, restaurants, and motels which they will build and operate. This radical use of the "free enterprise" principle seems feasible enough in populous areas where the highway system is already good, but an enterprise that starts out with a set of dusty paths winding through a sparsely populated region will have no traffic to build a motel for and no money to improve the roads to bring in traffic. The plan is for local communes to prime the pump, but so far they have been slow to respond. As a result, in backward areas the roads are likely to be poor for some time to come.

It was a relief when we turned onto dirt roads. They were slippery from a rain the night before, but at least the surface was smooth. As we followed the country lanes I began to realize what Yugoslavs mean when they talk about the "interior" of the country. The mud grew deeper, the roads narrower, and the hills steeper. The houses were not packed close together into villages but spread out through the hills, each with its plum orchards and lush grass, its pigpens and rows of vegetables. We saw an occasional peasant on horseback or walking, but otherwise the lanes were deserted.

Our host greeted us finally at a bend in the road, and led us through several pastures, yards, and orchards to the farmhouse perched high above. We entered the upper story of the house, which was of half timber construction, with stables below and the living quarters above. A long table was set for us in a comfortable closed-in porch whose windows looked out over the wide valley below. The wife and daughters—one of them wearing a bouffant teased hair-do above her peasant costume—brought Turkish coffee with *slatko*—the sweet preserves the Serbs traditionally serve to arriving guests, no matter what the hour. Then came the hot plum brandy concoction called "Shumadiya tea." Straight brandy was served for the little speeches of welcome and gratitude, and then pitchers of white wine were brought with the meal, which began with mounds of fresh sheep's cheese, served with onions, hard-boiled eggs, and bread still warm from the oven. Soup, stewed chicken, and vegetables were followed by *gibanitsa,* a traditional Serbian cheese pie, and finally came the main course: a young lamb roasted on a spit since early morning. Then the toasts resumed as we were served more coffee, brandy, fruit, and sweets. We stayed so long at the table that we missed the village fair. Finally the women of the house left their work, and a young man appeared out of nowhere with an accordion, to accompany the whole group in the national folk dance—the kolo.

The hospitality of Serbian peasants is famous. They may live on bread and beans, but when a guest comes there is always the semblance of plenty. Miladin was more prosperous than most, and he had not allowed their reputation to suffer. Still, it was not a wholly pleasant celebration. Some of the city people were so annoyed by the roads they had had to travel over and so bored by the traditional peasant ritual of eating and drinking that they were hardly civil to their host, who in return became even more courteous and complimentary. His family looked on in bewilderment. It was curious to see this strain between city and country people, for in Belgrade people seemed to feel strong ties to their peasant past. Not only was this peasant far more sophisticated and cosmopolitan than most country dwellers, but his city visitors were hardly a generation removed from their peasant background; yet the gap between them was already too great to be bridged even by good brandy and overflowing hospitality. This is not one of the happier results of urbanization.

South of the hills of Shumadiya the mountains rise steeper. Here, where the watersheds of the Black Sea, the Adriatic, and the Aegean meet, a great medieval Serbian empire was centered. At its height—in the mid-fourteenth century—it included Albania, Macedonia, Epirus, Thessaly, and northern Greece. Before the Serbs were finally defeated by the Turks in 1389, they had developed a civilization which was already moving into the Renaissance, as the frescoes in the remaining Orthodox monasteries amply testify. But after the defeat at Kosovo Polye the country fell slowly into ruin, and today South Serbia is what the Yugoslavs call a "passive region," where the possibilities are few for economic development without help from outside. (And help from outside almost always means draining the resources of the more highly developed regions like Slovenia and the Voivodina, which are themselves rich only in a relative sense.)

Driving out to Studenitsa, one of the medieval monasteries hidden away in these hills, I passed a coal-mining hamlet at the foot of a mountain, with its peasant market set up on tables under the shade of half a dozen oaks. The wares were pitifully few, even at the height of summer. And the countryside was crisscrossed with dry gullies down which the soil had been carried away for centuries by roaring torrents, leaving little more than a thin crust to grow the peasant staples: beans, peppers, and corn. Though I had never seen them before, these denuded slopes were familiar, for in the publishing house in Belgrade I had translated dozens of articles on erosion in the South. The Yugoslavs are making heroic attempts to halt its progress, but there is little money for dams and earthworks, and it is difficult to force the peasants to terrace their fields and stop cutting down trees to make new plowland on steep hillsides where the soil will immediately be carried away. Some of this barren land is being reforested, and little pines are seeding in rapidly wherever the peasants have been persuaded to keep their sheep away. But the area is a long way from prosperity.

A peasant who had finished selling his produce in the market hailed me for a lift up the mountain to his farm near the monastery. I nodded, and he climbed in with his baskets. Then, curiously enough, he tried to dissuade me from picking up a small boy who was trudging along with his school satchel. "He'll talk a great deal and annoy us," the peasant insisted. But the day was so hot and the road so steep and empty of traffic that I couldn't turn the boy down. Far from a chatterer, he sat completely silent until we came to a spot with dense woods on either side, where the man got out. He said something to the boy, and he too got out. I went on the remaining mile or two to the monastery, set on the top of the mountain with a few houses round it and a tavern crowded with people listening to the radio. My wife and I were standing in a corner with our beer, wondering whether the peasant was simply a misanthrope or whether, expecting to pay for his ride, he had feared having to pay for the boy too, when the little boy came in and went up to a man near us. They whispered together for a few moments and then the man rushed over, tried to pay me for the ride, found a chair for my wife, and proudly pulled out the yearly report card his son had walked over eight miles to fetch.

"His grades are good and he'll get an education. My son will get out of this poverty no matter how far he has to walk to school," he told me.

So even in this isolated spot there was promise. The monastery held its promise too. Some of the buildings were in a state of near collapse, but the frescoes were being cleaned and the bearded priest who showed us around and served us brandy in a cool, elegant parlor was anxious to talk of their projects. They had a bit of land for orchards, the government was paying to repair the frescoes, and they had a new roof on the church. They weren't exactly rich, but at least the Turks (!) were no longer ravaging them and the buildings were no longer decaying from neglect and isolation. One day there might be a good road up the mountain and then a stream of visitors would come to make them famous again—and perhaps even prosperous.

To the east of Studenitsa the land slopes down toward the Morava River, a wild stream which has never found a solid bed and which floods southern Serbia every spring, taking away livestock and houses and leaving behind rich mud. The highway from Belgrade to Greece sets its course for Skoplje, the capital of Macedonia, through the Morava valley with its lush cornfields and plum orchards. In places the corn is being replaced by fields of potatoes, for one effort to rationalize the country's agriculture has been to encourage the farmers in the Morava bottom lands to leave corn and wheat to the plains of the Voivodina and replace them with potatoes and other vegetables more suitable to their fertile but narrow plots of land. Sheep are raised on the plateau to the southwest, in the high mountains to the east along the Bulgarian border, and in Macedonia to the south; cotton is also being introduced on some of the rolling wastelands of southern Serbia and central Macedonia.

The Yugoslavs like to refer to their economic development as "tumultuous"; when the changes of the last twenty years are placed in the context of the centuries the epithet is no exaggeration, but in itself the birth of economic energy is at best a slow process. But in the Morava valley towns like Leskovats, which has woolen and cotton mills and an international textile fair every summer, economic development does seem like a great storm. The center of town is like a sprawling construction site with the dust and noise of new buildings going up and the confusion of detours around street pavings. At one woolen mill I saw still serviceable but long-outdated looms laboring under many hands in an old three-story building. Next to it, in a new one-story building of concrete blocks, spinning frames imported from Belgium were operating almost unattended. The director, the president of the workers' council, and the superintendent who took me through the plant could talk of nothing but new jobs and apartments, raising labor productivity and increasing exports. "We even export to England," I was told. "And we get a laugh when some snobbish Yugoslav buys a suit in London and it turns out the fabric was woven right here."

To the east of Leskovats the mountains rise to the Bulgarian border. The dirt road which leads onto those mountains runs along the side of a long ravine, through a beautiful forest of first oak and then beech. Erosion—both natural and man-made—is obvious everywhere. All along the climb to the top we saw rockslides created by racing muddy torrents, though every few hundred feet there were dams, most of them built by youth brigades in the early years after the war. A friend in Belgrade who had worked in those brigades once told me of the tight security precautions observed here in the days of the break with Russia and its satellites—Bulgarian spies were everywhere, and one Yugoslav student arriving at the work camp late at night was shot by a sentry who took him for an infiltrator. Near the top of the mountain rusting tank traps stand as reminders of those uncertain years.

When we ceased to climb we came upon a grassy plateau dotted with flocks of grazing sheep. Couched among the gently rolling hills was Vlasinsko Yezero—the Lake of the Vlachs, a Rumanian tribe still numerous in eastern Serbia. The dark peaks of the Bulgarian mountains were clearly visible across the lake. Down below the day had been clear and sunny, but so close under the clouds which hovered over this chilly mountaintop the day suddenly seemed to be overcast. A cold wind swept over the lake. We rode several miles along the shore, past little groups of boys and girls playing soccer to wile away the afternoon when they must tend the sheep. Their books and umbrellas were piled neatly beside the road. Eventually we reached a handsome hotel, an example of the efforts the Yugoslavs have made to provide accommodations overlooking their picturesque spots. The hotel was an exception to the rule that restaurants never provide the delicacies of the locale, for the sheep in front of the terrace had obviously supplied the fresh white sheep's cheese we enjoyed with our coffee. But it was no exception to the rule that Yugoslav resorts are always crowded in July and August, for it was full of people from as far away as Belgrade, escaping the city heat; and we could not get a room.

We descended the mountain in the dusk and went on to Vranye, Serbia's southernmost town. Here, almost at the edge of Mace-

donia, the signs of long domination by the Turks become more
vivid. The dust and heat of the South mingle with Oriental slovenliness and languor. Whereas in Shumadiya the Turks ravaged the
land and kept the countryside in turmoil, here their way of life
dominated the people. They were dislodged from this area only in
the Balkan Wars of 1912 and 1913. During the long centuries of
occupation it was doubtless more peaceful here than farther north,
but today it is harder to break into energetic modern civilization.

We arrived in Vranye at the height of the *corso,* the traditional
evening stroll which plays an important part in the lives of young
people all over Yugoslavia. From five or six to nearly nine o'clock
they crowd the center of town and walk round and round in groups
of twos and threes; here they look over each other's new clothes,
exchange the latest gossip, meet new and old friends, and do their
courting. In the cities of the North the *corso* is slowly being replaced by movies and plays, jazz clubs, and meetings. But in the
smaller towns, particularly in the backward South, teen-agers pack
the main streets even on the coldest, dreariest evenings, and many
towns close the streets to traffic during the hours of the *corso.*

When we got to Vranye, a few minutes before nine, the main
street was still closely pressed with people and the restaurants and
sidewalk cafes were overflowing. I asked a man in the crowd about
hotels. "There are two," he replied, "but one you wouldn't want to
go to. The other is up the hill opposite the monument."

The hotel he recommended was not what his comparison had
led us to expect. The structure itself had the handsome lines of a
town villa. Tall potted palms stood on either side of the archway
that led into a garden where there was music and people were
dining. But the stucco had half-dissolved and the disorder inside
was reflected by the slatternly window shades, all cocked at different angles.

A sign over a door in the archway indicated that the clerk was
at readiness on the second floor, but we went first to a table
in the garden to order broiled pork chops and the southern specialty, roasted hot peppers. The rear was even more unkempt and

squalid than the front, but the musicians with their violin, drums, an accordion, and a long black pipe resembling a clarinet were so mixed up, outlandish, and intriguing that they almost made up for the slovenliness. A sensuous woman played the pipe with a concentration proper to the front row of a philharmonic orchestra. And a tall man took the violin through one absorbed improvisation after another with the same concert hall gestures, though the tunes were local folk melodies. Only the accordionist's repetitions of the Oriental theme from which they started kept the two long-hairs somewhere near home base. A third man, who sat drinking before the drums, invented nice background rhythms to accompany the improvisers, but then at the most untimely moments he would look pensively at his colleagues and at the audience, take a sip of his brandy, and pound the bass drum off beat with the force of an elephant. This interruption of pure noise would make the violinist wriggle as he played and turn the woman into a frowning matron; then they would settle into some other complicated and often discordant way of elaborating upon the long slow tune.

After supper I mounted the staircase toward the hotel desk. It was not evident where I should go from the top of the stairs but I noticed a light coming from an open door and went there. A man sat facing the door at a little writing table which had the ruled pages of the hotel register spread over it. I asked for a double room, and he said he was sorry but he had none.

"You're full?" I asked, wondering what could have attracted so many people to this dusty southern town.

"No, we are not full," he replied.

"Well, what do you have?" I asked.

"We have only rooms for six persons. If that suits you, I can give you accommodations."

I shook my head and thanked him.

"Well, that's the way it is, comrade," he said, smiling, having known from the beginning how the whole conversation would go. "It's my place to offer and yours to refuse."

So we drove to Skoplje in the middle of the night, for there was no other place to stop.

It was a morning in early July 1963 when I first went out to see the city of Skoplje. What stood out to the eye in those days was the great effort being made to catch up with the other parts of Yugoslavia.

The Vardar River, running broad and shallow through the city, was crossed by an ancient Turkish bridge linking the central square of the modern city with the old quarter where narrow lanes led away crookedly beneath the overhanging second stories of Turkish houses and stores. Two avenues cut through this quarter, one to the market and the other up to the old fortress, which had been converted into a museum and fashionable restaurant. The other streets meandered into great quarters of poverty and slums worse than anything I had seen in Yugoslavia. The shops selling sweets and handicrafts were quaint, but most of the living space was squalid.

On the other side of the Vardar the new city stretched up and down the riverbank. Apartment houses, schools, offices, restaurants, and stores were going up everywhere; whole quarters were having their streets broadened and paved; there was a sense of bustle and purpose. Skoplje was evidence that even in this poorest part of the country the way was opening up toward modern life with its possibilities for physical comfort, good health, and enlightenment.

The striking thing about Skoplje at that time was how much had been done. Three weeks later, the substratum rumbled and shook the city until almost none of its buildings could be used any longer. For a long time after that early morning earthquake the only thing to see was how much had been undone.

It was a catastrophic setback for Skoplje. Nearly 1,500 people were killed; most of the 180,000 citizens were suddenly homeless; and the whole workings of the city were in chaos for months. It will be the end of the decade before the people of Skoplje can rebuild to the point they had reached that July, even with help from abroad and from the more highly developed regions of the country. The destruction of Skoplje was so extensive that it means a setback not only for Macedonia but for Yugoslavia as a whole.

As the work of rebuilding proceeds, what stands out is the fact that the same effort and energy which in the years after the war brought Skoplje from a squalid, stagnant Balkan town to a rapidly developing modern city are clearly present today. Although many of the citizens of Skoplje are living in prefabricated houses and going to prefabricated schools and offices and stores, they are planning a new capital and building the industrial base to support it. In 1960 industrial production had already climbed from 19 percent to 35 percent of Macedonia's total output. New chemical plants, cotton spinning mills, and a steel mill are moving it up further.

Much of this energy is a direct result of the policies of the postwar Yugoslav government. Until the end of the Second World War the Macedonians living in Yugoslavia were not recognized as a separate people (as they are still not in Bulgaria). Macedonia was simply a backward part of Serbia, and the Serbs who ruled the Kingdom of Yugoslavia nowhere created more hatred for themselves than by their treatment of the Macedonians. Since the war Macedonian has become one of the officially recognized Yugoslav languages, and the Macedonians have their own republic. Decentralization of both government and economy has given them a good deal of autonomy, though this has not prevented them from receiving considerable federal aid for economic development. A good deal of dislike still exists between Macedonians and Serbs and the exuberant new sense of national identity sometimes causes friction, but the Macedonians have worked in recent years with more hope, energy, and solidarity than ever before.

A leading Yugoslav political scientist once remarked to me, "Decentralization has caused us tremendous problems and they have not by any means all been solved. When eleven different publishing houses set up the type and publish the same novel in one year, you wonder about the waste. But traveling through Macedonia and seeing how much the poor communes there are doing for themselves helps one to remember the other side. Decentralization has released a tremendous amount of energy that goes wasted under a system of centralized authority. And that release of human energy is more important than the waste of duplication."

In the Macedonian mountains many of the Moslem villages are so poor and wretched that it is hard to believe they are in Europe. But the energy of development is being felt here too. Now only the old women cover their faces from passing cars. The children are going to school to escape the poverty and backwardness which have been their people's lot for centuries. Large-scale reclamation projects are turning the rolling wastelands into cotton and wheat fields. The small farmers are turning to early vegetables for the northern European market to supplant their income from the traditional Macedonian crop—tobacco. Many are leasing their lands to cooperatives for vineyards and orchards and taking jobs in the city. Life there may be difficult at first, but it holds far greater promise.

One evening shortly before the earthquake I had a long talk with a remarkable woman who was a professor of sociology at the university of Skoplje and a member of the Central Committee of the Macedonian League of Communists. In her fifties, plump, not very tall or handsome, she looked more like a tired housewife than a lifelong revolutionary. Yet from her student days, most of her life had been spent in underground activities, in jail, and in struggling to put the program of the revolution into practice. Like all Yugoslavs, she was excited about the economic advances made in this region since the war, and she talked at length about the development of Skoplje and the problems and possibilities brought by urbanization.

What was striking about her, however, was not her revolutionary past or her love of material progress, but her democratic spirit. She was quite open about all the abuses, injustices, and inequalities she felt were still standing in the way of democracy in Yugoslavia. "Yet I don't understand," she added, "why Westerners judge my country entirely on the basis of Djilas' *The New Class,* which was written nearly ten years ago. In America last year I talked to many of your sociologists about what we were trying to do here, and I found they viewed everything I said in terms of Djilas' theory. At the time he was writing, there was much truth in what he said, but his book hardly describes the Yugoslavia of today."

Late in the evening, as we walked through the shaded streets of Skoplje, she summed up her own political views.

"In the early years we used to argue about whether we should move toward democracy at once or first build up the economy. It is possible that we would have made more efficient use of our resources by refusing to face the problems of democratic management. And there are still people who view democracy only as a function of economic development. But the more I see and learn about the rest of the world—about Russia and America in particular—the more I feel that economic development does not make it easier to face the essential problems of man and society. The standard of living rises, but the problem of giving the common man some power over his own destiny continues to be neglected. I feel that men can develop themselves fully only through exercising social power. And only men who have developed themselves in this way can cope with the new society created by technology. With every day that passes I am more grateful that we did not wait until it became easy to institute workers' councils; that day might never have come. Now there is hope that our councils and boards and assemblies will become solid enough to cope with the difficult problems of modern society in a human way. Meanwhile, we must criticize, criticize, criticize. . . ."

XII

Over the Mountains to the Sea

A NEW HIGHWAY is being built to link Skoplje with the Adriatic. But when I took the road to the sea there were stretches worse than any I had seen elsewhere in Yugoslavia. The first twenty miles outside Skoplje had no paving, and in the old roadbed there were holes ten feet wide and two or three feet deep. The traffic had doubled the width of the road by venturing into the fields, but there was no smooth track anywhere.

The road improved as we climbed west into the Shar mountains, but the land grew poorer and barer until there was nothing to be seen but windswept pastures. In the winter the snow cover is deep and the isolated hamlets of this mountain area are so plagued by wolves that when the children walk down the slopes to the village schools they must be guarded by fierce sheepdogs. In summer the grassy hillsides are dotted with flocks of sheep; when their young shepherds see a car coming from afar they run down the long slopes waving their arms to find out what time it is, though they surely have inherited enough woodsman's lore to know the time within a quarter of an hour. It is an excuse for conversation and they get little of it during the long days.

To our left were the forbidding mountains of Albania—its borders closed to Yugoslavs and Americans—and ahead lay the Autonomous Province of Kosovo and Metohiya, or Kosmet, a broad plateau where the medieval Serbian empire was crushed by the Turks and where a million Yugoslav Albanians are now centered. The largest minority in Yugoslavia, the Shiptars, as the Albanians call themselves, have been in this area since the sixteenth century. The province is rich in brown coal, lead, zinc, nickel, and magnesium; and the land on this great plain holds more promise for farming than many other areas of Yugoslavia. But centuries of accumulated poverty, ignorance, filth, and disease have kept it the most backward region of Yugoslavia. Twenty-five years ago there were three tractors and not a single combine in the whole area. Modern farming methods were unheard of. Roads and communications were almost completely lacking, and life in the isolated villages was still medieval. Even today many of the men must go off to the cities in order to survive. But few of them remain there permanently. In Belgrade they carry coal and wood for apartment dwellers and do other unskilled jobs. They sleep thirteen or fourteen in a miserable room (I knew of one apartment building where ten were camping in an unused elevator shaft), and when they have saved up some money they go home and buy a wife and an acre or two of land, and eke out a poor existence by growing tobacco and tending sheep.

This attachment to home is accompanied by the resistance to development which goes along with ancient customs and superstitions. Only a few years ago an epidemic of typhoid fever occurred in Prishtina, the province's capital, because the local authorities would not be convinced that their ancient sewer system was unsanitary. Many women still bear their children lying on the floor. Though the postwar government has forbidden women to wear the veil, many Moslem women still avert their faces when they see a car coming along the road.

Gradually, however, this region and its people are changing. Both the federal government and the Republic of Serbia (to which the province is officially attached) have poured in funds for development, and enormous efforts have been made to combat ignorance and primitivism. The literacy rate is rising rapidly, and the radio and TV are bringing new connections with the modern world. A university was opened in Prishtina a few years ago though there was no faculty to staff it. For some time Belgrade professors had to sandwich two train trips to Prishtina into their weekly schedule in the city. The university has since gathered its own faculty, and five thousand students are enrolled.

In the towns there are new textile, leather, and shoe factories, and the province's industrial production has tripled since the war. Though only about 30 percent of the villages have electricity, new thermoelectric power plants fed with lignite from abundant surface deposits are already producing fifteen times more power than in 1947.

Driving across the plain we passed enormous vineyards, orchards, and wheat farms that had new tractor sheds and administration buildings. One tract of some 10,000 acres, now managed by a local industrial farm, was parceled into 16,000 individual plots until a few years ago. Half the peasants were ready to sell their land, since it gave them no living and they had found jobs elsewhere. But the others had little or no income except what they eked out of an acre or so of tobacco. They could not live very long on the price they could get for the land. The industrial farm persuaded them to lease their land in exchange for jobs on the farm. Though there was no question of dividing up the land again, since the new farm would provide them with a much better living, the peasants were reluctant to see their boundaries plowed under. Finally, the farm sent up a helicopter to take an aerial photograph of the whole field and presented each owner with a copy. Though the photos had no legal value, they provided enough of a reminder of the past to embolden the peasants in a venture which would do away not only with backward farming methods and poor yields but eventually with the idea of private property.

With this rapid development the haste to build up funds for economic expansion is sometimes shortsighted. We arrived in the early evening in Petch, one of Kosmet's largest towns and a major tourist attraction because of a nearby monastery which was the Serbian patriarchate in the days of the great empire. I went at once to the town's fine new hotel. The clerk said he had double rooms but no single room for the friend traveling with us. I asked whether there was another place to stay and he directed me across the square to the town's other hotel, which was older and second-rate. Here the accommodations we wanted were available. But when we took out our passports and the clerk realized that though we spoke Serbian we were not Yugoslavs, he suddenly withdrew his offer, saying he had none of the forms foreigners are supposed to fill out.

"Aren't you supposed to have them?" I asked.

"We're out," he replied.

"Can't you get some?" I pressed, beginning to suspect some trickery was involved.

"Yes, from the police, but I can't leave."

I suggested that I fetch some from the other hotel. He frowned but said nothing. I returned in a moment with the forms, only to be told then that the rooms had been filled in the meantime. I began to shout in anger at this chicanery and the clerk began to shout back.

The outburst was, of course, fruitless. I wasn't going to get any rooms and the argument soon reached the point where I must either leave or fight. But I did learn from the remarks sandwiched between the clerk's curses that the two hotels were part of the same enterprise. I returned to the first hotel to display my dissatisfaction over there and then set off for Andriyevitsa, seventy miles distant through the Rugovo Gorge, which after dark is neither beautiful nor safe.

Though the practice of shunting foreigners to the best and most expensive hotels by refusing them at cheaper hotels is illegal according to the best opinion I could get in Belgrade, it is fairly common. The explanation is simple. The commune and the local hotel enterprise invest together in a fine new hotel. They share the financial interest in the increased tourist revenues. They both want the fastest possible return on their investment. In order to maximize the profits they force all foreigners to the new hotel and leave the cheap hotels for Yugoslavs who can afford the new hotel only when traveling on expense accounts. The hotel enterprise can get away with this because it is frequently a monopoly, and the local authorities wink at the illegality because increased profits mean increased tax revenues. But the tourist may go away bewildered at the highhanded treatment he has received in these backward areas, where quick money outweighs long-term business sense.

Our nighttime trip took us to Montenegro, and the next morning the air was clear and bracing as we climbed into the mountains of the smallest, most barren, and proudest of the Yugoslav republics. Unlike the rest of the country, Montenegro has always been independent except for the narrow strip along the Adriatic coast, and its history is one of great fighters and politicians. Montenegrins are not known as hard workers. For centuries the men raided the Turks at the foot of the mountains or fought blood feuds with other clans, while their women provided a miserable existence from the tiny patches of arable land found in pockets among the rocky hills.

Today the possibilities for livelihood are still few, but the mountain villages, with their white stone houses, are scrupulously clean and the gaunt peasant faces bear a look of fierce dignity. The women no longer do all the labor, though the old attitudes linger in amusing ways. A Montenegrin acquaintance of mine in Belgrade lived a city life much like that of apartment dwellers in any modern country; he helped with the shopping and the children and treated his wife as an equal. But when he went home to visit his family, he had his English wife walk behind him with the bags so that his parents would not think he had lost his manhood.

Driving through the high country, we looked across deep valleys to the dark slopes of the mountains opposite. When the gravel road snaked up a hillside it would point us up at their pinnacles, each with its irregular snowcap and a motionless cloud which clung to it. The rest of the sky was a perfect blue. In the occasional hollows there was a hayfield and an orchard and from time to time a sign pointed down a path to a ski lodge, but the early morning was deserted except for occasional peasant boys selling wild strawberries by the roadside.

As we passed through a settlement—we had seen three houses

in the space of a mile—a young man flagged us down. He climbed into the car and explained that he was just going over the mountain to spend the day with his cousin, but the bus would not be along for an hour.

We began to talk on the inevitable Yugoslav theme: economic development. "What do people up here do for a living?" I wondered.

"They clear out," he said simply. "There's nothing here but rocks, beauty, and clean air. A little tourism is beginning, but the roads are no good, we don't have the facilities, and nobody here has had any experience with tourists."

I thought of the hotel where we had spent the previous night. Built like a huge Swiss chalet, it was clean, the rooms were large, and the beds were comfortable. But it was being renovated at the height of the season and in the morning there were two busloads of tourists standing patiently in line before the only bathroom not being painted.

"And what do you do?" I asked him.

"I'm studying economics in Belgrade," he replied. "There are no jobs here for people who finish only high school. If you go to school at all, you have to go on."

Statistics bear out his point. Montenegro has a higher number of university students per capita than any other republic. Montenegrins who get any schooling at all go on to the university in a far higher proportion than in the most literate of the republics, Slovenia, where a diploma from a technical high school enables a boy to get a good job in industry. Except for the steel mill in Nikshitch Polye, built since the war with federal funds, there is almost no industry in Montenegro. The traditional skills of this republic are literary and political, not technical and industrial (even in the new steel mill, labor productivity is lower than in Slovenian mills built under the Austrians and still using the old machinery). The first Slavic printing press was set up in Montenegro in 1493, and in the last century this tiny country was ruled by a philosopher-king, Bishop Nyegosh, who in his twenty-year reign set up regular courts and established the first senate and the first elementary school in

Montenegro. At the same time he wrote Miltonic epics which make him still the most revered Yugoslav poet.

A truck was parked at the top of the mountain our passenger was crossing to reach his cousin. "Stop behind that truck," the young man said. "I want to honor you." I stopped without fully understanding, but when I saw a small hut behind the truck I realized that he wanted to buy us refreshment. Everywhere else in the country hitchhikers offered payment at the end of the trip, but this sensitive Montenegrin would not insult me by offering money he knew I would refuse. And I knew better than to think I could refuse his hospitality, though it meant he would pay several times the bus fare for the short lift we had given him.

Inside we came upon a scene reminiscent of Bret Harte's California in the days of the gold rush. Half a dozen men and a woman, all dressed like lumberjacks, were carousing, singing, and joking—at 10 A.M. I had this perplexing Montenegrin honor in my mind and told about a news item I had seen the day before. A motorcycle carrying a man and woman had crashed into a truck as it made a left turn on a city street in Skoplje. The truck stopped and the driver, a Montenegrin, jumped down. When he saw the bleeding couple under his truck he jumped back in the cab, took a pistol, and killed himself, though he had made the proper signal and was in no way responsible for the accident. The couple from the motorcycle were badly injured but both survived.

"Yes," the young man said grimly, "we still have some of that primitivism left. Only a Montenegrin would do such a thing. The fellow simply couldn't bear to think of himself as a murderer. I knew a similar case. An acquaintance of mine accidentally killed his brother when they were inspecting a rifle. The man immediately put the gun to his heart and killed himself. Awful primitivism!"

As we returned to the car, I remarked that this custom was certainly gruesome and regrettable, but that such delicacy and courage seemed to deserve a better name than primitivism.

"No," the young man objected. "It is a cruel custom with no place in this world. Only primitivism keeps it alive, the same primitivism which says it is manly to fight and sing ballads and womanly to work."

At the bottom of the winding descent from the roadside hut we came into a valley with narrow fields fenced off from the road. The young man pointed to the cluster of houses where his cousin lived, and we said goodbye.

Soon afterward we left behind even the rare cultivated fields and came into a world of bare gray stone. Folk tales have it that in making the earth the Creator distributed the rocks from a bag slung over his shoulder. When he got to Montenegro the shoulder strap slipped and the heavy load was dumped in a great heap beside the sea. The story fits perfectly the dark rugged mountains which enclose Tsetinye, the former capital of Montenegro. Only the black asphalt of the road belies the impression that these bare rocks tumbled down the day before.

Tsetinye is now simply a pretty white stone village filled with cultural monuments. The new capital, Titograd, has been built up since the war on a dusty plateau where airplanes can land and transport for future industry can be more easily handled. It has none of the charm of Tsetinye, but its other advantages are obvious to anyone who makes the long ascent to the tiny plain where the village nestles among the peaks.

I was followed around a dozen miles of hairpin curves by a small panel truck, apparently carrying the mail. Seeing the driver was in a hurry and could not pass, I did my best not to hold him back, though he had more power than I did. It became a sort of game. On reaching Tsetinye we happened to park on opposite sides of the square. Someone appeared to welcome him, but he shouted back, "Just a minute. First I must shake the hand of the comrade from Belgrade." And he came all the way across the square to congratulate me for having shifted gears "in perfect rhythm."

"I am always glad to see a man from Belgrade who can drive in our mountains," he said.

I explained that in spite of my Belgrade license plates I was an American. "Ah, well then, let me explain," he said. "You see, the automobile is the only piece of machinery we backward Montene-grins have had any experience with and we've learned from these roads to use it well. The rest of the Yugoslavs are terrible drivers; they don't understand cars, they don't pay attention to traffic signs or highway markings, and they have no discipline."

The incident reminded me of how a Yugoslav diplomat with several years' service in America had characterized the difference between our two nations. "You Americans are a highly disciplined people," he said. "When you drive down a deserted road you stop at the stop signs. No Yugoslav would think of stopping if he didn't see a car coming."

In the descent from Tsetinye to the coast, the rocks are left behind at the crest of the ridge where the road points down to the blue Adriatic. The strip of coast below this road is Montenegro's most flourishing economic asset. The reason is tourism. At few places on the Adriatic coast can one see such intense construction work underway. Hotels, motels, and summer camps are going up in two or three rows along the sandy beaches and in the groves of ancient olive trees on the lower slopes.

Budva, the principal tourist center, is one of the smallest of the walled Venetian towns along the Adriatic. Unlike most of the others, it has not been assimilated into the new town which has sprung up to handle the tourist trade. Built on rocks that jut out from the shore, a wide square separates its main gate from the hotels and restaurants lining the road. On two sides a steep wall of natural rock and square-cut stone faces the wind and waves of the sea. On the third side a stone landing stage stands outside the high walls and the town's other gate. The coastal steamers pull along-side this dock, which also serves as a terminal for the buses which careen along the curves of the coast or chug slowly up the empty road to Tsetinye. At the shore end of the landing stage a small tropical park borders the lagoon where fishing boats tug gently at their painters.

Only a small part of the crowd that fills the narrow streets of Budva on a summer day stays here to sleep. People come to shop, to see films, to drink wine, and just to enjoy the pedestrian leisure of a town without traffic. At night they depart to hotels spread along the beaches south of town.

Two of these hotels strike an anomalous note in this socialist society. One is at Milocher, where the villa that served the prewar royal family as a summer palace has been converted into an expensive resort. The spot was chosen with an unerring taste for landscape, and the immense and exquisite park surrounding the villa has added human art to natural accident. The estate fronts on two rocky coves; the villa and its formal garden occupy the shore of one, while one of the many guest houses occupies the other, whose steep rocky sides stretch farther out into the sea than one would ordinarily want to swim.

The regime of the hotel is what one might find in a small exclusive hotel in the West. The atmosphere is definitely not populist. The guests, who were German, French, and English when I was there, spent most of the day on the beach, read a great deal, conversed quietly over cocktails on the wisteria-shaded terrace, and retired at an early hour.

Milocher looks out to the beautiful island of Sveti Stefan (Saint Stephen), joined to the mainland by a short sand fill. Once a fishing village, it is now the most luxurious resort hotel in the country. Here the guests are accommodated not in rooms but in modernized fisherman's cottages draped with bougainvillea. Tucked in among the cottage apartments are a barbershop, a hair stylist, an American-style bar, a tourist bureau, and a gift shop. The restaurants are on open decks built out over one end of the island; here an orchestra plays for dinner, and there is dancing late into the night.

Milocher and Sveti Stefan are the capital assets of a thriving socialist hotel firm. The Yugoslavs call them their "dollar factories," because they provide the kind of service which brings in foreign currency. Yugoslavs cannot ordinarily afford the rates, which range from $8.00 to $14 a day for a room and three very fine meals. Presumably those Yugoslavs able to absorb the production of 32,000 small Fiats a year could afford a few days at one of these hotels, but then they couldn't buy the automobile. It is even said that Yugoslavs avoid such places for fear of being thought embezzlers. But though they cannot afford to register here, for fifteen cents the ordinary citizens can tour the island, eat in its restaurants, and dance on its decks. The same holds at Milocher. Everyone has the run of the beautiful park, the restaurant has an à la carte menu for dinner guests, and the swimming costs seven cents. The facilities of these expensive hotels for foreigners have in fact become one of the area's principal attractions for Yugoslav tourists.

The Montenegrin coast reaches only to the great landlocked Bay of Kotor, much of whose shoreline is dotted with tumble-down Renaissance palaces which can be bought for a song. Beyond is Dalmatia, a long narrow strip of fertile coast dotted with tourist resorts and fronted by hundreds of offshore islands. Just behind the coast the Dinarid mountains rise stark and gray. The porous limestone karst of the mountains will not hold water, and only a little heavy red soil collects in the cracks and pockets in the rock, which has been called "petrified sponge." The peasants build low stone walls in irregular shapes around even the tiniest of these pockets, to keep the soil from blowing away in the north wind which sweeps in from the sea. From an airplane they look like small round grave plots. There is little humus in the soil, and the peasants who grow a few grapes or a little corn and tobacco on these tiny fields say their land requires *"gnoy* and *znoy"*—manure and sweat.

The Dinarid mountains contain extremely rich bauxite reserves and aluminum production represents one of the country's greatest potential assets for raising itself to the economic level of the Western European countries. But there are still few aluminum plants and they process only one-tenth of Yugoslavia's ore production. The rest is exported. The lack of capital to build plants is one reason for this unfavorable situation; it is the old story of the underdeveloped country which must ship out its raw materials at low prices and buy back the finished products at high prices. But capital is not the only thing that is short. A great deal of electricity is needed to produce aluminum and the tremendous hydroelectric potential of the narrow Adriatic watershed is hard to tap, for there are few surface rivers. The karst is honeycombed with subterranean rivers fed by open holes on the surface, but in order to build dams and storage reservoirs the porous terrain has to be plugged with concrete so that the water will not leak away through the rock. Once the hydroelectric plants going up along the coast are completed, Yugoslavia could become an important aluminum producer and there will be lakes from which to irrigate the karst plateaus and give new life to the region's agriculture.

At present, however, the peasants of this area lead a dogged existence. During the night they bring their meager produce to market towns and in the late morning they stream back out into the mountains with the horses and burros. The first time I saw this procession I was surprised at the number of mattresses that were rolled into the large wicker baskets swinging against the flanks of the animals. But it is not so strange. This is the phenomenon we call "economic development" and "the rising standard of living." For the peasants those colorless terms mean something very definite: an end to sleeping on the stone floors of their huts. For them the first step of progress is literally "getting off the ground." The next most popular purchase is a radio. Perhaps in two or three years foreign travelers in the market towns of the karst will look at this late morning procession in bewilderment at the number of radios being taken up those stony paths into the gray hills. But if the mattress breaks one of the fetters holding the peasant of Hercegovina to the cursed stone on which he was born, the radio can build for him new bonds with a life far from these gray rocks, which are so bare, so niggardly, and so poor.

Much of the karst region is in Hercegovina, the southern partner in the republic of Bosnia-Hercegovina. When the Turks spread into this area after their crushing victory over the Serbs at Kosovo Polye, Mostar, now the main town of Hercegovina, was a tiny village clustered around the chain bridge over the Neretva River. The Turks recognized the importance of the village at the north end of the Mostar plain and they set their city there. In nine years—from 1557 to 1566—they built a magnificent bridge of cut limestone which arches so steeply over the rapid green current that even the burros slip on its steps and their drivers have to push from behind. The gray stone bridge, the same color as the cliffs of the Neretva and indeed the whole countryside of this barren region, is one of the treasures of Yugoslavia. The Turks did after all leave something from their centuries of occupation besides strong coffee and sweet cakes.

With this bridge to link Sarajevo in the north and the Adriatic to the west, Mostar grew as a trade center. Working with gold from the East, the goldsmiths opened little shops around the bridge; then in the eighteenth and nineteenth centuries, as the town became more important, larger tradesmen and merchants took over the Street of the Goldsmiths. But when the railroad came through near the end of the last century, the route across the bridge lost its importance and the tradesmen moved away. They were replaced by dealers in old rags and bones. The Street of the Goldsmiths became a place of stink and filth. Between the world wars many of the shops were abandoned and by the end of the Second World War the whole street lay in ruins.

In the last ten years the Street of the Goldsmiths has been transformed. The buildings have been restored and redecorated in their original style. One shop is now a coffeehouse with a shady terrace across the street where guests can take their little trays of Turkish coffee and contemplate the river or watch the bustle of the street leading to the peasant market. There is a secondhand bookstore (one of the few in Yugoslavia) and an artisan who makes inlaid wooden trays; plans are underway to bring in other artisans who can satisfy the desires of tourists—a goldsmith, a coppersmith, and a tailor expert with peasant patterns. Farther up the street the old bakery has been restored and put into operation making *lepinye,* the small round loaf of chewy white bread common in the central parts of the country. In a fine old half-timber building across the street a bar has been opened downstairs, where the menfolk play chess, and upstairs a coffeehouse has been furnished with Turkish divans and ornate coffee tables with carved legs. Slabs from the tombs of the Bogomils, a sect of medieval

Christian heretics which once flourished in this area, are set in one wall.

But the masterpiece is the restaurant in an old shop overlooking the river, where one sits in low-arched vaults to eat traditional Hercegovinian dishes and drink the local white wine, Zhilavka, which is famous all over Yugoslavia. The vine is sometimes grown elsewhere, but only on the limestone slopes of the karst does it yield a wine with the characteristic lightness and sharpness.

On summer evenings tables are set on a limestone ledge above the roar of the river and a young lamb is roasted on a spit. People come soon after sunset to drink wine and put in their orders for the roast lamb, which is served soon after dark and devoured so quickly that latecomers have to be satisfied with *chevapchichi* and *lepinye*. Downstream is the graceful Turkish bridge; across the river the hills are silhouetted in the dark starry sky; and upstream the outlines of slender minarets rise above the glow of the town.

The restoration of the Street of the Goldsmiths represents only one trend in the development of Mostar's tourist potential, which is in the hands of a single hotel and restaurant enterprise. After modernizing the old hotel in the center of town, they proceeded to erect a fancy new one directly across the river. Like its name— Hotel Bristol—it could be transferred comfortably to any city on any continent. Its only marks of local individuality are its site on the bank of the Neretva and the excellent local paintings hung in the dining room and corridors. One wonders why any tourist would be drawn by the Bristol to stay more than one night in Mostar, for no matter in which direction he set off he could find another Hotel Bristol waiting for him at the end of the day.

But if the Bristol will not detain the tourist, it has made it possible for many more of them to spend a night in Mostar, and most who come this way probably do. The investment, then, has presumably served its purpose of increasing Mostar's tourist income. But Mostar is also a town of painters and intellectuals, drawn there not only by its beauty but also by the sense that Mostar, unlike most provincial towns in Yugoslavia, is more than an overgrown village. It is a little city, with a city's sophistication and vitality. These people are perfectly aware of the damage the race for the dollar or the dinar can mean to culture, and they have fought to make their town unique. The restoration of the Street of the Goldsmiths was their idea.

They had no easy time convincing the businessmen that it was practical. For in Yugoslavia—like everywhere else in the world—the rush toward modernization with its chrome, neon, and plastic, is usually so fervent that individuality and tradition are apt to be forgotten. At first they could not get the hotel enterprise to invest a cent, and they got only a tiny sum from the commune. Larger but still modest sums were secured from the republic. Out of these they managed to fix up the coffeehouse, which required the smallest investment. "We wanted first of all to get people down there where they could sit and reflect and see the possibilities," one of that original group told me. "After the coffeehouse we got a little more money and fixed up an abandoned cave where beer and wine and brandy could be served with *chevapchichi* to a great number of people with little more preparation than setting up tables and chairs. At first the places didn't make money. But eventually the townspeople began to come and the new places entered into their habits. By that time everybody was ready to invest. Now the hotel enterprise has taken over the coffeehouses and restaurants and is managing them at a profit, because they get both local and tourist trade. But the Bureau for Protection of Cultural Monuments has opened an office down there to be sure commercialism doesn't get out of hand."

Restoration of the Street of the Goldsmiths would not have taken place or would have taken a different direction if Mostar were not enjoying an unusual influx of artists and intellectuals. Yugoslavia is already beginning to resemble the highly developed countries in that the best educated and most liberal people tend to gather in the largest cities, leaving the provincial cities and towns to their cultural poverty and stifling conservatism. The young people who go to the city universities do not want to come home to that atmosphere. And thus there is a constant drain of the best people from towns which need them to cities which have so little room for them that the competition for jobs, housing, and prestige is fierce and many minor talents are lost by the wayside. This is a problem in any country, but it is crucial in a country trying to institute decentralization, which requires that talent be spread around.

The smaller cities in Yugoslavia try to draw in doctors, engineers, teachers, and artists by offering them good apartments and better salaries, but this does not always work. Mostar's case is improved by its natural beauty, but more important perhaps is that the first wave has already arrived: every man who comes to the provinces makes it more attractive for the next man.

One of the people I met in Mostar was a young painter who was born there and stayed. "I'm nearly the only local painter of the dozens who now live here," he said. Mio made his living by working for 30,000 dinars a month (a modest salary) as a designer of sets and costumes for the local children's theater. Through membership in the Union of Painters he had free medical care and pension rights, and he had a new apartment through his job, though with a wife and two children he had so little space that he did his painting in the pantry. He had no important position, but he was deeply engaged in making his impression upon the society around him. A Bohemian intellectual, he had many bugbears to fight in the provincial situation. He felt the people now running the restoration project were pseudointellectuals who wanted to set themselves up as cultural authorities for the town but who were really pretentious, conservative, and vain, and in addition tended to operate politically as a clique. He was having trouble selling his paintings because they were too sombre to suit the current tastes. One of those I saw stacked against his pantry wall showed a group of emaciated peasant women in mourning and a thin girl in rags reaching for bread. "I know it looks pessimistic," Mio said, passing his hand over the purples, blacks, and blues, "but it is not without hope and humanity. Notice the flash of brightness here and there and this line which pulls upward."

"I'm a Communist," he explained, "but I'm not interested in celebrating what socialism has already achieved. Much is still undone. Unfortunately, my views make me an unpopular painter."

Though nothing about him indicated that he was a party member, his remark came as no surprise. It was particularly interesting that Mio was a member, because it meant not only that the party was liberal enough to include men who were full of criticism, but also that such men could think of the party as a promising lever of reform. In Yugoslavia this is important, for though one can affect policy where he works or lives without belonging to the party, the party is the heart of all political organization in Yugoslavia. Attempting to act politically without joining the party is much like going into business without capital.

One evening when my wife and I were visiting, a woman suddenly appeared in the open doorway of Mio's apartment and whispered to Yelena, his wife. "Come in and meet these people!" Mio shouted to her. The woman moved quickly out of the doorway without answering. Yelena went out and we could hear their low voices.

"Damn her," Mio said, "she came to the door only to have a look at you. Why won't she come in and talk? It's an insult for her to imply that my friends and I are not intelligent or human enough to understand and respect her and learn something from her. And it wouldn't hurt her to listen to our talk either. I like living here with these people, but they will be the death of me. Or perhaps I will be the death of them." And he clapped his hands and rubbed his thick reddish beard.

"Most of our neighbors are workers with a Bosnian or Hercegovinian peasant background. They have some stodgy notions about correct behavior. Sometimes I give them a fit and get them all confused. Not long ago Yelena went to visit her family. I have a brother in town who lives with my mother, and I told him he could bring his girl friend to the apartment when I was out. The women in the house happened to see the girl friend leave, and as soon as Yelena returned they made her miserable with their tales of my loose living. True, I often sit in the cafes far into the night, but I am a family man and not at all interested in other women. But my habits scandalize the neighbors. They are always saying that I'm the last one in at night and talking about how I get drunk, which doesn't happen often, for I love coffee and talk much more than wine and song. I tell Yelena that she must swear at them and tell them to mind their own business, but she says she cannot use the words I tell her to say. They even come into the drugstore where she works and make her unhappy with their pestering. But I fixed them. These people regard the equality of women as a sin equal to blasphemy, and the notion of a man's trying to make his wife's life a little easier seems mad, though many of these women bring home their share of the family income. The day before Yelena came home I went out and hired a woman to come and clean the apartment. I opened the door wide and told her to sing and make as much noise as she could, so they would all see what I was doing. You cannot imagine how they were shocked at my hiring another woman to come in and do my wife's work. But the day will come when they do understand, when they see that I did not want Yelena to come home tired from her trip and have to clean up the apartment when the next day she would have to go off to her job. One day I will make them understand. I love the provinces, but I can't stand provincialism."

North of Mostar the stark gray mountains give way to green rolling hills and fertile valleys. The change in landscape is so sharp going from Hercegovina into Bosnia that one wonders what unites the two halves of this republic. And indeed they have little in common except the history imposed by five hundred years of Turkish rule. During those centuries the well-to-do Bosnians and Hercegovinians became Moslems and joined with the Turks, so as not to lose their wealth and power. The peasants, who remained Christian, were kept in wretched poverty and backwardness. Often they were forced to hide out in the mountains or to flee to Serbia to keep from being killed or enslaved. The young boys were regularly carried off to Istanbul to serve as Janissaries. The Slav peasants deceived their masters when they could and occasionally rose up against them, but they never managed to throw out the Turks; that job was finally performed by the Austrians, who ruled here for forty years—until the Archduke Ferdinand was assassinated in Sarajevo and the First World War united Bosnia and Hercegovina with the rest of the Yugoslavs.

In Bosnia, Turkish rule left behind a strong tradition of Moslem culture among the well-off; ignorance and primitivism were the legacy of the poor. Although this area has excellent forests, some of the richest mineral deposits in Yugoslavia, and much land suitable for farming, Bosnia was until recently one of the country's underdeveloped regions. The villages in the more mountainous areas are still very poor, but the small towns are now developing rapidly on the basis of new industries and some of them are looking nearly as prosperous as cities to the north.

Zenitsa, one of the most heavily industrialized, is an "iron town," though its name in Serbian means "the apple of your eye." Once it must have been a country village with its picket fences making drunken lines over the bluff that stands on the west side of the Bosna River. The Bosna is broad and shallow and so clear that every pebble beneath the swift current can be seen from the new bridge. The bridge leads most honorably from one of the town's main streets, but on the other side of the Bosna there is still nothing but a wide meadow and a dirt path. Somewhere behind the far hills someone must be coming with a road.

Zenitsa emerged from the war with a small smelting plant and a population of eight thousand. But it was well located on the railroad line between Sarajevo and the junction with the Zagreb-Belgrade line. Nearby—at Varesh—is one of the country's two largest iron mines. The other—Lyubiya—is only a short distance to the north. Since the war Zenitsa has grown into the country's largest steel producer and has a population of over 40,000. Most of the building is of course postwar, but age matters as little in Zenitsa as in any steel town. Only the new hotel, the Metallurgist, standing tall and modern between the town and the Bosna, still shines with its original color. All else has been reduced to the timeless gray of heavy industry by the fumes from the smokestacks. The townspeople have tried every known filter, to no avail. They have done their best to provide greenery along the streets and in parks, but the greenery too is immediately transformed into just another feature of the dismal scene, which is one of the prices to be paid for the affluence of industrial society.

In a cheap restaurant on one of Zenitsa's side streets I saw the kind of drinking that Americans associate with just such dismal boom towns. The air reverberated with fiery accusations and tender pleas for forgiveness. Beer bottles were smashed to the concrete floor to provide emphasis. I watched two men escalate an argument from disagreement to accusation and then from swearing to blows. The drunker of them insisted that it was unjust that he should earn less when he had been employed in the mill two years longer than the other fellow. "Why should I get less just because I am a manual laborer?" He swore and stood up. He aimed a blow at the man opposite him but lost his balance and fell full onto the table, knocking some bottles and glasses to the floor. The young manager came over to calm him down. The drunk dragged himself up and listened repentantly to the manager's sermon. At length he began to caress the manager's cheek with the palm of his hand, saying he would never open his mouth in anger again. He paid a hundred dinars for the broken bottle and the incident was forgotten. He invited the manager to a drink, and the manager joined them. A man at the table near mine remarked, "A fellow who doesn't like to drink cannot be a good man, but it is our greatest fault that when we drink too much we get stupid."

City people consider Bosnians a primitive lot not only because of their love of drink but also because a great deal of federal money for development was poured into Bosnia immediately after the war with slight results at first. There was apparently a great deal of waste and mismanagement. But now the area is enjoying a great spurt of development and the standard of living is rising noticeably. With the rapid changes, contrasts between new and old abound. Outside the fence of a modern copper rolling mill in Sevoyno I saw women tending sheep and spinning yarn with distaffs. In small towns new apartment buildings are rising up beside dilapidated Turkish hovels.

Once I took a bus trip from Belgrade to southern Dalmatia. We were traveling through Bosnia on a dirt road and listening to Robert Casadesus play a Scarlatti sonata over the loudspeaker when the roar and dust of the bus frightened a pair of oxen coming toward us. The huge white animals wrenched their crude cart around until it blocked the road completely. For all his concern with the schedule and rivalry with a competing line, the driver was used to such emergencies and brought the bus to a halt. The peasant crawled out of the ditch where he had jumped for safety and thanked the driver for sparing his oxen. He hastened to pacify the animals, and we watched as he coaxed them off the road onto a rutted clay path that struck up the side of a mountain at a frightening angle. We waved as we set off again. Casadesus was still playing. Someone said, "Long live Scarlatti—down with oxen!" We cheered.

XIII

The Northwest

In Belgrade I was always conscious of being a foreigner, but when I traveled in the rest of the country I found myself looking with the eye and sometimes the prejudices of a man from Belgrade. This was an advantage in my visit to the Northwest, which is where a Westerner might ordinarily feel most at home. If one is to understand its significance for the rest of the country, it is important to approach this corner from the east.

The small farms spread comfortably over the green hills of Slovenia show a tidiness and order which one does not see elsewhere in Yugoslavia. The fences stand up straight. The rows of beans and potatoes are free of the weeds and grass which often choke the straggly vegetables of both cooperative and private fields in the South. The stone farmhouses and outbuildings are solidly built and well kept up. When one comes from the east, these neat cottages with their window boxes and flower-bordered walks, their luxuriant apple orchards and kitchen gardens, make it hard to believe one has not crossed the border into Austria. It is too lush and green, too prosperous and comfortable, to be the Balkans.

Even traveling is easier and more comfortable here. In some of the other republics long-distance buses must cover long stretches of narrow dirt roads to get from capital to capital. But in Slovenia even the secondary roads are paved and kept in good repair. The

Serbs can be quite ironic about the orderliness and efficiency of the Slovenians, but occasionallly they make the comparison at their own expense. They point out, for instance, that the Slovenians repair their roads from winter damage in the spring, while they themselves get around to it only in the fall, just in time for the renewed onslaught of winter.

An acquaintance in Zagreb once told me that I should travel through Slovenia if I wanted to see the real possibilities of socialism. "Those people," he said, "know how to put both things and themselves to use. There you will find farmers who manage to tend their crops, work as carpenters, and buy and sell potatoes, all at the same time. They have the culture and discipline which we lack in so many other parts of the country, particularly where the Turk has been. The centuries under Austrian rule made the Slovenians into Westerners like you, not Mediterraneans and Orientals like the rest of us."

And indeed, when I traveled through Slovenian villages I felt that the difference in standard of living derived substantially from the difference in culture. There are no obvious sources of greater wealth here. Much of Slovenia is in the Julian Alps, with the highest peaks in Yugoslavia. The rest is rolling hills and narrow valleys. There is no rich, flat land like the plains of Voivodina or the broad plateau of Kosovo and Metohiya. But every inch has come under the hand of men determined to make the most of it. There are no signs that anything has been wasted. The hay is cut even from the narrow rights of way beside the railroad tracks. The hillsides are planted in orchards and vineyards which produce some of the best Yugoslav wines and jams, and the bare mountain slopes are used for summer pastures.

The picturesque spots along lakes and mountain streams have been turned into thriving tourist resorts where people from all over Yugoslavia come to escape the summer heat. My Belgrade acquaintances, returning from vacations in the Slovenian Alps, would talk with passion about the level of efficiency in Slovenia. "In our tourist resorts," they said, "you pay little and get less. The

Slovenians charge as much as they dare, but at least you get what you pay for. They do mind their business."

But the thrift and industry of the Slovenians are sometimes called penny-pinching and coldness by the Serbs, who pride themselves on their flamboyant generosity and warm sentimentality. A Belgrade friend of mine who had served in the army with a group of Slovenians liked to point out that they never shared their packages of food from home or bought anybody a drink. "Look at me," he said, "I am not rich like the Slovenians, but I will not invite you to a cafe and pay only for my own drinks. I would rather be in debt all the time."

The Serbs tell with great delight a story from the court calendar about two Slovenian peasants who had to bring home for burial a relative who had died in a TB sanitorium. In order to avoid paying the extra charges asked by the railroad to cover special precautions in transporting bodies infected with tuberculosis, the two peasants bought a casket and informed the authorities that their relative would be buried in the town where he died. Then they registered the empty casket as baggage and boarded the train for home, carrying the dead man between them as if he were drunk. The train was now crowded and they were able to install themselves and their dead companion in an empty compartment. They propped him in a corner and lowered his hat so that he appeared to be sleeping. When the train stopped at a deserted station, they dashed into the restaurant for something to drink. Meanwhile a new passenger chose to sit in the compartment with their relative. As the man was stowing his baggage the train started with a jolt and he dropped a heavy suitcase on the head of the corpse, whom he had taken for a sleeping man. Not one to hesitate, as soon as he saw the man was dead, he tumbled him out of the window while the train happened to be crossing a river. When the two peasants returned and saw their relative was not there, they asked the new passenger whether he had seen him. This man covered his crime by saying that their companion had just then stepped out of the compartment. The two peasants looked at each other, shrugged their shoulders, and rode home without inquiring further. Eventually the body was found, the police unraveled the "murder," and the peasants were fined for cheating the railroad.

In Ljubljana and other Slovenian cities it is obvious that the higher standard of living is the result of more than individual thrift and diligence. Ljubljana, the capital, is a bustling city on the Western style. Turning a corner one need not fear any sudden glimpse of the Orient or any shocking leftover from an untidy past. Here the old is deliberately preserved for its charm or cultural significance and it fits in easily with the general atmosphere of continuity and prosperity.

There are more automobiles on the streets than in other Yugoslav cities: one for every eight inhabitants. People are better dressed, and the clothes in the shopwindows are smarter. The service in hotels and restaurants is more efficient, and private living quarters are more comfortable. A few years ago the rest of the country was shocked by a Slovenian film which showed a young man living in a luxurious penthouse apartment in Ljubljana. The fact is, however, that the Slovenians would live even better were they not pouring much of their surplus money into the development of southern Yugoslavia. After the earthquake in Skoplje in 1963, it was common to hear people say, "The poor Slovenians. This will cost them a pretty penny."

The fact that 40 percent of the Slovenians work in industry and only 30 per cent in agriculture (as opposed to over half the population for Yugoslavia as a whole) provides a telling indication of the basis for their higher standard of living. They began to develop an industrial base even under the Austrians, along with a good network of roads and an electric power system. Now they have not only the industrial base but the industrial traditions to use it efficiently. In addition, their schools are turning out skilled technicians at a higher rate than anywhere else in Yugoslavia. The end result is that Slovenian industry is livelier and more sophisticated than the industry of the rest of the country. Labor productivity is high and workmanship is excellent. When the publishing house I worked for in Belgrade despaired of the Belgrade printers, the director would throw up his hands and say, "Well, we'll have to go to Slovenia." Slovenian equipment is much older than that in Belgrade, but they do the finest printing work in the country.

Along with the efficient industry come higher wages. The translators I knew in Ljubljana were paid over a third more than their colleagues in Belgrade, and they still considered themselves underpaid. The per capita income in Slovenia is 50 percent above the Yugoslav average. But I heard it said that the industrial traditions of the Slovenians, which are so much of an advantage in putting out good work and raising the standard of living, are a disadvantage in the system of workers' management. The Slovenians are said to be so used to discipline that they are hesitant to stand up in workers' councils and fight their directors. This is a gross exaggeration; but it is true that a few years ago many Slovenian directors were getting salaries five times higher than their Serbian counterparts, though Slovenian workers were not enjoying an equivalent advantage. It was not the Slovenian workers who put a stop to this, but a general campaign against high salaries originating from Belgrade.

I also heard that capitalism was stronger in Slovenia than in the other republics. And it is true that Slovenia shows certain elements of a mixed economy. Private owners manage a higher percentage of the forest land than in other areas; individual craftsmen and artisans seem to be thriving; and fewer peasants have leased their land to cooperatives. These things are to be expected, however, in a region where people are accustomed to making the most out of their resources. Many of the peasants, for example, can make a good living solely by farming, without being forced to supplement their income by taking factory jobs. Until they can do better by leasing their land to cooperatives they will go on tending it as private farmers. This is not to say that Slovenia has no cooperatives; indeed, those along the Drava River Valley are among the most efficient and prosperous in the country.

All the major areas of the Slovenian economy are socially owned and managed, just as in the rest of Yugoslavia. The transition to socialism looks less revolutionary here because it is not "operation bootstrap," as in many other parts of the country. The changes are less spectacular because they are not mixed with sudden development after centuries of stagnant backwardness. The Slovenians not only have an industrial base and individual discipline to build on, they have a traditionally high level of culture and sophistication. They publish an extraordinary number of books, journals, and newspapers, although Slovenian is spoken by only slightly over a million and a half people. The illiteracy rate is 1.8 percent, far below the Yugoslav average of over 20 percent, and indeed below that in most countries in the world. The population in the cities is highly educated, and adults go on studying. A middle-aged woman I knew from a village near Ljubljana was fairly typical. She had held reponsible jobs in the city for most of her working life and was soon to retire on a comfortable pension. But she was studying English in a very demanding night course and reviewing her German and Italian in order to work in a hotel on the coast. She would have no great need for the money, but she wanted to keep busy, see new people, and go on learning.

Istria, the peninsula that bulges into the Adriatic between Trieste and Rieka, is partly in Slovenia and partly in Croatia. The traveler from Belgrade, however, is apt to feel that he has left the Land of the South Slavs. The rounded hills which slope gently to the sea resemble northern Italy, with their neat stone walls, their rows of poplars bordering the roads, and their vineyards and olive groves. The little towns strung out along the coast display the marks of the Renaissance and the seal of Venice. Some of the inhabitants speak only Italian, and the Slavs, who are in the overwhelming majority, speak with an Italian intonation.

Like most of the Adriatic coast, Istria was ruled by Venice for centuries and then by the Austrians. Its permanent incorporation into Yugoslavia came only after World War II. In addition to the historical and cultural influence of Italy, this area is also subject to a more general Western influence which is primarily economic. It is inevitable that where the standard of living is high enough to make room for luxuries, Western-style consumer goods and offshoots of Western popular culture will be in evidence. This influence receives a direct impetus from the foreign tourist trade, the bulk of which penetrates no farther into Yugoslavia than the northwest corner. Encouraging foreign tourists to spend more money means providing them with more of their kind of service and entertainment. Everywhere in Istria one sees attempts at Western cosmopolitanism. Koper, a beautiful old town just below Trieste, has a nightclub, strippers, a band that specializes in Dixieland, and floor shows as late as 2 a.m. There is nothing in the atmosphere of the place to distinguish it from similar cabarets in Western Europe. The young generation of socialist Yugoslavia—the girls with their teased hair-dos and the young men with their narrow trousers—appear perfectly at home in this atmosphere. And the hotel clerks, the waiters, and the shopkeepers are as fluent in German and Italian as in Serbo-Croatian.

I spent a week in Istria, looking out at the Adriatic from the sunny terraces of hotels and restaurants where waiters plied back and forth with *risotto* and *scampi* and where the guests spoke every language but Serbo-Croatian. After two years of fascination with the part of the country which was furthest from my previous experience, I now found foreign the part that ought to have been most familiar. Had I come to Istria in midsummer, the change would not have been so abrupt, for at the height of the season these resorts draw as many vacationers from Zagreb and Belgrade as from over the border. By October, however, there were only Germans and Italians. The Yugoslavs had turned to the city to engage in the autumn spurt to fulfill annual production plans, and few signs were left to remind me of the social adventure I had felt in other places.

Though the pace of economic development is perhaps more rapid here than in most places in Yugoslavia, it is not so readily apparent. The new apartment buildings and hotels were not going up beside ancient hovels but in the midst of towns that had progressed steadily over the years. Since I did not speak Slovenian, I rarely heard remarks like that of a waiter in Skoplje who asked me to pay before I had finished my coffee and explained that he had to rush off to a workers' council meeting, or the woman in a Zagreb cafe who replied to my remark that the beer seemed expensive, "It will only be different when we stop pampering our directors and really pay people according to their work."

But one day, driving along a poplar-lined road through the hills just behind the sea, I saw something which was enough to remind me that these people were still Yugoslavs, with a Communist revolution behind them. The sound of a band playing a dirge reached me from around a bend, and I slowed down the car. Around the curve I came into a settlement of perhaps a dozen houses. The mourners were walking four abreast in the early afternoon sunshine. There were many more of them than could have lived in the village, for the head of the procession was a quarter of a mile ahead of us. I followed at a snail's pace. A car from Ljubljana pulled around, blew its horn, and attempted to pass, but a "man in charge" suddenly appeared from nowhere. Evidently a little tipsy, he walked directly toward the car until it was forced to stop and return to its place. Thereafter he kept glancing back to be sure the Ljubljana car did not attempt another rudeness. Meanwhile he moved up and back alongside the procession, wiping his forehead desperately and weaving from side to side, all the while shouting to keep the stragglers in line and never losing his control over the whole ceremony. The odd thing was that his drunkenness, comic gestures, and total seriousness with the mechanics of the funeral conveyed a sense of deep grief. At one point his maneuvers puzzled me. Scurrying forward, he brought the procession to a halt and silenced the band. Then he went into a house and brought out a priest, who embraced several of the mourners. Shortly afterward, when the procession turned off the road toward the tiny cemetery in a grove of cedars, I saw the explanation. The procession was led, not by a priest bearing the cross, but by a man in a gray flannel suit carrying the red star of the Partisans.

Rieka, Yugoslavia's largest port, lies at the head of the island-studded Bay of Quarnero, the body of water lying between the Istrian peninsula and the Dalmatian coast. Between the wars the city was cut in two by the Italian-Yugoslav border. In some cases next-door neighbors had to take half-hour detours around the walls of the frontier to reach each other. Neither side prospered. Sushak, the Yugoslav part, lacked any important share in the port facilities, and Fiume, the Italian part, was a port with no hinterland to serve.

Since the war Rieka has been one of the pacemakers in Yugoslavia's economic development. Its prosperity comes from three of the country's most successful economic activities: shipbuilding, petroleum refining, and shipping. With the emphasis now put on shaping the Yugoslav economy toward international trade, its importance will unquestionably increase even more. When I was in Rieka a Russian ship was drawn up for repairs; a Japanese ship was transferring frozen tuna to a coastal boat which would take it to canneries farther south; and Yugoslav, American, and Dutch freighters stretched in both directions.

Just around a turn in the coastline lies the country's oldest and most luxurious tourist resort. In the late nineteenth century Opatiya was a pleasure spot for the Austro-Hungarian nobility and the wealthy of Central Europe. Today ornate hotels stretch for miles along both sides of the one street with the mountains rising behind them and luxuriant gardens extending down to the rocky shore. At one end of the strand is the village proper, with its neat stone houses and narrow streets winding down to the quay where the fishing boats dock.

I spent a good many hours sitting in the autumn sunshine by the quay at the one outdoor table of a tiny seafood restaurant whose menu depended entirely on what the catch was that day. There were nearly always fried sardines and squid, for along with mackerel these are the most plentiful fish in the Adriatic. Other varieties were only an occasional treat; for all its three hundred-odd species, the Adriatic is poorly stocked with edible fish. Seafood is a delicacy even on the coast, and Yugoslav tuna fishermen must go as far as the West African coast to get enough tuna to keep the canneries going.

Little restaurants like this one, which are privately owned, were rare in Yugoslavia until recently. Although individuals can rent out rooms, and private craftsmen, tradesmen, and farmers are allowed to hire up to three workers, the government has consistently discouraged private ownership of restaurants and cafes. But the demand has risen so fast with the rising standard of living and with more and more foreign tourists pouring in every summer that the socialist sector has not been able to keep up with the business. Also, investments in restaurant facilities by the socialist sector have usually gone where the business was heavy enough to give a rapid return. As a result, little towns and out-of-the-way tourist attractions have been neglected.

Now, with their typical pragmatism, the Yugoslavs have decided that if the socialized sector can't handle the demand, it is better to give some of the business to the private sector than to let it go begging. They have passed a new law encouraging private individuals to open small cafes, restaurants, and family boarding houses, and even allowing them to rent small restaurant facilities from socialist enterprises and manage them independently. This is the sort of thing which makes dogmatic socialists cry out that Yugoslavia is betraying its revolution and reinstating capitalism; the Yugoslavs reply that in this developing society there are many things the socialized sector is not yet able to handle and it would be unrealistic and puritanical to insist that no cafes are better than private cafes, when the reverse is so obvious to everyone. After all, they say, a socialism which cannot face the realities and deal with them without depriving people of the good things of this world hardly stands a chance.

The long costal strip of Dalmatia, with its hundreds of offshore islands, runs south from Rieka to the Bay of Kotor. Dalmatia is now a part of Croatia, but for centuries it was ruled by Venice, and the traces of Venitian influence are everywhere evident in the tiny walled seaport towns tucked into coves and bays of the shoreline and on many of the larger islands. Unfortunately, the Venetian shipping that built up the gracious inheritance of these lovely walled towns also denuded the slopes of the hills behind them. All the trees were cut to build ships. Valiant efforts have since been made to reforest the slopes, but no real hope came until the end of the war, when the new Communist regime outlawed the goats which were devouring the tender seedlings. Foresters say that only an authoritarian regime such as Yugoslavia had immediately after the war could have overcome the peasants' resistance to the ban. Though many countries need such legislation desperately, few have been able to banish the goats effectively. Now the results are so clear that resistance to the policy has died out.

In the mile-wide strip of fertile land right beside the sea the peasants grow vegetables and grapes. But the agricultural population numbers between seventy-five and one-hundred for every four acres of gardens, orchards, and vineyards; and the peasants are hardly well-to-do. In many villages the men become fishermen or join the merchant fleet, and those who stay behind supplement their income by taking in tourists in the summer, or they migrate to the towns to work in factories or in the rapidly expanding tourist industry.

The biggest tourist center in northern Dalmatia is Split, which spreads around a broad bay fringed with Mediterranean pines. The steamers that carry tourists up and down the coast tie up at one end of a broad promenade lined with palm trees. At the other end, the hill of Maryan rises up from the sprawling city, and in the center stands the emperor Diocletian's palace, the walls of which are honeycombed with apartments, for the Dalmatians long ago took over the palace for living quarters.

With its huge shipyards and tourism, Split is one of the busiest cities on the coast. But as soon as one gets beyond its suburbs, the countryside becomes very quiet. On one side of the highway rise the bare gray slopes of the mountains; on the other, tiny villages lie scattered among the vineyards; and beyond is the blue sea.

Trogir, just north of Split, is one of the old walled towns with narrow streets channeling between tall Renaissance buildings of yellowish-white stone. Though it is less famous than Dubrovnik or Split or Kotor, this tiny seaside village jutting out into an open bay is one of the most beautiful spots along the Adriatic coast. Its cathedral square alone is enough to exempt the town from all comparison. In taking the thirty or forty sunlit paces across this quiet square—with the graceful columns and rounded arches of the old town court at one end and the intricately carved portals of the cathedral at the other—a man feels encouraged about human capacity for wisdom and clarity. Reason denies that a town whose every citizen must pass daily through this noble arrangement of stone and space should have a column in its vital statistics for suicides.

I did not inquire about this, but in my few hours in the town I did learn that the blessedness of Trogir's stone was not sufficient to ward off the madness of even its longest-established inhabitants.

My wife and I went with a friend to call on two elderly ladies who came from an old Italian family and resided in a tumble-down palace filled with dusty antiques, sketches, snapshots, and piles of rags and filth. The ladies paid no allegiance to Communist Yugoslavia but considered themselves Italian countesses and preferred to speak Italian. I discovered that they made more mistakes in Serbo-Croatian than in French. Before the war they owned much of the fertile coastal strip between Trogir and Split, but afterward the land was taken away through a law expropriating the property of collaborators. No doubt the countesses also suffered some resentful treatment from their fellow citizens, who remembered not only that this family was once rich in the midst of general poverty, but also that they had a heyday during the wartime occupation of Dalmatia by the Italians. Little love was lost on such people after the war and revolution, but they were of course the last to understand why, preferring to see themselves as the victims of persecution. In the confused heads of these ladies their real loss of wealth and the general dislike they had been made to feel had been reduced to the same dimensions as the fiction that the Communists had stolen from them a huge vase and taken it to grace the garden of the presidential palace at Split. They even gave my wife a snapshot of the vase, showing one of the sisters and two gentlemen in Edwardian dress tumbling about in it.

Their persecution complex extended beyond Yugoslav communism. A year earlier, they told us, a third sister died at table while eating cheese and apples, the victim of an unnamed Italian who had done the deed by remote control. His purpose was to make them abandon their suit in the Italian courts against Premier Fanfani. They were suing Fanfani because the Italians had abandoned them to the Yugoslavs after promising that Dalmatia would never be abandoned while one Italian family was yet living there. The sisters felt that the Italian government should make up for its bad faith by granting them compensation for the land the Communists took from them. Even the Americans had a place in their fantasies. At the end of the war, they said, the Americans had decreed that everyone should stay where he was, and since this was clearly unfair, the American government should rescind this dictum and grant them a visa, not necessarily to go to America, but to leave Yugoslavia.

Their fantasies were endless and what treasures they had left were being sold off to pay for indulging them. Our friend was there to buy an elegant old dining room suite. The old ladies would use the money for a trip to Zagreb to beg the American consul for an exit visa and to continue their court suits against miscellaneous Yugoslavs, Italians, and Americans. While our friend bargained with one sister, the other harangued us with her cause, until at last we escaped into the autumn sunshine with a promise to do what we could with the American government.

Outside, a steady wind was sweeping the bay, making whitecaps and giving the Adriatic the cast of dark blue ink. The belvedere where Napoleon's Marshal Marmont played cards during the few years that Dalmatia was under French rule sat near the edge of the water. From its slender marble columns clotheslines were strung to a row of small pines along the shore. Beyond, a medieval tower stood at the edge of the canal separating the small island of the town from the mainland. The water of the Adriatic, which had been such a deep blue out in the bay, was a murky green as it slipped through the canal. It should have been a pleasant place to pause, to look out over the bay at the distant hills, to glance behind us at the squat fortress of the same yellow stone as the town, to watch this emerald-green water slide silently, like a ribbon, between the exactly parallel walls of the canal.

Yet the scene was disquieting. We were standing on a blind side of the tower, but at the bottom of its wall there was a small drain running blood. The lungs of a large animal had passed through the opening and then caught on the lip of the wall. The blood streamed far down the canal like a long red blot on a solid green carpet.

The tower was obviously being used as a slaughterhouse, and the slaughter of animals should not disquiet a man who goes on comfortably eating his meat. But some accidental association made it seem as if we had come upon a naked spot of the primitive and barbaric instincts which burst out in this country only twenty years ago, when the Croatian fascist Ustashe murdered whole villages, collected the blood of their victims in barrels and drank it from dippers. They were not like the Germans, whose executions in Yugoslavia, as elsewhere, resembled a huge industrial operation. The Nazi administrators who organized the process of killing and kept it running smoothly had to calculate to the last detail the space in which to shoot people, the bullets and the time to fire them, the trucks to carry the corpses away, the fields in which to bury them, and the capacity of equipment like special ovens and poison gas chambers. The Ustashe, however, were not scientific and calculating but passionate and disorderly. They literally butchered their victims, piercing the heart and then slitting the throat. They passed wires through the brain. They gouged out the eyes. They threw babies into the air and caught them on their bayonets. They did things to women which make rape seem civilized. Then they threw all this defiled humanity into pits and went off in their drunkenness, failing even in that minimum of decency which requires a man to cover his victims with dirt.

We set off around the tower and came upon the large open door. Inside, the floor was hollowed into a shallow basin and in its center an enormous white ox lay balanced on the ridge of its backbone, with its stiff straight legs pointing askew. A young man and a mustachioed old peasant were moving about in the misty light of a small electric bulb. When we stopped for an instant to peer in, I discovered that my associations were not so outlandish after all. My thoughts had apparently wandered in a channel which was natural here. For the young man glanced up and said with a smile, "It's all right, folks, we're only slaughtering the innocent."

The road inland from Rieka climbs straight up from the sea and then crosses the same barren mountains which plague the lives of peasants farther south. Beyond the gray karst are higher mountains covered with pine forests where the snow lingers until late spring and nothing is plentiful but trees. Nearly all the houses are unpainted, for the peasants find it easier to cut lumber for new siding than to acquire the cash to buy paint.

Beyond the ridge of this southern spur of the Alps the land slopes gradually down to Zagreb, the capital of Croatia and the second largest city in Yugoslavia. Zagreb is the political and cultural center of a people who come from the same racial stock as the Serbs. But the Serbs are Orthodox and the Croats Roman Catholic, and their religious differences have been compounded by centuries of political separation. While the Serbs were under the Turks, the Croats were dominated first by the Hungarians and then the Austrians. When the two peoples were finally united after World War I in the Kingdom of Yugoslavia, the Serbs dominated the new country and the Croats suffered both economically and politically. Their resentment against the Serbs was fierce. Now decentralization and the federal government's policy of equal treatment for the republics, along with strong measures against flare-ups of old nationalist hatreds, have eased the tensions between the Serbs and Croats. But there are still great differences between them. The Croats have a higher standard of living and strong cultural ties to the West.

Zagreb is a thriving industrial city set in a broad bend of the Sava River. The sprawling factories and new housing developments on the outskirts are indistinguishable from other growing Yugoslav cities, but the center has preserved its Austrian look. Tall gray buildings press close against the narrow sidewalks thronged with shoppers. Every few blocks the streets open into squares ringed with heavy government buildings left by the Empire, or tiny parks shaded with old oaks, with a statue commemorating some Croatian patriot or poet in the center. In the cafes the coffee is thinner and weaker than to the south; the pastries are Viennese and one is likely to hear the sedate strains of a Viennese waltz over the buzz of conversation.

One of the most amusing indications of Austro-Hungarian influence I came upon was a draft program drawn up by the Communists at the Zagreb Medical School. They presented a very sensible plan for improving the education given to doctors through more emphasis on practical training and fewer formal lectures. They were critical of the Austro-Hungarian character of the medical faculty. The professors, they said, did not like equality. They did not want co-workers—only assistants. The time had come for men to be judged by their work and responsibilities rather than their titles. It was of course important to maintain high standards, but this end was not necessarily served by holding back the younger teachers. The program concluded with an almost pathetic complaint: "Communist teachers should of course have no special privileges, but neither should they be snubbed and discriminated against, as they sometimes have been in this medical school."

A friend of mine from Zagreb, who was himself a doctor, laughed when I told him the story. "In my hospital," he said, "there are only three party members. They aren't snubbed, but they aren't very influential. Two of them are not even much respected. But I don't think the solution is to improve the quality of the party's membership. I prefer to see the party wither away, and I believe this is also the intention of the party leaders. It's becoming possible because I and my colleagues who are not Communists support their ideas. Decentralizing the medical service and putting it on a business basis has been a great boon. The people in our hospital have become interested in the hospital's financial condition and they turn out the lights when they aren't being used. I'm impressed by the practicality of the system the Communists introduced. I would not join the party, however, for I am too much devoted to my work and my private life to take on other responsibilities. But if I do my share in the management of the hospital and support their programs, then there will be less and less need for activists who must take on a double or triple share of civic responsibility.

"And then," said this man who had grown up in an old bourgeois Catholic family, "they are introducing something new. The minister of health of our republic is a doctor who comes once a week to work in my department. Imagine, he is a minister in the government but when he comes to our hospital he is just a doctor working under my direction, since I'm the head of the department. In the middle of the morning the nurse makes coffee, and the three of us sit down together for a few minutes to rest. The poor man! You should hear the way the nurse goes after him. She has ten minutes in which to criticize and castigate the government policies, and she doesn't waste a moment. Here he is an important official and she but a nurse, but she makes him account for every policy decision he makes. You know, I was brought up in the old style and could never speak as she does, but I find it exciting."

XIV

New Forms

and Old Contradictions

T<small>HE</small> Y<small>UGOSLAV</small> C<small>OMMUNISTS</small> say they are building a new kind of democracy. They describe it as direct self-government by individual citizens wherever public decisions are being made. When the system is complete, they say, apartment houses will be managed by their tenants, businesses will be run by their workers, and government affairs will be handled by ordinary citizens elected for limited terms by an alert population.

The men who established this goal of direct democracy as the leading idea for Yugoslav development are the Communist revolutionaries who in 1945 established a complete monopoly over politics in the country. For twenty years the policy of the League of Communists has become government policy. The policy of the party's Central Committee has been the policy of a million and a half party members, who occupy almost every influential post in the country; the policy of the party and government is the policy of the League of Unions, whose membership extends to virtually everyone working in the socialist sector of the economy; it is the policy of the Socialist Alliance of Working People, a political organization so broadly based that on paper it encompasses the whole adult population; it is the policy of the Youth League, which is the only large-scale organization for young people; and it is the policy of every means of public communication.

How do we square the vision of direct democracy with this reality of this exclusive hold on political power? We are accustomed to speak of the vision as a front and to call this Communist political monopoly a dictatorship. But Communist rule in Yugoslavia does not fit the usual ideas we have of dictatorship. We expect dictators to justify their power on every possible ground and to make consistent efforts to preserve and consolidate that power. We do not expect them to stir up the population with promises of self-government. The Yugoslav dictatorship not only promises a new, direct democracy but it justifies its own existence on the basis that only Communist leadership can take the country toward that democracy. Communists in other countries talk a good deal about the "withering away of the state," but they never mention getting rid of the party dictatorship. The Yugoslavs, however, have made it clear in their Party Program that they mean for the party to wither away along with the state. The disappearance of both is presumably a long way off, but the Yugoslavs do see it as their goal. They say the party is necessary now, "in order to defend the present," and to lay the foundations for the future. When there is no longer any need to defend the socialist revolution against those who would like to return it to the old order, and when the new system of direct democracy is ready to become the sole and sovereign political system of the country, then the dictatorship—and the party itself—will disappear.

The dictatorship's two functions—defending the revolution and building a new democracy—do not mesh easily; they involve real contradictions. A revolutionary dictatorship defends its revolution by consolidating its own power, centralizing the apparatus of government, restricting civil liberties, limiting public discussion about ways and means, and using a secret police to disarm possible "enemies within." In its stance as defender, the dictatorship inevitably shows a pessimistic attitude toward the people, and voices arguments like "our people still lack the skills and culture for democratic self-government," "the people's social and political consciousness is still so low that too much freedom might undo the revolution," or "democracy must wait until we reach a higher level of economic development." Building a new democratic society, on the other hand, requires optimism and trust in the people. The monolithic power of the state must be broken up, civil liberties must be restored and strengthened, more open discussion of ways and means must be encouraged, and the security of the regime must depend on the consent of the governed, not on the operations of the secret police.

One of the most important characteristics of the Yugoslav leaders is their admission of these contradictions. They know that their revolution can go sour if too much emphasis is put on defending it and too little attention is paid to making the transition from dictatorship to democracy. They are aware that if they cease moving forward, there will come not a halt but a move backward. My conversations with government and party officials convinced me that the majority of them believe in the promise and possibility of their plan for democracy. But their actions are more indicative than their words.

In the past ten years the Yugoslav dictatorship has done a great deal to cut the ground out from under its own feet. Since the early fifties there has been a consistent and deliberate transfer of power from the central government to the lower administrative levels, to the individual enterprises of the economy, and to representative bodies, which are increasingly open to the influence of the ordinary citizen. Workers' councils, managing boards, assemblies, committees, and house councils have taken on larger and larger decision-making responsibilities; and the sphere of activities of the party and government officials has diminished greatly from the authoritarian control of the early postwar years.

This is not to say that the Yugoslavs now have all the freedoms considered basic to democracy. There are still very real restrictions on the political activities of ordinary citizens. They are not allowed to act politically except through the established forms. The established political organizations—the Socialist Alliance, the union, the Youth League, the many and varied professional associations

—all support party and government policies and in many respects resemble mere mouthpieces. The party remains the real political force in Yugoslavia.

Non-Communists find it difficult to get elected to any important office or to rise to a position involving real power. Party members are given the advantage because they are generally considered more solid and responsible than non-Communists. A Communist editor I knew complained to me one day that though his non-Communist staff members were competent, he could not expect the devotion to duty and self-sacrifice from them that he might expect from party members. "When I hired the staff," he said, "I deliberately didn't ask whether they were party members. Now I'm sorry. I can't count on the non-Communists to give up their free time to get an issue out on schedule; I can't expect them to carry on if I have to be away. The one party member among them is the only man I can absolutely depend on." There is doubtless something to what he said. Party members *are* often more responsible than other people. But this is not the whole truth. Frequently, Communists simply trust other Communists first and foremost. This is particularly true when sensitive jobs are involved. My friend the industrial psychologist made a study of workers' management in his factory, and his superiors were so impressed by it that when the Central Council of Trade Unions decided to do a broader study along the same lines they recommended him for the job. He was apparently refused because he was not a member of the party. My friend's reaction was: "It's still early. When another five years have passed I don't think this will happen any more. The party just hasn't learned to trust outsiders yet."

There are also limitations on civil liberties. When an individual appears publicly—in print or giving a lecture, or on the radio or television—he dares not call into question the government established by the revolution or the ideological framework established by the party. It would be unthinkable to call a public meeting to oppose the League of Communists or to make a speech denouncing Tito or to publish a book which questioned the rightness of socialism. Freedoms of speech and assembly do not extend that far. In exceptional circumstances the police can legally open a man's first-class mail or search his apartment without a warrant. There is freedom of religion, but a religious man, like other non-Communists, is unlikely to advance to any position of power, and sometimes subtle pressure is exerted on young people to persuade them of the disadvantages of religious belief.

Today, however, the country bears little resemblance to the classic police state where citizens are constantly afraid of being watched and thrown into jail for reasons they cannot discover. I knew a good many people who had been in jail for political reasons in the past, but they were completely agreed that it is almost impossible to go to jail as a political prisoner now.* In 1964 there were 198 political prisoners in Yugoslav jails, most of them old-timers (and Stalinists). This is a far cry from the 7,000 held in 1953. The harsh methods used in those years are gone. The politi-

---

* However, they all made an exception for Milovan Djilas. Once considered the second man in the Yugoslav government and Tito's likely successor, Djilas began to quarrel with the regime in 1953. Interviews given to the *New Leader* and *The New York Times* in 1956 and publication of his well-known anti-Communist book *The New Class* led to his imprisonment. He was freed in 1961 after signing a statement saying that he would desist from his provocative activity. In 1962 he was returned to jail for arranging American publication of his book *Conversations with Stalin*. Except for an unflattering portrait of Khrushchev, the book contained little which had not been published years before in Vladimir Dedijer's biography of Tito. Djilas' apparent purpose was to cause as much damage as possible to Yugoslav-Soviet relations at a time when the exclusiveness of the Common Market made better relations and more trade with the East seem an economic imperative for Yugoslavia. This explains in part why he was put back in jail, though he was actually charged with publishing state secrets. But his conviction and incarceration remain indefensible even when one can understand why they happened. My guess is that in this whole tragic history of Djilas, a good deal of hotheadedness and irrational behavior has occurred on both sides. What is most tragic is that Djilas, who was one of the first Yugoslav leaders to champion respect for law, liberalization, an end to favoritism for party members, more open discussion and criticism, and more freedom and responsibility for all citizens, should have left the framework of Yugoslav thinking and politics and become discredited with his fellow citizens. Ironically, he is sitting in jail now, while others are making progress toward the very goals he first proposed and then ceased to believe were possible in Yugoslavia under Communist leadership.

cal atmosphere is already more relaxed than it has been in thirty-five years, and the increasing relaxation is bringing more liberty.

This is immediately clear to foreigners. Yugoslavs have told me that in the early and middle fifties every tourist was suspected as a possible spy. Today Yugoslavia is as easy to get into and move around in as any Western country. I can testify to this from my own experience. During my two years in Yugoslavia I always went wherever I pleased, and I had good reason to believe that no one kept up with my movements. Twice I neglected to inform the aliens section of the police of a change of address. On one of these occasions a friend in the government called the police in order to locate me, and the police calmly said they assumed I was somewhere in Belgrade but they didn't know where.

The feeling of a relaxed political atmosphere is general. I saw only a few Yugoslavs who were afraid to speak their minds openly. In most cases their fear was clearly a vestige of earlier years, when careless words could actually land one in jail. (People still recall the joke about a government-sponsored contest for the best political quip. The first prize was ten years, the second five years, etc.) Private citizens make every imaginable criticism in conversation, even in public places. Shortly after I arrived in Yugoslavia I heard a man on a crowded Belgrade thoroughfare curse loudly at the luxury of a long parade of limousines filled with Yugoslav leaders escorting some visiting dignitary from the airport. I was surprised to find that strangers who thought I was a Serb from Belgrade would tell me they were totally opposed to the regime. I heard complaints about specific mistakes from everyone I met: "Out of sheer love of modern machinery we import building cranes we don't need"; or, "The peasants were pressured to grow Italian wheat and now it turns out that it isn't good for bread"; or, "We invested all our money in Bosnia and half of it's been wasted." Everyone criticized the failures of everyone else, including the leaders, to live up to their ideals.

Generally speaking, the private criticisms against mistakes and abuses are insistent and thorough. Public criticism is something else. The Yugoslav press, radio, and television are not unrestricted. No editorial page will carry a denunciation of the regime, the one-party system, or the top leaders. An official censor is supposed to check what the papers publish, but I was told by newspapermen that the real censorship is imposed within the newspaper itself. A reporter who makes political blunders might find himself unemployed. It is possible for non-Communists to move up to important editorial positions, but the chief executives are Communists and even fairly important political figures, and the party has a firm hold on the decisions of the editorial board. The same situation exists in radio and television.

Citizens are free, of course, to rely on foreign newspapers and periodicals for their opinions. A number of these are sold on the newsstands in the cities. City dwellers also have access to the British, French, U.S., and Russian reading rooms, and city-owned public reading rooms subscribe to foreign papers and journals. The daily news programs beamed into Yugoslavia by the Voice of America are not jammed, and many people listen to them regularly as a supplement to the local newscast.

The Yugoslav papers report world affairs with reasonable objectivity, and they are not mere parrots of the government on domestic affairs. But where they excel is in their criticisms of local abuses and errors. In the spring, when vegetable prices are dropping, a reporter makes the rounds of the city's most popular restaurants and produces astounding calculations of the profits made on cabbage by simply chopping it up into slaw. If vegetable prices are high in midsummer, the consumer can count on a denunciation of the distribution system in the newspaper. The papers always keep their readers up on which restaurant managers are watering the wine and brandy, how local factories are wasting scarce foreign currency by buying too many foreign licenses, and how the communes are pressuring successful firms to merge with unsuccessful ones. Cases of embezzlement are reported in great detail, and the articles on corrupt directors and how they run their workers' councils play a great part in the constant campaign to strengthen workers' management.

But popular journalism, which must be one of the principal

foundations of any democratic experiment, still has a long way to go in its treatment of broad social themes. Although plain speaking is more common every day, journalists, like novelists, poets, film-makers, literary critics, sociologists, and political scientists, face a problem: how far should they go in their criticism of a country which they know has glaring shortcomings but which they feel is moving in the right direction? A Western socialist who was a journalist in Belgrade summed up the problem very well. "When I first came to Yugoslavia and saw the attempts to put real life into the theories of workers' management and democratic decentraliza-tion, I thought I'd like to spend the rest of my life here," he said. "But now that I've seen all the things that go wrong, I need to go off to Spain or Portugal every year where I can comfortably take a position of complete opposition. Here I'm always both for and against. If I praise things, it looks as if I'm blind to the wrongs. If I criticize too much, I appear to oppose things I approve of."

At the same time, critics of society know that while the way is open to treat the life around them more freely, they still risk something in breaking new ground. Perhaps their efforts will be supported and encouraged, but it is always possible that a new venture will be rejected, even harshly. I heard one panel discussion over the radio in which several of the country's long-established writers criticized themselves for being too timid. And it is true that most novelists write about the war, whose themes and moral prob-lems are safely in the past, or they ignore politics and treat the universal themes of contemporary life: restlessness, boredom, absurdity, and loneliness. But the responsibility is by no means all theirs; from time to time incidents occur to remind them that however broad the freedom enjoyed by the arts, journalism, and the social sciences, that freedom still has limits. A film called *The City,* a disaffected but realistic portrayal of certain discouraging aspects of present-day life, was suppressed in 1963 after a contro-versial court case, because "it gave a distorted picture of contem-porary Yugoslav reality." A Slovenian poet, in spite of protests from the literary community, was jailed in 1964 for writing too critically. In 1965 Miograd Bulatović, a well-known young Yugoslav novelist, found it impossible to get his latest novel published in Yugoslavia, though he had a contract with a Belgrade publisher and advance copies had already been printed before publication was called off. The ostensible reason for the halt was the book's lasciviousness (which is surprising considering the frankness with which Yugoslavs usually treat sex); the real reason was apparently the novel's sympathetic portrayal of some Italians during World War II. Some things are still hard for the Yugoslav Communists to admit in public. And it is always easier for a party member to say them for the first time than it is for a non-Communist like Bulatović.

One perplexing problem is that no one seems to know exactly where the limits to freedom lie. In early 1965 a young Yugoslav historian named Mihajlov published two articles in which he not only sharply criticized some of the distressing facts about present-day Russia, but also discussed the appalling history of concentration camps in Russia in the twenties and thirties. After the publication of the second article, an official at the Russian embassy was quoted by *The New Yorks Times* as saying, "No American journalists have written this critically." It looked for a moment as if there were no longer any limits to freedom of speech in Yugoslavia.

Then things began to happen. The magazine which published the articles was taken off the newsstands. One of its editors was reprimanded by his party organization for accepting the articles and temporarily dropped from the staff. The author was attacked by one of the big weekly papers. A few weeks later Tito himself made a speech denouncing him. Finally Mihajlov was arrested, held for questioning for several weeks, and then charged with damaging the reputation of the U.S.S.R., an offense carrying a minimum sentence of three months. Many things appeared inexplicable. But then it turned out that during his 1962 visit to Russia, Tito had made a compact with Khrushchev that each would prevent the publication of criticism of the other's country and the Russians had rather sharply reminded him of his promise; this at least explained why Tito became personally involved in the incident.

Milovan Djilas' last arrest also had to do with injured Russian feelings. *Conversations with Stalin* contained nothing adverse about Yugoslavia. But though Tito mentioned "Djilasism" in his speech denouncing Mihajlov, the case was handled quite differently. Djilas was put in jail long before his book was ever printed. The American publisher offered to abandon plans for publication if Djilas was released, but the offer was not accepted. Mihajlov's articles, however, appeared in two successive issues of *Delo*. Nothing at all was said about the first issue, and the second was on newsstands five days before it was withdrawn. The later steps taken against Mihajlov came slowly—and apparently under strong Russian pressures. Mihajlov himself behaved differently from Djilas. Where Djilas readily published in the West and made statements to the Western press, Mihajlov left unanswered the inevitable requests for interviews from Western journals and newspapers. He continued to insist that he was not anti-Communist. When he was sentenced to nine months in jail (the maximum penalty was four years), he announced that he would appeal to a federal court. Spectators at the trial made no secret of their distaste for an affair in which political pressures were exerted on the legal system to punish a man for writing what everyone acknowledged as the truth. Meanwhile in Zagreb a public controversy continued in the press between certain philosophers and politicians over the most profound questions of Yugoslav society. Mihajlov was caught anachronistically in a door that was already ajar and opening wider.

One of the frankest statements on the problems of artistic freedom and social criticism was made a couple of years ago in the Zagreb daily *Vjesnik* by Dobrica Ćosić, a Serbian novelist whose Marxist commitment is beyond doubt. It was made in direct response to Tito's pronouncements on the artist's "responsibility to society."

By his nature the literary artist grants conditional acceptance to every social reality; . . . he usually accepts social realities and negates them at the same time. Understanding the nature of the relation between art and society depends on a capacity and readiness to understand this fact about the artist and the creative act. I can understand and accept only an art which negates and supersedes existing human reality—an art which in the name of higher or different visions opposes any given socio-historical situation. . . . For by definition there has never been, nor can there ever be, any social reality which deserves to be kept the same forever.

Ćosić's ideas were of course not new; his statement belongs to the tradition of artists who have had the courage to say that "freedom is the essence of art." His proposal for solving the art versus society controversy was admirably mild and simple: "There would be fewer misunderstandings and life would be a lot more bearable in this world if society . . . would ascribe much less socio-political and outright ideological significance to art."

In theory this is certainly the wisest policy for the society to follow. And the Yugoslavs have found it easy to do so with their painters and musicians, who have rarely been troubled by pronouncements on "social realism." But with writers it is not so simple. A conversation with the director of a large Yugoslav publishing house gave me an insight into why it will still take time for full artistic freedom to become established. It seemed to him wholly inexplicable and even ridiculous that Ćosić, a committed Communist, should make such a fuss about the principle of artistic freedom. This director, who had considerable authority in deciding which books his publishing house would publish, was totally unprepared to understand that a committed artist could be interested in the freedom of other artists to choose commitment or noncommitment and might not wish to impose his own commitment on them.

Still, there is reason to believe that the skirmishes over the issue of freedom to criticize signify ebbing resistance by the old guard to the increasing independence of artists, rather than any new suppression. The efforts of bold individuals to discredit the old clichés are so frequently welcomed that sometimes the self-censoring writers and journalists seem overly cautious—more conservative than the government. Even in the official party journals I have come upon sharp criticisms of the remaining limitations on freedom, attacks on the failures of the system of self-management, and even suggestions that it is time for Yugoslavia to supplement Marx with more comtemporary thinkers like John Dewey. In this case, as in so many others, the metaphor of thawing ice is apt, for it takes more than a sudden rise in temperature to thaw ice: it also takes time.

The whole process of political development since 1950 has been like a gradual thaw. Decentralization of the economy and government, and the institution of workers' management have greatly loosened the hold of the dictatorship and begun the process of building up power from the bottom. In 1963, over a decade after workers' councils were established, the new constitution set forth the basic civil liberties necessary for political democracy and established new forms for self-government in politics and public business. It thus marked a new stage in the transition from revolutionary dictatorship to democratic socialism.

The constitution proclaimed the principles of privacy of the mails, inviolability of dwellings, habeas corpus, due process, equality before the law, and the right to legal aid; and it set up a constitutional court to see that no laws violated constitutional guarantees. Although exceptions were made to some of these guarantees of civil rights for cases involving "national security," the exceptions were described precisely, and all the violations of the guarantees were made punishable by law. Freedom of speech, freedom of the press, and freedom of association and assembly were also proclaimed, though with this important limitation: they may not be used to "destroy the bases of the democratic socialist system established by the constitution."

In addition, the constitution replaced the commune people's committees by elected assemblies, and it reorganized the republic and federal parliaments to make them more responsive to the needs of the electorate. They now have five chambers. One is elected by all the citizens, but the other four have specialized functions and are each elected from a different part of the working population. The Economic Chamber represents those employed in industry and commerce; the Chamber of Health and Social Security represents the staffs of hospitals and social security agencies; the Chamber of Culture and Education represents teachers, employees of publishing houses, and members of opera companies, artists' guilds, and theater troupes; and the Chamber of Organizations and Policy draws its members from workers' councils and officials of political organizations, i.e., the League of Communists and Socialist Alliance. The idea is to combine the various chambers in joint session according to the scope of the legislation under debate.

Though the first elections to the reorganized parliaments were strictly under party control, they swept away old members to whom rubber-stamp obedience had become habit and put in new men with better education, newer ideas, and a more liberal attitude. Many of the people elected to the specialized chambers were not professional politicians. Yugoslavia's most famous opera singer, for example, went to the Federal Parliament, and one of the country's best short story writers, who is also the director of a publishing house, went to the Serbian Parliament. The pattern of electing specialists was so general that a friend of mine, a mathematician who himself went to the Federal Parliament, remarked that Yugoslavia was moving from bureaucracy to technocracy. Actually the parliamentary reorganization represents an interesting experiment to try to solve modern society's problems with the specialist, whose powers as an adviser are sometimes inordinate, often poorly controlled, and always screened from the scrutiny of the electorate. If the specialists themselves go to parliament, they must face problems in their whole context and argue their positions in the open, instead of behind the scenes. Furthermore, they help to loosen the hold of professional politicians and bureaucrats on public power.

One innovation made by the constitution is going to encourage this trend away from professionals. This is the principle of "rotation." Hereafter a man may be elected to office for no more than two four-year terms; the principle applies also to important appointive offices. Though an exception is made for President Tito, who may be re-elected indefinitely, all future presidents will be limited to an eight-year maximum, just like everyone else.

The conception that Yugoslavia is some sort of personal dictatorship under President Tito is too widespread to be ignored. But at this point one must distinguish between Tito the legend and Tito the active politician. Tito became a legend during the war; his name became a symbol of the Partisan resistance, when many were uncertain whether he was a man or a woman, a Yugoslav or a Russian. There are Partisan poems which represent him as some sort of deity—ubiquitous and supernatural, marching at the head of every contingent as it went into battle. This is the stuff on which cults are built, and there has been a Tito cult in Yugoslavia. At least after 1948 it touched every part of the population, and this image of Tito was deliberately used to unify the country and resolve antagonisms in the most difficult postwar years.

In the years when the victorious revolutionaries were starting from scratch, Tito's leadership did apparently have elements of personal rule. I am told, for instance, that emergency relief to victims of floods and other natural calamities once came out of Tito's personal fund. But even in the early years major policy decisions were usually made in the frequent informal discussions which Tito had with his top lieutenants. Now, twenty years later, the revolution has received its explicit and detailed definition in laws and ideological documents like the Program of the League of Communists. With the 1963 Constitution the general definition of the society which is to emerge from the revolution is complete. Although it will be some time before all the features of that self-governing society become solidly established, many are already realities. The power to make decisions has begun to spread outward and downward and Tito's active role—at least in domestic affairs—has grown relatively small. As one official told me after a trip through the United States, "For Americans there is apparently only one man in Yugoslavia: Tito. While we respect Tito very highly, we keep in mind the hundreds of thousands of people who have become involved in the business of running this society."

The developments brought by the new constitution are going to spread the power around to many more people. They represent a further commitment to a society in which self-government brings the socialist workingman and citizen to a clear awareness of his own and the general interest and makes him willing and able to participate in public decision-making. But new forms are one thing and a new atmosphere something else. For some time, as official statements admit, old wine will inevitably be served from the new bottles.

This was obvious in some of the pre-election meetings I attended. At one meeting to nominate candidates for the Economic Chamber of the commune assembly, the nominations were clearly prearranged by the directors and party committees in the enterprises. The whole affair was lifeless and staged. A secretary sitting next to me was surprised to hear her name read out on a list of people wishing to second a nomination. She concluded that her boss had simply used her name without bothering to ask her whether she supported the candidate in question.

However, at a precinct meeting of citizens in my neighborhood the prearranged nominations for the commune assembly were presented frankly as the candidates of the Socialist Alliance and the party. Individual citizens then added other candidates to the list. The tone of the nominating speeches was refreshing. Instead of recommending candidates simply on the basis of party work or heroic exploits during the war, the emphasis was on activity in workers' management and community affairs. Though in these first elections to the new assemblies most of the candidates were still party members, the voters had more say than ever before. In time the emphasis on active participation in the public business of the society will probably make it harder for party members to get into office solely on the basis of past efforts, and it will become easier for active non-Communists to be elected.

It is still early, of course, to say how much these changes mean or how long it will take the new forms to develop. A great many difficulties must be overcome. Bureaucracy may be harder to uproot on the local level than in Belgrade. Out-of-the-way communes may suffer because of the low level of culture and the shortage of expert knowledge. People caught up in the revolution of rising material expectations may prove indifferent to opportunities to enter into the business of the society.

Probably the painful efforts to get the communal assemblies and the reorganized parliaments functioning with real power will fill the next decade, as the last decade has been filled with the development of workers' management. Not that the development even of "economic" democracy is complete—it is only now, for instance, that the workers' councils are beginning to get a firm grip on the purse strings and a real say in hiring and firing directors. The Yugoslavs continue to emphasize the need for stronger and more independent workers' management as the basic form of direct democracy. But hereafter the two processes of self-government in the economy and in politics will be developing side by side. Thanks to its late start, self-government in the commune will probably develop faster than workers' management did in its early years. For the workers' councils and managing boards have already given many thousands of people some experience in parliamentary procedures, in examining the background of decisions, and in taking on the responsibilities of management.

One essential difficulty, however, is already apparent from the experience with workers' management. This difficulty lies in the contradiction between the Yugoslav vision of democracy and the power, organization, and methods of the League of Communists.

At one time there was no doubt about the party's control of all government bodies and all factory workers' councils. In recent years the party has ceased to give orders to the workers' councils but its hold over government bodies has not loosened. And in most factories the party organization has continued to discuss specific issues ahead of time and instruct its members on how to vote in the workers' council meetings. Frequently this has merely meant the substitution of indirect control for direct control. And it raises real problems. The non-Communist members of the workers' council are naturally annoyed when their Communist colleagues come to meetings with instructions in their pockets. And the

Communists themselves are not always comfortable discussing matters on which they are not free to change their minds. Besides, the Communist's dual allegiance—to the party and to the people who elected him—is bound to lead him into conflict with one group or the other. And the fact that his first allegiance is to the party contradicts the very basis of democracy, for the party is not the people.

These problems have never been clearly solved for workers' management; but as workers' councils have grown more independent and more and more non-Communists have begun to participate, more pressing problems, such as lowering production costs, expanding facilities, and increasing exports, have pushed the question of the party into the background. When the new commune assemblies were set up, however, the old question was brought into the open again, this time with a new sense of urgency. All during 1964 the problems of how the local party organization should behave toward the commune assembly and how the party organization in the factory should behave toward the workers' council were discussed, argued, and solved in a hundred different ways in conversations, speeches, newspapers, and journals.

This is a knotty problem and it has no easy answer. On the one hand, it was the party which set up the workers' councils and assemblies, and the party has also been the main force in trying to give them independent existence; on the other hand, the time must come when the commune assembly and workers' council are free of any control by the party, or else people will cease to expect any real life from them.

The problem of party control over legally independent representative bodies cannot be solved without solving the problem of party control over its own members. The party is organized with its power at the top. General policy is made by a few leaders and passed on by the Central Committee. Broad directives are then issued downward. The party committees at lower levels discuss more specific issues, but their directives always move downward, not upward. The individual Communist is responsible for following the party line on all issues on which the party has taken a stand, whether they are decided on by the Central Committee or by his own little factory organization. This structure of the party not only limits the freedom of the individual Communist to decide independently on matters before an assembly or workers' council; in itself it contradicts the principles of direct democracy proclaimed by the League of Communists. (As one party member put it, "It's getting so the only citizens unable to enjoy freedom of speech are the Communists".)

The question of the party led to the Eighth Party Congress in December 1964, after several months of discussion. The Congress did not settle the question; it only took a position on it and established the "line" for the time being. Its position was that the party's role is to provide guidance and leadership in the area of political ideology. It is not to interfere with the workers' councils or commune assemblies by taking a position on every matter to be decided and then applying pressure for the acceptance of its position. Individual Communists who are members of these bodies are to further the goals of the party as individuals, not as agents of an organization which has already made their decisions for them. In other words, they are not to receive directives from their factory or commune organizations about how to vote in the short run, but their activity will be expected to serve the broad goals of the party in the long run.

The party itself is to be democratized to a certain extent. Individual members are to be allowed more participation in formulation of policy, and decisions are to be preceded by open discussion. But once a decision has been made, it must still be accepted and supported by all members. The minority shall not have the right to continue its opposition but must accept the view of the majority as if it were its own. The democratic principles of direct democracy are not, in other words, to be applied to the party and its internal structure.

Both the pre-Congress discussion and the arguments made in support of the Congress' decision were highly theoretical, but behind both lay the practical question of how much democracy is possible at the present stage of development. In a sense all important political questions in Yugoslavia can be reduced to this question of tempo. How soon should workers' management be made independent? How rapidly should the apparatus of the state be dismantled? When should the commune become the country's principal political and administrative unit? To what extent should civil liberties be broadened? How much should non-Communists be allowed to move into responsible positions? And finally, how rapidly should the party relinquish its domination over political activity?

Some party members feel that democratization is going too fast and too far. They say that decentralization and the market economy undermine the goals of a rational planned economy. They point to the fact that ordinary workers do not seem inherently anxious to take on the responsibility of business management, and ordinary citizens show little spontaneous readiness to take on the duties of formulating public policy. And they say that the liberals in the party overestimate the readiness with which people will comprehend and further the general good.

At the opposite pole, the liberals in the party are pushing for more democratization, faster development of the system of self-government, elimination of inequities associated with position and influence, and broader public discussion and criticism. They insist that men cannot become more responsible except through being given more responsibility. They point to the fact that the greatest problems in the economy and government occur precisely in those places where there is least democracy.

Political events rarely develop according to the logic of ideas. If the liberals seem to have the most solid arguments on their side, it is nevertheless not inevitable that they will win. Yet one cannot follow Yugoslav developments without believing that ideas do have some political force in the long run. The ideas espoused by the Yugoslav Communists are pushing them toward more freedom and democracy, and every step in that direction makes it harder and harder to call a halt without contradicting the Party Program. There is no turning back. The only choice is between a faster or a slower rate for the democratization already underway.

The debates between the two extreme views on the question of tempo usually end with the party leadership plotting the "line" in the middle ground—liberalization at a moderate, deliberate pace. Perhaps Tito's most important function now is in plotting this middle course. As the head of the party, he manages to adjust the process of liberalization to the conflicting ideas of its members: democratization is too slow to frighten the conservatives into a strong-arm reaction but it is not so slow as to disillusion the liberals. The two tendencies in the party have been held together long enough to lay the foundations for direct democracy, to retire many of the old guard, and to give the young liberals a solid sense of the problems involved in adjusting their ideals to practical realities.

There is a popular joke which tells something about Tito's political style. Before they installed traffic lights at one main intersection in Belgrade, motorists would signal to the traffic cop with their horns. A single blast meant a request to go straight, two blasts a turn to the left, and three blasts a turn to the right. This makeshift system fascinated a visiting Englishman, and he stood on the corner for an hour trying to catch the traffic cop in a mistake. At length he heard sirens and a long black limousine approached the intersection at great speed, blowing its horn in groups of three blasts. The policeman stopped the other traffic and signaled for the limousine to make a left turn. The Englishman saw the mistake and went up to the policeman. "You know," he said, "I've watched you an hour and you didn't make a single mistake until that limousine blew for a right turn and you directed it left." The policeman smiled and shook his head. "I didn't make a mistake. That was Tito's car. He always toots one way and goes the other."

Foreign observers like to speculate on the eventuality of Tito's disappearance from Yugoslav political life. My own guess is that Tito will be missed more as the unifying head of the party than as the charismatic leader of the country. Imperfect and incomplete though it may be, the system of self-government seems strong enough to continue without a legendary leader. If this is true, it may well be Tito's greatest accomplishment.

The principal question, then, is how the wings of the party will be kept together as the ideological disputes and criticism become more thoroughgoing and frank. Perhaps the opposing camps will become formally organized within the party or perhaps Yugoslavia will be the first Communist country to institute a two-party system. The soul-searching discussions of 1964 did not cease with the Party Congress, and as they continue, the idea of a faster pace for democratization seems more and more realistic as a political, not just a theoretical, solution.

Index

Index

AUSTRIA
Maribor
H
Lake Bled
Julian Alps
SLOVENIA
LJUBLJANA
ZAGREB
TRIESTE
Piran
Koper
CROATIA
Karlovats
BROTHERHOOD-UNITY HIGHWAY
Opatiya
Rieka
ISTRIA
Sava
Krk
ADRIATIC HIGHWAY
Brioni
Pula
Tsres
Bihatch
Banya Luka
Travnik
Yaytse
BOSN
Zadar
Zenitsa
Dugi Otok
DALMATIA
Dinarids
Y U AND G
Shibenik
SARAJ
HERCEG
Trogir
Yablanitsa
Split
Brach
Mostar
Neretva
Hvar
Ploche
Korchula
Mlyet
Dubrovnik
Bay of
Milo
Sveti St
Petro
ADRIATIC SEA
ITALY